NAKED AND MAROONED

ED STAFFORD was named European Adventurer of the Year in 2011; he was also a finalist for the National Geographic Adventurer of the Year in 2010, and he is a Guinness World Record holder for his incredible feat (feet?!). Ed started running worldwide expeditions after retiring from the British army as a captain in 2002. When not leading trips, he worked alongside the United Nations in Afghanistan, assisting with the running of their first-ever presidential elections. Prior to this journey, Ed was in production with the BBC on its conservation series *Lost Land of the Jaguar*. In August 2010, he became the first man to walk the length of the Amazon River, accompanied by forestry worker Gadiel "Cho" Sanchez Rivera, for all but four months of the twenty-eight-month journey. Ed was married to Amanda in a traditional Aboriginal ceremony in the Daintree Rainforest. They live with her two kids in central London. He is planning future projects with the Discovery Channel, and he travels the world speaking about his adventures. To follow Ed, visit his website: edstafford.org.

ALSO BY ED STAFFORD

Walking the Amazon

NAKED AND MAROONED

One Man. One Island.

ED STAFFORD

P

A PLUME BOOK

PLUME
Published by the Penguin Group
Penguin Group (USA) LLC
375 Hudson Street
New York, New York 10014

USA | Canada | UK | Ireland | Australia | New Zealand | India | South Africa | China
penguin.com
A Penguin Random House Company

Previously published in the United Kingdom by Virgin Books, an imprint of Ebury
Publishing.
Published by Plume, a member of Penguin Group (USA) LLC, 2014

ISBN 978-0-14-218096-9

Printed in the United States of America
10   9   8   7   6   5   4   3   2

Set in Dante MT Std

Penguin is committed to publishing works of quality and integrity.
In that spirit, we are proud to offer this book to our readers;
however, the story, the experiences, and the words
are the author's alone.

To Frederick,

Without whom I would never have met your mum

I love you, mate

CONTENTS

Prologue 13

Introduction. 15

SURVIVING
Day 1 25

WATER
Day 2 to 6 45

FIRE
Day 7 to 14 115

SHELTER
Day 15 to 28 167

HUNTING
Day 29 to 42 221

THRIVING
Day 43 to 60 261

Epilogue. 311

Acknowledgements. 319

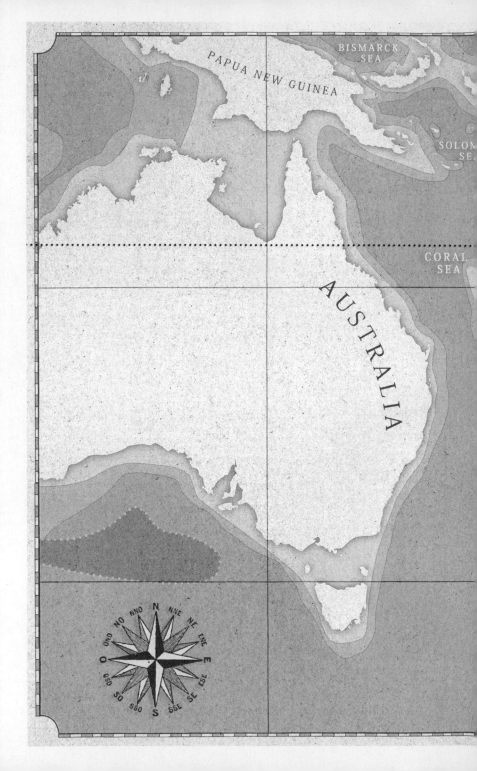

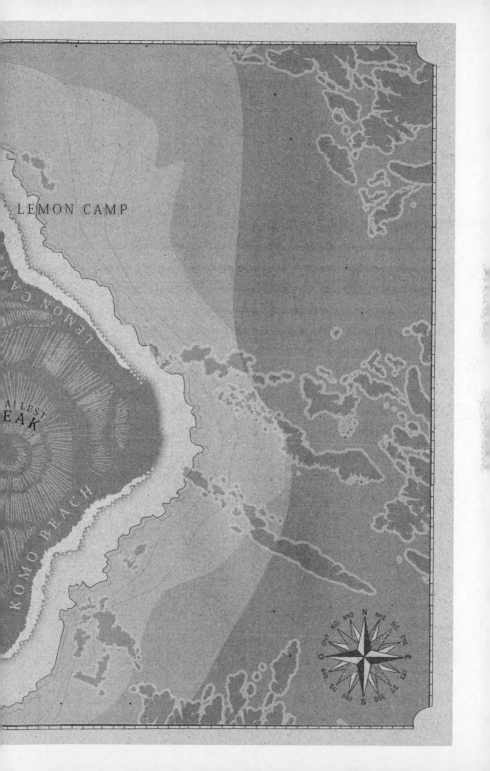

PROLOGUE

'It's time, Ed. Take off your shorts and get out of the boat.' The bubble of apprehension that had been growing for weeks moved up from my guts into my throat. This was it – the doors to the exam hall opening, the driving test beginning, first date and first parachute jump all rolled into one.

My fears were compounded by feeling utterly stupid and vulnerable taking off all my clothes in front of a TV producer and two warrior-like Fijian clansmen. The latter's wide faces scrutinised me and, without uttering a word, their eyes told me they thought all westerners were fucked in the head.

Nakedness. Nobody likes a willy waver. There are some men, especially those from military or rugby backgrounds (I qualify for both), who can think of nothing better than getting drunk and taking their clothes off for the thrill of it. I would say I'm the opposite. My earliest recurring nightmare was of turning up at school without either trousers or underpants, and the feeling of ridicule still haunts me now if I think back on it.

Completely naked, I climbed down into the waist-deep tropical water to feel my toes settle on the sandy seabed and my balls shrink against the new, wet, exposed world. Camera in hand and at arm's length, I knew I needed to record my emotions – every crevice of my brain needed to be laid bare to engage disbelieving people wedged into their armchairs in front of the TV. This was real and I wanted to document it all.

I couldn't figure out how I felt and confided to the shiny black lens how overwhelmed I was. I padded slowly up into the warm shallows and on to the beach in a state of shock.

I watched the small metal fishing boat loiter inanely for a minute or two before the Yamaha outboard coughed up some brown phlegm into the turquoise water and began to back away from me, gradually shrinking in size and influence. As the vessel slipped out of sight, the life-affirming drone of the motor was snuffed out with a huge fluffy pillow of complete isolation.

Utter silence.

I stood on the beach truly alone for the first time. This golden lip that encircled the rainforest-clad island was my doorstep to an intimidating new world. I would not see another person for sixty days. I was on an uninhabited tropical island and I had nothing with me to help me survive. No food, no equipment, no knife and not even any clothes. All I had was my camera kit so that I could intimately record my self-inflicted sentence.

An emotional attack helicopter rose from my belly, rotors lacerating my chest until it smashed violently into my ill-prepared brain. Logical thought was the victim and I was left stunned like an impotent witness of a brutal, bloody crime.

INTRODUCTION

I had been travelling for over twenty-four hours – London, Hong Kong, Sydney, and now the capital city of Fiji, Nadi. My clothes felt greasy and my skin had acquired a layer of scum that made me feel grubby and in need of a steaming hot shower and a good soapy scrub, neither of which I was going to find at the end of this journey. We were being weighed along with the baggage to ensure that the total weight was OK for the single-propeller plane that we were about to board. I weighed in at eighty-nine kilos – deliberately not too trim – with surplus fat to shed. The Cessna would fly us over the volcanic Fijian mountains and onwards to the outlying tropical island of Lakeba.

We touched down on the wet grass runway of Lakeba and hung around for a few hours eating cheap white coconut biscuits and drinking sweet tepid coffee until our tin boat was ready to ferry us on the four-hour crossing to the remote tribal island of Komo. With bruised bottoms and balls sore from the boat slamming down into every oncoming Pacific wave we groggily and nauseously flopped out of the boat to meet the Komo clan.

Komo is on the very eastern outskirts of the Fijian islands and is closer to Tonga than mainland Fiji. It is home to a tribe of Fijians who are gentle giants. Women stand taller and broader than the average European male and wear their hair in large round Afros that accentuate their presence. Komo men, who have never heard of a dumbbell, have legs the size of kegs of dynamite and faces as wide and kind as you could possibly ask a child to draw. As we picked our way through the wood and tin village of small self-built huts we were greeted with broad smiles, waves and genuine interest as to what we pale, unhealthy, looking white men might be doing in this colourful corner of the world.

I was travelling with two men, Steve Rankin, a gentle, short, slightly balding TV producer from England, and Steven (with an 'n') Ballantyne, our local fixer, a tall, well-spoken and charming expat who lived in Hong Kong with his Chinese partner. The two physically contrasting men seemed to share an under-standing of the resigned struggle of surviving in the suburbs of TV World and they had already struck up a close friendship fuelled by late nights and hard liquor. Together we had around thirty-five cases of cameras, laptops, hard drives and bottles of hand sanitiser and we unloaded all this into the house of the village chief who had moved out for the next two and a half months. The house's sole occupant would be Steven, and he would remain on the island, administrating the filming and coordinating any emergency evacuations. Steve, on the other hand, would return to England shortly after I started filming and oversee the entire event from afar. He would return in two months to film my extraction.

The simple house consisted of two small rooms. The first had three single beds adorned with colourful nylon mosquito nets and the other contained a wooden table and four sturdy chairs. I lay among the black camera boxes on my yellow foam mattress. I didn't need to unpack anything – that was for the others to organise. All I had was a tiny fifteen-litre day sack with one change of shorts and T-shirt and some toiletries. Where I was going I wouldn't even be allowed to take those.

I looked up at the ceiling and knew that my job over the next two days was to soak up as much information from the locals as possible and get myself mentally prepared for what I was about to undertake. Don't worry about anything else, Ed. The self-coaching voice had already begun to make itself heard.

After an hour or so, huge-haired women started to fill the crude wooden table with steaming plates of rice, chicken and fish fresh from the ocean. This was accompanied by colourful heavily iced cakes and sweet white biscuits. I was apparently expected to eat and eat. The walls of my stomach felt as if they had passed their elastic limit as I struggled to digest the mass of sugar and flour. Visibly straining, I escaped the nervous gorging to explore the island.

A dusty path rose through the village, past the communal generator and behind a small wooden school. I followed it to the highest point I could find. As I crested the hill behind the village the sun was setting low and orange in the west. Before me was a familiar shape that I had seen before only in photographs. Olorua: my home for the next sixty days. The uninhabited island had three topographical peaks and, from my viewpoint, two distinct saddles. With no scars from clearing or logging she was entirely cloaked in thick lush rainforest standing alone in a vast ocean. Although she was only eight nautical miles from where I was standing on Komo she seemed far more remote and isolated than all the other islands in this forgotten corner of the world. She looked bigger than I was expecting and, for some reason, with the warm evening sun lighting up her western side, she seemed peaceful and welcoming. But first impressions can be deceptive.

I passed out that night, having eaten my way through an evening of apprehension, with an uncomfortably stretched belly.

The next day I was introduced to Rama, the brother of the chief, whose job it was to answer any questions I had about local plants and methods. Rama seemed enormous and yet, when I stood beside him, he was only about six foot tall. I was an inch taller than him but he must have weighed four stone more. Well into middle age, his frame was powerful and muscular but softened by a comfortable layer of fat. Rama was clearly a kind man and had that aura about him, and an absence of ego, that allowed him to be entirely himself. I could tell by the affection in his eyes that he was genuinely flattered to have been given the responsibility of being my teacher and that we were going to get on well.

Fire by friction was the subject I wanted advice on from Rama. I could light a fire back home with materials and methods traditionally used there, but how did they do it here and with what? He said the best tree was called 'tangalito' – it had a black stem and there was plenty on Olorua – on this side (south-east), on the shore that faced Komo. He grabbed a couple of pieces of wood from a tree and, without any preparation with a knife or any other tool, he sat down and started to rub one against the other as if he were setting to with a chisel, fuelled by an over-dose of amphetamine.

I recognised the simple fire-plough method of lighting a fire and witnessed the wood turn black and emit a little smoke and powder. 'I'm unfit!' he declared and gave up trying to build an ember. It was enough for me to know that this wood was good. I probably wouldn't use the fire-plough method, because I wasn't confident that I could consistently get an ember that way, but I could see that this wood was suitable for making fire and I left it at that.

I mentally ticked fire off my jumbled list of things to cover before my deployment and immediately flitted on to other worries. No pause, no consideration, no deep breath – I just pinged on to the next subject like a pinball. If I'd been less stressed about my impending ordeal I might have registered the ease of testing wood like this. Even if it was not yet a skill in my armoury I should have seen just how useful it was in itself. All you had to do was rub one piece of wood backwards and forwards on a flat surface of the other – there was no carving involved – and if the wood was good it would heat up quickly, turn black and start to smoke. But, blinkered by my apprehension about what lay ahead, only the tried and tested methods that I'd *learned* could possibly be an option. Everything else was stressing me out and so I let a valuable lesson slip through my sweaty fingers.

I spent much of the two preparation days relaxing. I was about to do something really hard and I deliberately allowed myself some down time. I lay on my bed, ate copious amounts of food and even played touch rugby with the local men and boys. The one further skill for which I did pick up the basics was plaiting coconut palm leaves so that they could be used to thatch a shelter. I hadn't mastered it but I had seen it done well and had a go and felt that I could figure it out if the need arose. Notably, and slightly worryingly, I *didn't* identify many edible plants that I would find on Olorua; I *didn't* ask about a single method of fishing (or ask when or where they fished); and I *didn't* even ask about how they used coconuts in their cooking. All in all, I squandered some very valuable time with local experts and instead put my feet up and relaxed.

I was so daunted by the enormity of what I was about to do that it made me feel uncomfortable even to dwell on the things that I didn't yet know. Rather than preparing for the future by putting some work in now, I opted to go for immediate gratification – food, rest and play – in the knowledge that my times of hardship had not yet arrived and I should make hay while I could.

What an idiot.

Still, in a way it added to the veracity of the whole adventure. Viewers of survival programmes inevitably ask themselves the question: 'Could I do that?' But they don't take a man full of pizza and tea whose idea of wilderness is the back of a garden centre and drop him unsupported in the middle of nowhere. They take someone like me who, nominally at least, knows what he's doing. So, in failing to make the very most of my time with the locals I was actually moving closer to the sort of challenge that might face someone suddenly shipwrecked and washed up on an alien shore. When people find themselves in survival situations many of them have no preparation whatsoever. It was more honest simply to arrive on the island and work things out for myself. That was my excuse, anyway.

In fact, mentally I was already in a mess. I was already failing to cope with taking complete responsibility for my own welfare. I was already fast becoming out of control – reaching for any excuse to avoid putting in the work and grasping at superficial distractions. I wasn't being honest with myself and, although I knew it deep down, I hid behind layers of self-deception that I would be fine. 'Another cake? Ooooh, thank you. I shouldn't but I will!' The sugar would keep me happy for another thirty seconds.

The truth, of course, is that I would not be fine at all. I was about to undergo the most unsettling, soul-searching and frighteningly disorientating two months of my life.

*

On the morning of Saturday 18 August 2012 I woke up charged with adrenaline. It was game day and I was up for smashing some people. Except this wasn't a rugby match – and aggression was not going to get me through this challenge. Yet my mindset was simple and focused – let's get this started now. I just want to get stuck in.

I was going in by boat but I had to wait for a helicopter to arrive that would film the insertion from the air. I sat on a wooden chair outside the flaky purple walls of my hut and wrote letters to my fiancée, Amanda. I wanted her to know how much I cared about her and for her to have a constant reminder that I was thinking about her. I knew that I wouldn't have any contact with her for the next sixty days and that would be hard for anyone to cope with. I felt selfish that I was putting her through this and yet I knew she was supportive of what I was doing and so I just tried to stick to the positives.

The mechanical beat of the helicopter's heart pulsed through the air towards my soft eardrums. The flying machine drew louder and closer, attracting an excited crowd on the rugby pitch in the centre of the village. I exchanged pleasantries with the Australian pilot and tried to be as sociable and normal as possible, but in my head I was already on the island and everything else was now just getting in the way. When Steve and Steven were ready, I walked through the village for the last time down to the metal boats and waved goodbye to these kind people who I had hardly made time to speak to. Camera in hand, I began to talk to the lens as if it were my true confidant. 'Come on – stop fannying around – let's go.'

The bashing of the hull against the waves didn't bother me as we slipped out of the reef. I relaxed almost to the point of sleep. Then, as we circled around Komo, Olorua came into view. The small island was utterly compelling on the horizon and I could not stop evaluating, thinking, imagining, wondering. What would these next sixty days be like? I could envisage a magical jungle world under the canopy: giant spider webs the size of a man and troops of apes to live alongside. My imagination latched on to Tarzan stories and I allowed myself to dream of an elaborate tree house with a veranda overlooking the reef nestling into the top of the tallest tree on the island. It felt good to be excited and playful about the idea of this contrived stay – it made a refreshing change from the ominous default feelings of fear, discomfort and dread.

As we approached the coral reef that encircled Olorua the ocean changed from a dark metallic blue to a brilliant turquoise. Steve needed to film me making some opening observations. I sat in the bow of the boat with the island visible behind and Steve fed me questions designed to elicit the dramatic answers he was looking for. If he didn't get the answers he wanted he simply told me what to say. 'This is the biggest challenge so far of my whole life!' I found myself mouthing to keep Steve happy. That's what he wanted to hear. I couldn't allow myself to see it that way. I'd walked the length of the Amazon for two and a half years through drug traffickers, defensive indigenous tribes and communist terrorists – an expedition that so many people considered suicidal. This wouldn't be more challenging than that, would it? Surely this TV project had to be a walk in the park in comparison to a walk along the Amazon.

This simply wasn't the time for me to be acknowledging fear – far too close to the bone as far as I was concerned – and I was allowing false bravado to distract me. I cringed as I found myself giving Steve the sound bites that he wanted – to me they seemed full of hype and an exaggerated sense of danger – for the opening sequences of the film. Paradoxically simple honesty would have provided him with feelings of more genuine anxiety than he could have dreamed of – but I was now far too scared to be honest about them.

'I cannot wait until I'm on my own. Nothing personal – but it's time for you all to bugger off now.'

CHAPTER 1

SURVIVING

1

The drone of the motor now long since receded, I walked up the beach to where my case full of camera equipment had been dropped in the shade of a coconut palm. I allowed myself to fall to my knees in the sand and clicked open the four chunky plastic latches. The case opened to reveal the only remnants of civilisation left to me: two video cameras, two head-mounted point-of-view cameras, a very stripped-down medical kit (just one course of antibiotics and a trauma dressing), an emergency satellite phone and a GPS locator device. If ever there was a moment for comfort eating, this was it. But there was no food in the box – nothing to help me survive at all.

I snapped into autopilot and tried to take charge by doing something that I did have control over. As I rigged up the cameras I was immediately aware of my first oversight. I had nothing to clip the radio mic box to. I was naked! 'It's ridiculous, isn't it? The silly things that I'm already starting to flap about.' I tried to joke to the camera and yet inside I wasn't laughing. I tried to clip it to the camera, which completely defeated the purpose of having a remote radio mic. I was flapping. Calm, logical thought was almost impossible to hold on to.

Sand was already finding its way into everything. Deep breath out. Having rigged up the second camera and radio mic, I sat down to make a plan. 'I'm up and running filming-wise. I just have this nervous energy circling round my chest at the moment. I think every part of me knows that this is not messing around – that I'm very much putting my money where my mouth is. If I can survive – on my own – for two months – fantastic. But I've never done this before! Am I going to go mad without anyone to talk to? Oh Christ.' My sentences were just streams of consciousness – there was no perspective or reason, just raw disjointed emotions and thoughts.

'OK, what's the situation, Ed? What are your priorities? What do you need to do first?'

I am a former British Army captain who has been leading expeditions and operations to remote parts of the world for more than a decade. I have been in very high-risk situations before in Afghanistan working alongside the UN and I've taught survival courses to people about to embark on jungle expeditions in Belize. But a menacing truth suddenly loomed in front of me. I had never had to survive before *from scratch*. You might think that would have occurred to me before but I felt a little sick as it dawned on me that I was making it up as I was going along.

Think about it. Expeditioners, even those at the most extreme level, all carry kit and supplies to help them. They will have food and a means of cooking it; navigation equipment; some form of portable shelter; water and a means of storing and purifying it. If things go wrong they will often still have a lot to help them get themselves out of trouble. They will have a well-thought-through casualty evacuation plan that would hopefully ensure that they are never in a survival situation for very long.

Consider this too. In prehistoric times cavemen would have been very unlikely to have been in a situation in which they started with nothing. They would be born into a tribe or family that had tools, animal skins, a fire, and they would probably all be cuddled up in a well-chosen cave. They would acquire all the skills that they needed in order to live in their world as they grew up. They would usually only have to deal with one problem or situation at a time. 'We need some more firewood/mammoth meat/sabre-toothed tiger skin.' Delete as applicable.

My eyes were suddenly opened to the fact that I'd just volunteered myself for the absolute worst-case scenario with an acknowledgement that I would have absolutely nothing to help me survive, and a sure certainty that the situation would not change for a very long time. I would be sending an 'OK' message every day from the locator device but if I fell off a rock and cracked my skull in the interior of the island it might be too late by the time they found me.

My brain, used to self-deprecation to help me muddle through such times, looked for someone to share a black joke with about the absurdity of my predicament. A chill shudder ran through me as I realised another absolute truth: no one was going to share this with me. No one would laugh or cry with me. No one would give me any encouragement. No one would advise me or warn me of danger. I had absolutely nobody to turn to or to comfort me in any of this. I had to take complete responsibility for myself in every respect – probably for the first time in my life.

'What the fuck am I doing here?' I asked myself all too late. What would make anyone volunteer for such a lonely yet totally public self-examination?

Rewind two years and I was running down a sandy beach in northern Brazil into the Atlantic Ocean surrounded by international press teams. Exhausted and yet as high and magnificent as Mount Everest, I stood in the crashing waves allowing the moment to flow through every vein in my body. I had completed an expedition that everyone had told me was impossible – I had walked the entire length of the Amazon and it had taken me nearly two and a half years. Pride surged through me to the point of tears – I had done something that no one had ever done before – and nothing would ever take that feeling away from me.

Or would it?

Imperceptibly, I immediately started to get side-tracked. The media attention made me feel good. When I returned home to a hero's welcome I found that I was being treated differently. I liked it. People wanted to hear what I had to say; people wanted a slice of me. The attention made me feel good and, without realising it, my internal glow of self-worth, one that had taken over two years to germinate and nurture, began to get lost in a fog of insincere compliments.

TV interviews gave way to radio, radio to motivational talks all over the world. My story was real and seemed to inspire people, and so I tapped into my pain and my elation time and time again.

'What's your next expedition?' was the question asked more than any other. I found this fascinating in itself; you do something that no one in the history of mankind has ever done before and then, because we are so used to consuming and spitting out information, people want something new.

Have a beer, Ed.

My Amazonian candle of self-worth now all but extinguished – a thin wisp of smoke the only sign of my evaporating self-belief. I listened to what *other* people wanted because they *appeared* to be my source of happiness. What would the Royal

Geographical Society think of this? Would Sir Ranulph Fiennes approve? Would this island adventure capture the hearts of the masses? Would that one make good TV?

Have another beer, Ed.

I fought imaginary battles between my perception of other people's expectations and my own lost sense of direction. Where was I going? What had this all been for? How could I once again get back to that place in which I was overflowing with real confidence?

Another beer, Ed?

I needed a sequel. I needed to stay *current*. I needed people to see me achieve something else. I needed to prove that the first time hadn't been a fluke ...

In the modern surroundings of a sophisticated basement flat in Streatham, south London, I sat with Craig, my loyal friend and TV contact, and, over a cup of sugary white Lady Grey, brainstormed what to do next. We'd gone through every expedition that we could possibly conceive and independently acknowledged that I'd probably done the biggest one I was ever going to do. Unless I wanted to commit four years of my life to circumnavigating the earth manpowered via both poles – the apparent 'Holy Grail' of modern-day adventure – everything else seemed unworthy.

I needed to think laterally. What could I do to step sideways from what people expected in order to pit myself against nature in a more intense manner? I wanted to sift out the exploratory filler, the boring bits, and just be left with one raw challenge after another. I began to dream about an event or a test rather than a conventional expedition. Something incredibly hard, outside my comfort zone; something at which I genuinely would not know if I could succeed.

Craig and I began by eliminating every factor that would make my life more comfortable. The first to go was any assistance. 'I need to do the next one alone,' I said to Craig, tapping my mug with chewed fingernails. The help I'd had in the Amazon had been incredible but had left me wondering. Could I have done the expedition without my loyal Peruvian friend Cho who walked much of the journey with me? I wanted to find out if I could stand on my own two feet and be put to the test truly alone.

'What if you were to be on a desert island and had to survive with only the basics?' suggested Craig. I allowed myself to imagine the scenario and then, as a glow of excitement began to spread in my belly, I slowly proposed, 'What if I was to have absolutely nothing to help me survive? No food, no equipment, no knife – not even any clothes?'

'Could you do that?' asked Craig.

'I have no idea,' I grinned.

'Get a grip, Staffs – deal with practicalities.' The video camera was my best friend and my mirror and meant that right from the start all my thoughts were verbalised. I caught the look of fear in my eyes in the flip-out screen and immediately realised the obligation to look after this frightened reflection of myself.

I ran through the textbook priorities that I had taught to others so many times. Water, food, fire and shelter. I knew that water was the only one that I really needed on day one but, even as I acknowledged that, a wave of panic rose in me. I had little knowledge of the island and no idea whether there would be any reliable water sources. What if I couldn't find water? Despite the inherently contrived nature of this experiment, it was now absolutely real and it was happening. If I couldn't find water quickly I was going to fail, and fail quickly.

'Stay calm, Staffs. You can delay this problem and give yourself some breathing space by using what you've already seen.' I was my own coach, my own adviser – I held my own clammy hand as I took the first steps on this daunting voyage. Glancing up at the green coconuts I told myself that without even moving from where I was I would be OK for one or two nights. I could throw rocks at the coconuts to dislodge green ones and I could drink the coconut water that I knew was full of electrolytes. That would hydrate me well enough for now.

My knees clicked as I stood up stiffly and brushed the sand off my bare bum. I looked up and down the beach for an obvious coconut tree that was low to the ground and immediately identified one that was only a couple of metres above my head height. I found a rock the size of an apple and threw it overhand at the inviting source of natural single-portion drinks.

I felt peculiarly self-conscious – like something from a kid's dream – scrumping naked. I threw and I missed. I missed again. Bollocks. Underhand … Missed. And again. Just as I was becoming exasperated I connected with a satisfying thud. 'Yes!' The coconut landed, making a soft crater in the sand.

Having never opened a coconut without a machete I held the rough globe in two hands and tried to think laterally. I found a large sharpish rock that was half buried in the sand and held my coconut aloft. Using the weight of my arms and the fibrous fruit itself, I brought it down hard on the edge of the rock again and again to break through the husk. After perhaps twenty strikes coconut water spurted on to the rock and, panting hard, I held the coconut over my mouth expecting copious amounts of liquid to flow into my parched mouth. A pitiful amount trickled out. 'That's amazing!' I fibbed, faking a smile to match. Then I realised what I'd done and laughed at my immediate instinct to cover up the failure – admitting to the camera that, despite all the effort, I'd hardly drank more than a few drops.

This frantic rigmarole was repeated with low-grade coconuts until I felt that I'd had at least enough liquid to keep me going and I decided to begin to explore the beach.

The long golden beach stretched out below its classic palm-tree fringe. If they were filming a Bounty advert here, you wouldn't be surprised. But neither would you be surprised to find a few skeletons clutching rotting treasure maps. That popped into my head, too – pirates used to maroon people, didn't they? I'd become my own Blackbeard, ordering myself off the ship to die in the relentless sun. Not a particularly helpful train of thought.

As I followed the water's edge I noted small details: where the high tide had left a dirty ring on the beach last time the water had risen; that the sun was about three fists (at arm's length) from hitting the horizon; and how blood on my foot told me that I'd cut my foot on the coral. I tried to smile and enjoy the beauty all around me. I felt no happiness at all and took zero pleasure in the now irrelevant aesthetics of my physical surroundings. It was day one: I could feel my shoulders burning, my saliva was already viscous and stale. There was so much unknown, so much to do, and so little to hold on to. I took shallow rapid breaths as if breathing deeply would take too much time.

'Time spent in reconnaissance is time seldom wasted,' I repeated a few times to reassure myself that this was accepted army wisdom and that I was making the best use of my daylight hours. I felt a strong sense of urgency and a need to get on with things. On reflection I had all the time in the world to relax into my own little private world that had no rules other than those that I imposed, but, ever conscious of my commitments to Discovery Channel and fear of looking like a failure, I immediately began to pile on the pressure.

Then the first of my cartoon double takes occurred. 'That's ridiculous,' I said out loud.

Before me, crudely carved out of the vertical rock face, was a cave. Not a small cave that I would struggle to get into, or a damp, low cave that would be wet at high tide, but a large, spacious cave cut high into the cliff above the highest of high tides with its back conveniently turned to the prevailing winds.

My checklist of survival priorities resurfaced from the swamp of tasks in my head and I smugly ticked 'shelter' off the list with child-like excitement. This was a gift on day one and I knew it. As I clambered up the rock on all fours to inspect my new home the musky smell of animals that reminded me of London Zoo hit my nostrils. The cave was about four metres wide, three metres tall and four metres deep. The sill at the front sat a good two metres raised from the beach below. The well-protected dry floor sloped significantly from back to front and consisted of a dirty brown powder (from the crumbling rock) mixed with a substantial amount of animal shit.

'Do they have rabbits in Fiji?' I asked myself. No – it had to be something larger. Sheep? Goat? Deer even? This was too many ticks at once and I whooped a little self-consciously to the camera to convey my surprise and joy. The prospect of animals to eat was one of my ultimate dreams for the evolution of this project and on day one I was already identifying that meat was a definite possibility.

Like many men I've never been one for multi-tasking; my brain has never liked the stress of lots of things happening at the same time. Despite the fact that my discoveries had been very positive I could feel a need in myself to sit down and consolidate.

I decided that the cave would be my base, at least initially, and went to get the big camera case from further up the beach. As I collected the case from the tree line I realised that if I wanted to film myself carrying it to the cave it would, absurdly, require leaving one camera behind filming me and thus would involve a further trip up the beach to collect it.

I was aware what a peculiar sight I must have looked walking down the beach, stark naked and white-bummed, with the big black suitcase. I could feel the camera's eye watching me from behind. I began to carry the case up into the cave and then fretted that I might slip and fall with the weight. I flapped and decided that a slip or a fall was too risky and instead put the case at the top of the beach in the tree line. I had a whole load of trivial decisions to make in one go. What was the right decision? Who would confirm this to me? No one. Great. 'It's funny, isn't it?' I confided to the camera. 'I need to keep trusting my gut feeling. My brain said take it up there and my gut said – Stafford, get a grip.' I consoled myself that I had made the correct decision, then immediately doubted myself and changed my mind. Finally, I told myself to stop messing around, and hauled the case up into the cave and sat down heavily on the hot plastic, giddy with indecision.

I mused that if the animals were big and they lived in the cave I might need a small rock by me to throw at them when they returned.

'Stafford, you always said that whenever you felt unsure you'd sit down and calm yourself down. First day you were bound to be all over the place.' I went through the positives.

'You've had a drink of coconut water and will be able to eat some coconut flesh tonight, and you've found shelter. The only remaining survival priority is fire and that isn't essential on day one. You're doing really well.'

✓ But I couldn't help but be unsettled by the continued look of panic in my wide, white eyes in the flimsy screen on the video camera. I could see the tension in my temples and my forehead looked like a nail bomb wrapped in crêpe paper. I tried to calm myself with words of reassurance – I had the experience and the capabilities to survive well on this island. I needed to trust in that. Unconvinced, I returned to immediate practicalities. 'Crikey,' I sighed, 'let's get some more fluids down me before the end of the day.'

The rough rocks kneaded the soft soles of my bare feet as I climbed down to the beach. I noticed several plate-sized giant clamshells I could use to hold water and mentally recorded them. The surface changed to soft sand, which felt kinder, but I was going to have to try to make some sandals if my feet weren't to be cut to ribbons.

In the tree line at the top of the beach was a much shorter coconut tree with some very green fruits on it. I shimmied a couple of feet up the trunk like an overweight chimpanzee on opiates and hand-picked two small coconuts. I smashed them on another sharp rock with all my might (being careful not to trap my fingers underneath) and sank two long, cool, sweet drinks that spilled down my chin and chest. I glugged and glugged and then panted, grinning at the simple pleasure.

In the Amazon I had struggled to stay positive and resorted to NLP (neuro-linguistic programming) tricks to keep me on track. When I had felt the onset of mental weakness I had deliberately envisaged people in my life who were inspirational so that I didn't slip into unbecoming behaviour. When confronted with bad situations I had learned to select more appropriate mind states than anger or frustration, neither of which helped at all. But this experience seemed very different from the outset. For a start the Amazon walk hadn't been done alone, and that seemed key. Isolation is a technique used by people – hermits, monks, yogis – looking for a mystical experience. In my self-created world of avoidance getting in touch with my inner self was the last thing I wanted.

I had anticipated that this challenge would need more than mind tricks. I knew it would push me to places of painful honesty and I had to confront them rather than artificially control them. My strategy here, to ensure that madness didn't take over, was one suggested to me by two Aboriginal Australians I'd met through Amanda and become close friends with – Harold and Jeremy.

Harold is Jeremy's uncle. They are mixed-race Aboriginal and white Australian and have feet in more than one world in more ways than one. Harold, who is about sixty, is so lacking in ego, so unimposing, in fact, that often his presence goes completely unnoticed. But to miss him would be a mistake as he is one of the most powerful Aboriginal healers who exists today. A man of few words, he has been a strong and calming influence on me ever since I have known him.

Jeremy is a completely different beast, younger than me, and with the exuberance of a youthful travelled man he boasts the wisdom of somebody far older. A powerful spiritual healer, talented artist and phenomenal musician, he has helped guide me to become a stronger, more conscious person.

On a recent trip to the Daintree rainforest in Queensland they had warned me not to underestimate my forthcoming sixty days in isolation. That is a very long time to cope with by your-self, they told me – plenty long enough to go mad. 'That's a long time, brother. You could get proper fucked up.'

Aboriginals have traditionally spent extended periods of time alone on walkabout. Their whole existence is a connection to the land and nature. They have a belief that we all have three brains – the biggest and most important is the gut, the instinct; the second is the heart; and the smallest brain is the logical mind that most westerners use solely to run their lives. Incredibly the same phrase, *'ngan duppurru'*, Yalanji Aboriginal language for the mind, also means 'tangled' – or more crudely, 'fucked'. They would use the same word to describe a fishing net that had become knotted up beyond repair.

Seeing my not so uncommon tendency to worry and analyse they explained to me that if I stayed in my logical mind for my time on the island it would be a long, hard fight to stay sane. I would face an onslaught of apprehensions, fears and uncontrol-lable thoughts that would test my strongest resolve.

Instead, they advised, I needed to come from a deeper place – a place of soul, a place of surrender to what is and where I wouldn't, couldn't, overcomplicate things.

To do this they gave me the simplest of tools. They told me to make a simple circle of stones big enough to sit in. Whenever I felt myself at risk of overactive dark thoughts, panic or undue worry I was to stop whatever I was doing and go and sit in this circle. There I would be safe, they told me, protected from the island and from any external factors. I sincerely hoped it would work.

My thirst quenched by coconut water I decided it was time to make my stone circle. I selected eight rocks the size of grape-fruits from the upper beach and, cradling them in my arms, I wobbled up the rock face into the cave. Ever the army captain, I mocked myself for wasting my time on such mumbo-jumbo. Nonetheless I laid out the twelve and six o'clock stones – then nine and three. I used the last four rocks to fill the gaps to make a symmetrical circle just over a metre in diameter in the pungent dust of the cave floor.

As with a new car, I wanted to try it out – to sit in it and take it for a spin. I lowered my buttocks into the circle and sat up with my arms resting on my knees and let out a long transformative sigh. I smiled and, to my genuine surprise, felt immediately relaxed inside the circle. I looked up in order to appreciate the magnificent view from the cave for the first time: the vast expanse of bright blue ocean, the waves crashing on the reef in the middle distance and the soft clouds cushioning the sun above the horizon. I didn't have to try. I was composed immediately. The transformation was extraordinary in its power and its speed. I felt safe, calm and peaceful. I could think calmly if I wanted but, more importantly, I could *feel*. I could appreciate beauty and I could feel humour again. I chuckled at just what an amazing tool this stone circle was. The need to analyse why just wasn't there. I felt good again – for the first time that day – and that was all that mattered.

With the sun a fist and a half from the horizon I decided that I had achieved enough for day one and turned my attention to sleeping. With a dried branch I swept out the cave floor and cleared my bed space of animal faeces. I did feel ridiculous housekeeping naked but at least no one could see me doing it.

I knew I would surely be cold with no bedding on the cave floor and looked around me to see what was available. It had not rained for some time and all over the cliff face were clumps of dry, coarse grass. My plan for warmth was hatched immediately;

in the daylight that was left I would gather as much grass as I could and sleep like a horse in a hay-filled stable. The grass had shallow roots in the rock face and came away easily in my hands in big clumps. The warm light of the evening sun watched over my last activity on that first day until I was content that I had enough grass to cover me and keep me snug.

As the sun brushed the horizon I sat in the dusty poo, spooned out some gelatinous immature coconut flesh with my fingernails and ate like an ape. I allowed myself to think of home for the first time. Of those I had left behind: Amanda, my beautiful new fiancée, and her two kids whom I had so quickly found myself loving so much. Immediately I became homesick and again asked myself what had possessed me to commit to such an absurd challenge. Why was I doing this? Why wasn't I at home reading Roald Dahl stories to the kids or sharing a bottle of wine with Amanda? What was I trying to prove and to whom?

As the light faded I realised that I had to stay in one place. I had no torch and no fire and would be restricted to the cave until dawn. The cool wind stirred and circled around the open cave. I turned the camera on, flicked it into infra-red and immediately realised that I had in fact got a sort of a torch. At first I questioned the morality of using the 'torch' when I wasn't actually filming but quickly ditched any such concerns; why make my situation harder than it already was by imposing silly rules?

Feeling very much like an animal cowering from danger, I lay down in the dirt and tried to pull the grass over me so as to stop the sharp draught chilling my exposed skin.

After five minutes of adjustments I lay perfectly still looking up at the blackness. I ran through my checklist: I was dry, warm(ish), hydrated and protected from the elements if the weather turned bad. I hadn't eaten much but I wasn't hungry.

Food seemed less essential for the moment and I was filled with a feeling of 'so far so good'. I felt too overwhelmed to be happy. There was simply too much to think about – all my plans for tomorrow. I wasn't sad, though. Today had been kind to me and I was in a better position on the first night than I had previously thought possible. I was functioning – that was all that mattered.

The idea of falling asleep immediately was always going to be an optimistic one. Don't look for hay bedding in Marks & Spencer's; you won't find it, and for good reason. It's incredibly itchy. But it's a trade-off: itch or freeze. The floor was gritty, hard and inconveniently sloped. I'd just got as comfortable as I could when I sensed a large spider crawling over my chest. I kept a stick beside me to beat away intruders. Paranoid, but comforting.

It was a time to sleep and build up my energics but, in my physical stillness, questions and worries came flooding into my brain.

I went over all the things that I knew I had to do the next day but, as the blackness thickened, my thoughts became more complex and fear-laden and I resigned myself to the fact that this was going to be a long dark night. Could I survive on my own? Where was my composure? Where would I build my camp? What was the rest of the island like? Had I only got through the Amazon because of the assistance that I'd had? Was I mentally strong enough to deal with the intensity of my situation? Had I finally committed to something that I was not able to deal with? Why were there so many questions? This may seem a little bit of an overreaction – I'd only been there a few hours after all – but sixty days! Two months! If I'm honest I have to admit I wanted to go home right there and then.

With my back bare to the gritty floor of the cave I tried in vain to switch off and fall asleep. I snuggled deeper into the corner of the cave and rearranged my hay bedding over me as the anxieties ran round my head.

I must eventually have fallen asleep because I awoke in the night shivering violently. My bedding had gone and I was completely exposed to the night and to the gusts of cold wind that eddied around the back of the cave. With no idea of the time, I felt around for the grass and rearranged my bedding, then tried to go back to sleep. As I lay awake, staring into the black night, the wind grew stronger. My grass became less effective as the ferocity of the gusts increased and my sense of being in control in the safety of the cave disintegrated and blew away with the dust.

In a snap I decided I needed to be out of the wind and so I felt my way down to the beach and tried to bury myself in the sand. I had remembered an Aboriginal story about some of them being caught out late and burying themselves in the surface layer of the sand to cut out the chill of the wind. My sand was damp, however, and as I dug myself a trench with my hands I became anxious that this was the wrong choice. I lay in my self-dug grave and heaped the damp sand over me from my toes upwards until I was covered up to my nipples. The wind was not detectable on my lower body but I was cold and I could feel heat being conducted away from me by the wet sand.

I deliberated, worried, gave myself time limits and subsequently talked myself out of them. After at least an hour I admitted defeat and broke the wet sand cast. I felt tired, inexperienced and unsure of everything. Gibbering with cold, my jaw shaking uncontrollably, I climbed back into the cave where I questioned not only my situation but also myself. Doubts crept into my head and gnawed at my confidence and sense of worth. I worried and turned and shivered all night. There was no way out – no fire, no blanket, no warm clothes to pull on. I felt exposed and utterly helpless.

Reflecting on that first night I was no more comfortable or composed than a lost animal. All I could do was lie in the dust and wait for morning. It was so much more than unsettling – I felt like I was unravelling – hopelessly out of control and seemingly without the ability to compose myself. But I was dry and alive. That would have to do for now.

CHAPTER 2
WATER

11

Through my closed eyelids I started to become aware that the darkness was diminishing and the sky was filling with light. I could hear the waves crashing on to the beach below me. I could also make out another set of waves crashing on the reef about 400 metres offshore. The background static was irregular and unrelenting.

I allowed my eyelids to raise – the only curtains to my open-air world. No other part of me moved as I slowly absorbed the scene before me.

What a view.

My rocky doorstep touched down into a front lawn of soft sand speckled with small crab hills and their corresponding wispy trails. Cushioned between the gently lapping white water on the beach and the coarser defences of the outer reef was a breathtaking lagoon. Protected by the reef's fortifications, the surface ripples shimmered peacefully. Beyond the reef, the darker waters didn't look so inviting.

For the first time, the thought of a storm struck me. That'd be fun. A calm night had been difficult enough. If there was a proper tropical storm, there'd be no prospect of help from anywhere. 'Let's not think about the things that might happen, let's concentrate on the here and now,' I told myself.

I propped myself up on my arms. Two starlings chatted politely as they darted in and out of a tiny nest above my head.

'And it begins,' I thought to myself as I registered that I had made it through the first night. Only fifty-nine to go.

Brushing the coating of fine dust and straw off my goose-bumped chest, stomach and legs I stood up and stretched. I reached for the camera, flipped out the screen and flicked the power on. I was still shivering as I began my daily monologue.

'Just put some clothes on!' was my first instinct of the day. 'But I haven't got any.' Despite the fact that there was no one there I felt naked and exposed. I felt distinctly uncomfortable and needed to do something about it. I picked up a rock that was whiter than the walls of the cave and etched two vertical lines to indicate that this was day two. My half-eaten coconut was covered in tiny black ants.

I powered on the Spot tracking device and pressed the 'All OK' button. The communication seemed inadequate. I wanted to write a long letter about how I'd fared on night one. I wanted to sit down and have a good natter with the production crew about how surprised I'd been by my own periods of near-panic, at how apprehensive I felt, about how real and unpleasant this all seemed. But I was on my own. That desire to be understood or to be listened to would remain unfulfilled for the next two months.

OK, introspection time over, Ed – get started. Have a drink. I gingerly climbed down out of my cave, ever conscious that if I cut my feet I had no antiseptic or plasters. I made my way to the coconut tree that I'd depleted the day before and easily dislodged another green fruit from the tree. After the routine twenty seconds of primal smashing like a gorilla I held the husk to my lips and drank the sweet fluid.

As I came up for air I looked around me and noticed that the rocks were covered in small black sea snails. 'I can eat those,' I thought. As long as they didn't make me sick I'd found myself a good protein-filled meal for breakfast. Excellent.

I picked a handful of snails from a rock the size of a cow that was half buried in the sand. I then took a smaller rock – the size of a tennis ball – and brought it down with a crack on the first snail shell. The rock disintegrated on contact but the snail was completely unscathed. 'That's not a great sign,' I thought to myself as I examined the ruins from my attack. I was very aware that I had no knife and that I would have to make myself some sort of basic cutting tool in order to be able to carry out the simplest of tasks. The fragility of the first rock worried me and I searched for a more solid alternative.

As I weighed up my options I began to realise that there were two main types of rock – a porous and brittle one that looked like dead coral, and a denser volcanic rock of which the island appeared to be composed. I found myself a similar sized piece of the latter and tried once to separate my first snail from its home. The shell shattered. I picked the body clean of the eggshell-like fragments, popped it into my mouth and swallowed. Not so bad, I thought – so I tried a second.

At that stage common sense coughed politely to attract my attention and put forward the proposition that it might be wise to wait a little while to see if I had any reaction to these first two snails before eating a whole housing estate of them. I grudgingly conformed to good sense.

Head up and looking about the beach, I decided to explore again. Where I was, the island rose directly out of the back of the beach behind me in the form of huge vertical cliffs that were shielding me from the hidden morning sun. I ventured round the island with the ocean on my left and the steep cliffs on my right. Reassuringly, there were *lots* of snails. Even if I didn't find anything else to eat I suspected that I could live for sixty days on coconut and snails alone, so this was comforting. It offered a more balanced diet than many students manage.

As I walked further I noticed an obvious crack in the face of the rock on my right. Below the crack the rock face was darker. As I moved closer my instincts picked up on something important and I started to smile again. Camera on. Lens cap off. Press record ...

'This is exciting.' My gut instinct immediately told me what I'd found. I am a geographer and I knew that a fault in the rock like this could only mean one thing. Fresh water. As I inspected the crack it became obvious that a small hollow had been chipped out of the rock by visiting islanders so that the water collected in a shallow recess. Of course I'd known there had to be a source of water on the island and that I just needed to find it – but this could not have been a more important find. Fears of failure in the first few days because of dehydration disappeared as I tried to get my mouth into the small rock pool. With a short slurp I got a slug of water that was definitely not salty. 'That is fresh water!' I announced. 'But something tells me I'd better clean that out first,' I spluttered as I spat out sediment and sand.

I could immediately see the potential for using some cordage to act like a wick and draw the water into a container, but for now I picked up the biggest giant clamshell I could find and took it down to the water's edge. I filled it with seawater and gingerly carried it back to the seep to use as a flush to clean out the stagnant water. Once it was cleaned, I stood back and savoured the importance of having found a source of water. Granted it was not actually flowing – rather, it was an imperceptible excretion of dampness into a hollow – but it was fresh and my spirits were duly raised.

My mental tick list came back into play and I pondered my current state of affairs. I had found a fresh water source. I had drunk a mouthful and cleaned it out. I'd also eaten two snails and, as yet, had no negative reaction to them. I'd drunk the contents of a green coconut and I'd eaten some jelly-like goo from inside it. For a first morning on an island things were looking not at all bad.

Ever conscious of the need to record the intricacies of how I was coping with the event mentally, I spoke a monologue to the camera: 'It's funny how my mind works. I just walked past the cave and my urge was to go and sit in it, as already it is my base, my home. But I had to tell myself – you don't need to go and sit down – you have things to do. But all I wanted was to just go and sit.' On reflection, I think there is a natural urge to make a home and to delineate a space that is your own. Once established in this unknown and unsettling new world, my instincts made me want to withdraw into my safe shell where the possibility of danger was lower and the variables were limited. But fight this instinct I must.

It was time to do something both utterly essential and yet, from a survival perspective, completely gratuitous. I decided that my nakedness needed addressing and that I would look to make myself a grass skirt. Having been to Australia to visit Harold and Jeremy only recently I knew that I could make a grass skirt and that all I needed was to find a beach hibiscus plant. I walked back towards the cave and then beyond so that the ocean was now on my right and the interior of the island to my left. The rock face soon gave way to a tree line of coconuts and other green foliage. As I drew closer I could easily recognise the large round leaves of beach hibiscus. It was the predominant bushy plant beneath the palm trees.

Beach hibiscus is amazing because the bark is so flexible and yet so strong that it can be used as cordage without any processing at all. I simply removed a branch, bashed the bark with another stick until it loosened it from the wood and then I peeled away the bark as easily as skinning a banana. No plaiting or modifications of any kind were needed, and each inch-wide strand was strong enough to tow a car. When split longitudinally into thinner strips, beach hibiscus can be used as cord and knotted very easily due to its flexibility.

Making a grass skirt is easy. You take a strip of bark long enough to go around your waist and string it between two branches like a clothes line. You then take more strips and tie them on to the clothes line with a simple overhand knot, the type of knot a child would automatically do without ever having been taught anything – simply the very first stage of tying your shoes – but pulled tight around the clothes line. You do this until you have tied enough strands of bark on the line to cover yourself. Nothing could be more straightforward.

What happened next is therefore perhaps a good indication of how all over the place I was at this stage. After tying about twenty strips of bark to my clothes line I came to the conclusion that this was taking too much time and that I should be doing something more 'essential' to my survival. The skirt would so far definitely not cover anything and so I panicked and grabbed some grass and decided to knot the grass into the bark, as if making a grass blanket. I was mixing two methods and was now trying to create a solid front to the 'skirt' so that my cobs could not be seen through it. What resulted was essentially a square grass sporran that sat in front of my tackle and coarsely scratched at it and my thighs. I looked like Ed McTwat.

It was uncomfortable, it was difficult to walk in, it exposed me whenever I sat down, it did not cover me from behind at all, and most importantly – when you are filming a documentary for Discovery Channel to be seen in two hundred countries around the world – it looked bloody daft. This was to be my first badly thought through and poorly constructed project of the day.

'That's ridiculous, Ed,' I reported as I did a silly hip-wiggle dance for the camera to pretend that I was happy and didn't mind that it looked stupid. I did mind, a lot, but I had rushed it (and bodged it) and now felt ever more pressured to get on with something else. I believe it was about two or three days before I regained the composure to fully admit to myself that my skirt was terrible and to make another one. To make a good one in the first place would have taken only fractionally longer than my absurd sporran attempt; and in the end I spent far longer because, of course, I had to make *two* skirts. The whole episode offers an insight into my mental state at the time. Rather than calmly solving a problem, I created more worry and conflict for myself.

This state of indecision and doubt made me afraid that I didn't have the ability to cope and this made me think more and beat myself up and get down and depressed. I was listening to the thousand dissenting voices in my head – the noise of the tangled brain – instead of listening to my one true voice, my gut instinct. But in this state I hadn't the perspective even to identify what was going on.

I tiptoed through the decaying coconut shells and into the island's jungle perimeter. Inside the tree line I immediately spotted several red-topped plastic bottles standing out against the leaf litter. As I scanned the forest floor I saw perhaps ten or fifteen bottles that had been washed up by the last spring tide. The scene was unsightly and a disgusting reflection on the cleanliness of the oceans but it was also very obviously fortunate for me.

Every bottle had a top on it as clearly only the bottles that had trapped air inside would float. This meant they were intact and could be used to store water. As I began to collect the bottles I threw them into a small cleared area of forest floor. One bottle, two bottles, three bottles, a broken flip-flop, four bottles, a polystyrene fishing float, five bottles, a plastic hair gel tub. My Womble treasures stacked up fast. I allowed myself to bask in the comfort of a dream-like situation where I could be sitting in my cave and smugly glance over at twenty or thirty litres of fresh water reserves. I cannot describe the sense of reassurance I derived from such a seemingly boring discovery.

To boot, one of the Coke bottles had a plastic straw in it. Like a kid finding the free gift in a packet of cereal, I smiled a wide thank you to the skies. I could see that it could be used for drinking water from the otherwise inaccessible rock hollow at the bottom of the seep. This old plastic straw was valuable and I would treasure it.

Back on the beach I squinted through the burning sunshine wondering where to go next. I didn't know what was on the far side of the vast rocky headland and so, with the ocean still on my right, I made my way over a slippery as glass wave-cut platform. Crabs scuttled out of my way and under rocks. They were everywhere. I knew that eating raw crab meat was an invitation to serious food poisoning but it was going to be crab soup heaven if I managed to get a fire lit.

The soft wind gently played at the hairs on my bare chest as I came round the cliff face and on to a stunning smaller beach

– the sand glaring white. It was picture-postcard beautiful, as if that mattered. I quickly checked the height of the palm trees to see if the coconuts were accessible and then returned to the cliff face to check for fresh water seeps.

The flat expanse of rock that made up the big platform at the base of the rocky outcrop was incredibly slippery. A fine coating of dark green slime meant that I could have almost ice-skated across it. Standing was hard enough, let alone walking over it to search for fresh water. I tried to work out geologically how the water could be channelled down through the rock to a further seep. Inevitably my bare feet eventually shot forward and I fell hard on my bare bum and jarred my hips on the unforgiving surface. My sense of humour didn't enjoy the particular slapstick comedy. I felt sorry for myself lying pathetically on the slimy black rock and decided that my explorations were over for the day. At least I hadn't seriously injured myself.

I returned to my own rock seep near the cave and sipped water using a small spoon-shaped clamshell as if I were eating a bowl of soup. The fresh water tasted healthy and clean as it ran down my dusty throat. The sky darkened and I looked out to sea. A grey wall of rain was approaching and it made me realise that I had no means of harvesting it.

In the Amazon, a heavy downpour had saved us on several occasions when we had run out of water and there were no rivers in sight. We had simply erected our bashas (tarpaulins) between the trees and put improvised collection pots (anything that would hold water) under the corners to collect the rain that fell on this large surface area. Using my camera's rubber dry bag I had collected thirty litres of water one evening in only about ten minutes. But here I had no tarp or any other water-proof material.

On earlier expeditions to Belize teaching jungle survival I had made rudimentary rain collection devices by using palm leaves to make a large surface area on a simple wooden frame and collecting the run-off water. I decided to use this principle and adapt it to local vegetation.

As ever, the coconut palm was the obvious candidate. When I looked at an individual palm branch I could see that each one had a natural gully that led to the main stem. If I could position the palms so that the rain would flow down the leaves to the stem, and then down the stem to the tip where it would drip or pour into a clamshell, I would be on to a winner. In theory.

Without a knife or machete I looked around for something with which to cut down a palm branch. By now I had established the nature of the rocks on the island – either soft and crumbly or hard and volcanic – but I could see immediately that neither could be knapped like flint into an axe or primitive cutting tool. It would have been like trying to make a blade out of a concrete paving slab. I had been told by one of the Fijian boatmen that if they are stuck without a machete they smash a giant clamshell and use the fragments as a crude blade but I had not seen this method in action.

I took a clamshell about the size of a standard casserole dish and slammed it with all my might down on to the rocks at my feet. It emitted a dull clunk and remained in one piece.

Try again.

This time I held the shell above my head and with all the force I could muster I hurled it on to the ground. This time the shell splintered and broke into two bits, each as blunt as Old Harry. I took one half and again slammed it into the rocky beach. It fractured again and splintered into something resembling a blade. With enough applied force I might be able to use it like a hand axe to cut through a palm.

Using this most primitive of tools to cut palms I soon managed to skin my knuckles. The edge was dull and required considerable effort – it was more tearing through the palm than cutting – but it worked, especially if I bent the palm back to apply tension to one side first before striking it. This made removing quite large palms manageable.

As I was catching my breath between palms a small gecko moved on the bark of a tree directly in front of me. Without hesitation I snapped my hand forward and trapped the little animal between my fingers and the bark. I was surprised how easy it had been to catch and found myself standing with the gecko in hand before I'd even had the chance to consider whether I actually wanted it.

I had set the camera up a few metres away in the sand and I moved towards it and lay down to show the little creature to the camera. 'It's obviously meat,' I thought to myself. 'I can eat this.' Clearly I'd never eaten a gecko before but it would be a good source of protein and so I decided I would. I briefly deliberated about whether it needed gutting and then just opted for squeezing it from the neck downwards to force all the excrement from its anus. Don't look for that in a Jamie Oliver cookbook, you won't find it.

I wiped the mess on a leaf with my fingers and then chucked the lizard in my mouth. It took a bit of chewing before swallowing and tasted more like I'd bitten my tongue than I'd eaten food. The little tail was still wriggling on the ground so I brushed off the sand and ate that too.

My structure for trapping rainwater reminded me of the little pigs' house that was built out of straw. Badly thought through and poorly constructed, project number two looked pathetic really and I doubted it would still be standing in the morning. But I'd made something and I'd eaten a gecko so I tried not to be too hard on myself about it.

My rainwater trap wobbled unsteadily in the wind and reminded me that I wasn't really much closer to getting a constant supply of water. In the meantime I needed a long pole with a Y-shaped fork at the end to help me dislodge coconuts from trees. My new clamshell was put to use once more. I found a tree that was long and thin and that forked at a height that would be useful for me. I then set about cutting down my first tree with a clamshell.

To reiterate, this was by no means a knapped blade such as you could produce from flint. It was simply a break that produced an edge that was less than ninety degrees and could be used with force to chop at things. It was about as sharp as a spoon and if I hadn't been worried about my teeth it might have been quicker to try and bite the tree down.

Each clean strike would do no more than dent the tree. Each miss would take yet more skin off my knuckles. I attempted to work my way around the trunk, creating a ring of dents, that then became a ring of deeper wounds, that then became a tiny trench around the tree, until it was eventually damaged enough to put my shoulder to the trunk and snap it over. This first tree took me about fifteen minutes and used all of my energy. Once it was felled, I trimmed off the branches by snapping them with my hands until I stood tall with a short, crude Y-pole in my hands.

I stood beneath a tree from which I'd previously not been able to reach the coconuts and positioned the fork at the point where the green stalk joined the coconut itself. Then I shoved upwards with two hands ... and watched the coconut rise up and flop back down again like some extremely resilient green, floppy testicle. I shoved again, applying force as sharply as possible so as to jolt the fruit free. By now, sweat was running into my eyes and I was being showered with bark and dead wood. Each thrust felt like valuable energy lost and I began to become frustrated and short-tempered. Eventually, however, I had some luck. The stalk snapped and a coconut plummeted into the sand with a hard thump. My first castration completed, I moved on to the next until I had five green fruits ready to drink.

I found a sharp edge in a small cliff that was at chest height and used it to smash the coconuts in order to be able to access the water while still standing up. These fruits were the best so far, with plentiful clear liquid inside. For the first time I felt like I was properly hydrating myself.

With fluids inside me I decided to eat ten snails. I'd not reacted at all to the first two and wanted to keep my energy levels as high as possible. I stood by a rock and cracked each little shell, peeled it like a hard-boiled egg and swallowed it whole. They were a bit gritty but seemed to do the job. I felt as if I was slowly taking control back from the island. I might have expended more energy collecting and preparing them than I got from eating them but there was protein and animal fat entering my body and that was reassuring.

Before I did anything else, I stowed away my precious plastics stash in my cave. In a world in which I felt so much at the whim of fate I strove to regain control and grab hold of the reins when-ever possible.

I took the flip-flop and examined the broken thong part around which the big toe goes. The rubber had perished and become brittle but I could easily see how I could replicate it with nylon cord from one of the fishing floats that I'd collected. The result was uncomfortable but at least the sole stayed on my foot. I now had one shoe and a grass sporran, the kind of things people get forced to wear on stag nights. Ironically, for me it was a step towards dignity.

I shovelled down some brown coconut. For some reason I didn't like the flavour or texture. Along with the snails this was the first proper ingestion of calories after the slippery coconut jelly of last night and yet I could only manage to eat a third of the fruit before abandoning it in the sand.

Feeling the sun overhead, I registered that before I explored more of the island I needed to protect myself from its rays. The fine powder on the floor of the cave might make a paste and I could smear myself with that. It was probably the result of the degradation of decades of animal poo and rock fragments falling from the ceiling but it would have to do. I carried a clamshell full of the powder to the water's edge, mixed it into a paste as best I could and rubbed the odorous lotion all over my shoulders, neck, head and face in one large mud pack, or, rather, poo pack. It definitely wasn't clay – but it would be better than no protection at all from the burning sun. I swivelled my itchy sporran around to cover my increasingly red bottom.

The plan for supporting my filming for sixty days without anyone contacting me in any way was as follows. There was a 'dropbox' on the east of the island in an old disused campsite that I named Lemon Camp for its being the site of two medium-sized, but out of season, lemon trees. This dropbox had been built by the clan and comprised a small ring of rocks with a wooden board on top to keep the worst of the rain off. The crude lid was held in place by two more heavy volcanic rocks. The dropbox was my only non-emergency access to the outside world.

The plan was that once a week – on prearranged days – I would walk over the island to Lemon Camp and leave all my used compact flash cards and dead batteries in the dropbox. I would make sure I was then free of the area by mid-morning. The only crew member, Steven, who was living on Komo, would then come in and collect the items at midday, by which time I would be well clear of the camp. In their place he would leave fresh batteries and clean memory cards for the video cameras. If essential he would also leave production messages such as 'The sound on camera two is on the wrong setting. Check that it is set to "External mic".' No messages of support or encouragement were allowed, only those necessary to ensure the footage coming back was usable in the edit suite.

Who'd made these rules? I suppose I had; they were driven by me. I was adamant that this was going to be a reputable survival project that would stand up to scrutiny. Would anyone have known if I had received support messages? Probably not – but the rules made me feel like we were doing things properly and honestly.

In the middle of the afternoon I would then return to the dropbox to collect the items that would enable filming to continue. This system also meant that the production crew back in the UK, and, in theory, survival experts all over the world, would be able to start to view footage while I was still very much going through the ordeal on the island. The other use for the dropbox was that if a camera developed a fault I would leave it in there and hope that Steven, the one-man crew, could fix it or replace it.

As I had never been to the island before, initially I had no idea where Lemon Camp even was. I did not know the shape of the island or upon which shore I had been dropped. I did not know how long it would take me to walk over the island or even whether I could find a route across it as there were no paths. I decided that the best option was to walk around the coast on my first visit to Lemon Camp. That would also give me a feel for the size and shape of my new home.

This first drop was only a drop-off of cards and dead batteries – I didn't require a new supply so soon. It was scheduled so that the very valuable first-day footage could be whisked back to London and so that the production team could correct anything that I was doing wrong – filming-wise. It was Sunday and the first actual weekly exchange was scheduled for Tuesday.

The tide was fairly low and I set out around the south of the island, land rising to my left, sea on my right. Past the vast rock headland at the south of my beach was the one I had already scouted once. It was shorter than my beach and crescent-shaped, giving it a neater, more contained feel than my long sprawling mass of sand. At the southern tip of this beach I was forced into the shallow waters by the sheer rocks and waded around a craggy point where large coloured fish darted through the most perfectly blue sandy ocean pools. The water lapped my grassy sporran at the deepest point and then began to get shallower again as I broke on to a further expanse of yet more golden sand.

The significant difference on this new beach was that I could now see Komo, the closest island to Olorua, where Steven and the Komo tribe were living. This shouldn't have surprised me as I had seen Olorua from Komo, but I had forgotten this, and so it did. As I saw the friendly green island I was hit by a bleak wave of isolation. The idea that just eight nautical miles across the sea was a warm community that was chatting and fishing and cooking together made me feel distinctly lonely. I wanted to be among them. For the first time I thought of Olorua as my captor. Her shores and the sea beyond were my prison bars and my minefield respectively. To have a conversation all I had to do was swim eight miles through tiger-shark-infested waters. Yeah, right.

Why did I find being alone so sorrowful? It wasn't as if I was here for ever.

The beach ran out and I clambered over sharp rocks and loose pebbles. I turned half left again to be presented with a much harsher view. A shore of large jet-black rocks was being assaulted by a prevailing weather system from the south-east. The wind was stronger and the waves were taller and darker as they crashed into the crumbling coastline. With a chill on the exposed skin of my torso I leaned to the right into the gusts and battled on up the beach until I was halted by an appreciable interruption in the tree line to my left.

Standing in the break of the tree line at the top of the rocky beach with my back to the ocean, Lemon Camp may as well have had a big sign directing me in. I faced a pleasant flat clearing tucked into the forest, partially rimmed by thorny lemon trees. There were obvious signs of human activity – a long length of bamboo had been wedged between two tree forks to act as a ridge pole for a tarp that had long since been folded up and taken home. There was litter: buried crisp packets and old fizzy drinks bottle tops. There were small lengths of perished rubber half buried in the soil. In the centre was what looked like a cairn with a lid – I had found my dropbox.

The area was large and flat but it was exposed to the prevailing wind on this side of the island and so I was surprised that it had been chosen as the camp that the Fijian clan had used on their visits in the past. There must have been some marine advantage for mooring boats here. Although I'd already acknowledged that I could not camp there (because the no-human-contact dropbox system required that I stay away) I was happy because I would not have wanted to anyway. My cave was better protected. The lemon trees bore no fruit but I broke a leaf and held it to my nostrils. The scent was powerfully fresh and lemony. I knew that if I could get a fire going these leaves would make a wonderful clean, zesty tea.

The two rocks on top of the lid of the dropbox thumped to the ground one after another. I lifted the piece of flimsy plywood to reveal a yellow rubber dry bag. Squeezing the chunky plastic clips I unrolled the watertight bag and tipped the contents on to the packed earth. In the bag was an empty cool box – an Esky.

Nothing else. I should not have been surprised as I knew how the system was going to work but somehow I had thought that there would be a note saying that I was doing really well, or perhaps a nice packet of chocolate biscuits. But, no: the box was empty.

I placed my only two dead batteries and my blue nylon wallet of used compact flash (CF) cards into the cool box and flipped the white plastic lid shut. As I did so I wanted to reach out for help. The fresh water source – as positive as it was – was bugging me. *'Was that it?!* Was that really my sole source of fresh water?' I wanted reassurance that there was another, more plentiful source – or perhaps a forecast that it would definitely rain tomorrow.

I had a momentary fit of anger at the production team. What a bunch of idiots, stranding me on an island with no water! I suspected they'd first come to recce the island after there had been a sustained period of rain. My worry was that they thought there was sufficient water here – the tiny flow I'd come across had probably been a veritable waterfall when the team visited. What if they didn't know that they had inadvertently put me in a much more difficult situation than they'd intended to?

First drop done, I continued around the coastline in the same direction so as to complete a full lap. At this stage I had no mental picture of what the island looked like. I had a rough idea of east and west, and therefore north and south, from the sun and so I knew I was walking from the east of the island back round to the west via the northern tip. I did not know how long it would take or whether the height of the tide would allow passage.

With the shore on my left, the crashing waves on my right and jagged rocks under foot I ventured once more into the unknown. The end of the beach was a buttress of the same volcanic rocks that had blocked me and forced me into the shallow water. I held the camera high so as not to get any of the salt water inside and slowly felt my feet along the rigid coral seabed. Sometimes I was in the water, sometimes there was a section of sandy beach, sometimes I was climbing over big rocks. I registered everything I saw: sections of washed-up bamboo, more old bottles and fishing floats, huge pieces of driftwood.

After squeezing around a headland and over an expanse of flat coral I arrived on a bigger beach and was shocked for a moment to see footprints in the sand. A sense of annoyance that someone else might spoil the purity of my experience, and an infantile hope that I might bump into a friendly face, swept through my mind. Could this be a fisherman? A local from another island? Steven? Had something gone wrong? The suspense was unceremoniously deflated as I realised they were my own footprints and I'd almost completed my first circuit of the island. I glanced up to the left and saw the rock seep; fifty metres further on I knew was my cave.

I'd completed a successful circumnavigation of the island and I was happy for a further box to be ticked in terms of amassing more information. But my baby steps frustrated me and I wanted to be in control of my new world. I now knew there were no watercourses or streams coming down to the shore. There was no escaping the fact that my one source was not really big enough and my hopes of others were fading. I felt the need to find out more but caught a glimpse of my reddening shoulders and decided to get out of the sun. The last thing I needed was sunburn.

I was both fascinated and lifted to see that the seep had filled again in just a couple of hours. I extracted about 500ml of water which I rather elegantly drank like soup from the small shell. I calculated optimistically that, if it could fill 500ml in two hours, I had actually already found a water source that could provide me with all my water. My morale was propped up by the prospect of a constant supply of fresh water in return for a little careful management.

I wanted to ride this wave of positivity, to be constructive and make something to help me feel comfortable. I didn't have to deliberate as to what this would be because the thing I needed to master most of all was water. I had some – but I needed more of it.

The morning's drizzle had not returned but, prompted by the niggling at the back of my mind about how appallingly inept my first rain collection trap had been, I realised that I could make a far simpler rainwater collection system in about five minutes. I collected every large clamshell I could find, washed them in the sea and laid them all out on the sand above the high-tide mark for rainwater to collect in. That was it. It was so easy it was silly but I knew instantly that if we got rain I would have a guaranteed five to ten litres of water ready to drink.

I felt as if the list of things to tackle was never-ending. Starting from scratch meant that I couldn't focus on one thing and really sink my teeth into it. I had to flit from one necessity to another to build a sure footing in this unstable new world. I was being jack of all trades and master of none, but with no one else to trade with I had no option but to do everything myself.

The next essential that I wanted to address was the cold at night. I had to concede that a fire might take some days to light so I opted to make myself a blanket and started on badly-thought-through project number three. I stripped some more beach hibiscus for cordage that I would weave into a blanket. The method would be exactly that same as for my scratchy sporran. I would tie a length of the bark between two trees, attach several further lengths with simple knots and then tie the clumps of dry grass into the strands. As soon as I started it became apparent that the process would take a huge amount of both bark and grass and that progress was going to be very slow. In an hour I'd probably made a blanket that was six foot long, but still only two inches wide.

Fears and concerns about wasting yet more time caused further doubts and panicky thoughts. Was I deliberately trying to make a mess of things?

'You can't cut any corners, Ed – you need to put the effort in if you're going to survive,' I told myself. It might take me a long time to make this properly so I had to be patient.

I sourced more hibiscus poles, bashed them on a rock to loosen the bark and stripped them, producing loads more cordage. I made another little mission up to the top of Snail Rock (the spur where I sourced and smashed my snails – no point in overcomplicating the names) in order to collect more clumps of dry grass to tie into the strands. I sat back with my fledgling blanket and tried to be calm and patient as I wove in more strands of bark and more fistfuls of grass. In another hour and a half the blanket was a foot and a half wide and had the appearance and softness of a harsh-bristled doormat.

By now I'd spent the majority of the afternoon on this coarse blanket and decided that it was big enough for me to press pause for the day. I slung the scratchy doormat over my shoulder, gathered up the remaining grass in my arms to supplement the loose hay that I'd used the previous night and carried my bedding back to my cave. Knowing how important sleep was and that, so far, my blanket would only cover part of my body, I then set out back up the beach to cut more palm leaves that I could lay over my loose hay bed to help protect me from the piercing wind. I hauled back a huge armful to the cave in the gusty grey afternoon, leaving long sweeping trails in the sand.

I forced down some white flesh from a mature coconut and admitted to the camera that I wasn't bothered about eating and that all I craved was water. I also swallowed ten raw snails from the rocks. I was determined to ensure I had enough protein going in to keep my strength up.

'If I ever thought this was going to be easy I now officially take it back,' I told the camera as the last gritty gastropod passed my oesophagus.

I felt like I was an ant or a chicken. I was at that level, scratching around for the measliest amount of food and ferrying materials back and forth to try and make a nest to make myself crudely comfortable. I kept trying to do all this while not allowing myself to get dehydrated. It was bizarre – I'd already found a tree with which I reckoned I could make a fire, beach hibiscus, but there wasn't enough time in the day to investigate this further. Unless I got enough bedding in there I wouldn't sleep tonight. It was unbelievable how much effort was required to do all of this *and film it*.

Filming your own struggles is very weird. I think if I'd been dropped on the island with no camera I'd have fared much better. Without an audience I would be free to make my mistakes in private. I wouldn't dwell on worries or negative emotions as they wouldn't help me at all. But the viewer needs to understand the pressures and emotions in order to feel any empathy and so I had to make the invisible visible, and share every worry. Without such openness the resulting programme wouldn't only have been bland and superficial – it simply wouldn't have stacked up.

On the plus side the filming gave me a project beyond just surviving which at times helped to distract me. Talking to the camera could also be a consolation, a legitimate reason for speaking out loud when you're alone.

The pressure of not only going through the survival ordeal – the thirst, the hunger, the discomfort – but of producing, filming and hosting your whole programme was huge. As a result I never really relaxed unless I just said, 'Bollocks to it – I'm having a no-filming afternoon.' Then I would take off my grass skirt and just do what was needed to get by: collecting firewood, foraging, eating, etc. I felt indulgent, guilty even, having these times by myself. Bizarre, really, when I had sixty days entirely alone.

So as to be able to tuck the corners of the blanket in and ensure I got some sleep that night, I decided I needed to excavate a section of the cave floor so that I was not resting on a slope – constantly bracing myself from rolling down the hill and off the two-metre ledge was not the easiest thing in the world. I set out along the beach – and immediately forgot what I was doing it for. Halfway back I remembered that it was to get a stick and I cursed my lack of focus. A knife would have made things so much easier but I hacked the makeshift digging stick down with my clamshell fragment and shuffled slowly back to the cave, exhausted.

The shadows on the beach grew longer and the golden light warned me that my day was almost over. The sunsets on the island were spectacular, staining the sky the purples and reds of smashed fruit, the dying light deepening and darkening the blue of the sea. I'm not the first to have noticed that sunsets are a very romantic time. They seem sent to make you think of those you love and, inevitably, the transience of human existence, how lucky we are if we achieve a moment of connection with another human being. It's as if the day can only sustain such beauty for an instant and then, exhausted by the effort, collapses into night.

Practicalities drew me back to the present and away from the contemplation of my insignificance in the grand scheme of things and the woman I loved, Amanda, who I wished was with me.

I washed out my precious new straw with seawater and took it to the seep. The rock hollow had hardly filled at all since mid-morning and my heart sank at the sight. I was confused: I had been expecting another 400ml of fresh water before bed but I had barely 150ml. I gently positioned the straw so that it was at the surface of the water and sucked it but managed only a mouthful of sediment. After a day with some substantial disappointments this seemed to be a kick in the face.

With no option but to revert to coconuts, I used the stubby Y-pole to dislodge three that were greenish-brown. After expending energy smashing into them my frustration began to boil when I found they were all dry inside. I could feel the anger growing inside me about the water situation. Then I noticed another short coconut tree bearing very small green coconuts and reached up easily and picked them with my bare hand. Each small fruit yielded sweet liquid that I flushed down my throat until I was belching like a yob. They were amazing and could not have come at a better time. I even managed to leave the third for the morning.

Having gone from fierce anger to grateful elation in the space of thirty seconds I stood on the beach in the dying sun, almost feeling like dancing. This whole experience was bloody extraordinary.

I ate my ten snails in the cave. I had hoped that things might have gone better but as I sat swallowing those slimy, fatty mouthfuls I realised I'd actually achieved quite a lot. I flicked on the camera and recorded my thoughts: 'What most people don't realise is that when you've got nothing – absolutely nothing – your whole day is taken up maintaining your status quo. I'm going to have to set myself such small goals to achieve each day.' To help myself feel better I ran over the day's accomplishments. 'I've made a grass skirt of sorts, I've circumnavigated the island, I've made two rain-collection devices, the second of which may work, I've made a crude blanket, I've drunk green coconuts, and I've eaten coconut flesh and snails.'

On reflection, it seemed like a good day's work and I wondered at my tendency to focus on the failures. I seemed to be pretty hard on myself and was unreasonably expecting every-thing to be easier – a series of successes – to bolster my confidence in my own ability. Of course it was never going to be like that, and there were always going to be failures along the way as I'd never done this before. As a result my high standards had the detrimental effect of making me focus on the negatives because I wouldn't allow myself to enjoy the things that went well. I was too intent on punishing myself for my mistakes.

When you select a team for a tough expedition, you need to be very careful. Stressful situations make people fall out with each other – it's almost inevitable. The problem isn't the falling out, it's how you recognise what's going on and deal with it. You need to forgive and forget. When you're a team of one that's a little bit harder. And, let's face it, if you want to tear into someone and criticise them, you've got a lot of ammunition if the person you're attacking is yourself. It's not like you can hide any weakness or stupidity.

I was angry at myself and at the world. I was annoyed at not taking the preparations seriously enough; annoyed that I didn't recognise the tuberous roots here; annoyed that I didn't know the types of wood for making a fire; annoyed that I couldn't plait the palm leaves. I was annoyed that I didn't know if there were any alternative fresh water sources. I hadn't taken any genuine responsibility for what I was about to do. I'd just allowed myself to fall into a crazy idea with the lazy attitude that everything would be fine – it always was. Good things happen to me. But as I began to lose control I saw the gaping flaws in the way I made decisions and projected blame in my own life. I had to stop negatively lashing out at everything and start taking ownership of the situation I'd created. If not, my very own dream would mutate around me into a self-created nightmare.

As the last of the sun faded and the sky turned black I sat in my cave staring at the darkness. I hadn't enjoyed day two. I hoped I would enjoy day three more. Had my expectations been too high for this whole project? Was I actually capable of thriving and not merely surviving? I wasn't sure of anything any more.

The two starlings came in to nest for the night and did their best to reassure me that I was not entirely alone.

|||

I woke up at around 4 a.m. having been asleep since it got dark at six the previous evening. The bedding had come loose and the draught had woken me up but I'd slept for a body-and-soul replenishing *ten whole hours*. I groaned an indulgent half-smile as I stretched like a sleepy cat in the dust.

The extra bedding and excavating had worked and I had directly benefited from my efforts. By 7 a.m. I estimated that I'd remade the bed three times during the night but I considered that good in thirteen hours. No part of me wanted to move from my snug dark ball in the corner of the brightening cave.

I marked day three on the wall in chalky stone and watched the crabs scurry across the pristine morning beach. The sight made me want to focus on lighting a fire so that I could feast on roasted crab meat. But primal fear brought me back to the most important survival priority of all – finding sufficient fresh water. I could feel myself getting more dehydrated by the day. After all, the coconut water was not pure water – and I wasn't sure how long I should rely on it as my main source of hydration.

So I began my deliberations once more. Rainwater collection, on any significant scale, meant building a roof so that the expanse of waterproof material could act as an artificial catchment area that I could harness. So was the most sensible thing for me to focus on building a shelter? I considered this and was immediately brought back to the fact that I *had* a cave that worked well so that would be an unnecessary, and very time-consuming, task right now. So, with some relief, I decided to revert to focusing on finding the right wood with which to make fire.

This was already a survival situation, albeit one that I could have brought to an end at any moment, but that was a madness in itself. I didn't have enough water or food. I kept having to calm myself down but became exasperated with myself for having to sit in my stone circle time and time again. I couldn't sit down and calm myself down all day. I needed to do stuff – to be constructive – or I would never progress. Hence I started to slip into ignoring my feelings and busying myself in as many urgent tasks as possible to hide from them. 'I must make a plan for the day: I will enhance the seep so that I can collect more water; I will source and carve my fire sticks; and I will cover my body in clay so that I don't get burned. 'Let's go, Ed – let's go.'

On the face of it this looks constructive. I was taking positive action, after all. But there was unease and tension about everything I did. In a place where I should have been entirely in tune with what was going on inside me I either frantically sought distraction in physical tasks or otherwise seemed to latch on to frustration at others, belittling myself for my situation. I completely devolved responsibility and allowed my brain to take my frustrations out on something else rather than confronting what was really going on inside me with the intention of actually sorting it out. It takes a seasoned escape artist to hide from himself on an uninhabited Pacific island, but somehow I was finding a way.

I drank 500ml from the seep with the straw with the hope that I would get a further 500ml by lunchtime. That wasn't a bad start. I was in existence mode and this was raw existence. I took my remaining little green coconut and drank it with some brown coconut for flesh and ten snails. Once I had covered myself in the shitty powder from the bottom of the cave mixed with seawater I was ready to start the day. I laughed to myself. This was like some hideous reversal of a normal day. Get up, wash off the dirt in a lovely shower, dress and eat something nice. Here it was get up, cover yourself in shit, don't get dressed, eat something horrible.

By the time the sun was overhead I had collected several hand drill elements made from beach hibiscus and they were drying out on a rock in the sun. The long thin new stems would make great arrows and spears and, if left to dry out completely, I had been told they could even be used to make fire.

I felt my bowels gurgle. It seemed the most ecologically sound way of doing a poo was to go in the sea. It also meant that it would be washed away and not leave any dirty areas of the island, so it was hygienic, too. After I freed a reasonable-sized turd I realised that the sea was also a handy bidet. Nice one. With no soap, I would follow Islamic protocol and use one hand to eat and the other to wipe my bum. This would have to start tomorrow, though, as I'd just wiped my bum with my right hand and I didn't particularly want to restrict myself to eating with my left hand for the remaining fifty-seven and a half days.

At low tide I spent time looking for further fresh water seeps in the hope that I'd find one that wasn't too brackish. But every pool that I crouched down beside and lapped from like a dog turned out to be seawater. While out looking I also found a set of goat tracks on the beach – the tracks were too small to be deer. I ran through all the exciting options that catching a goat could mean: meat, fur, sinew ... I looked up the beach and saw something dark lying in the shallows. On inspection it turned out to be a dead kid goat. Its coat was soaked, matted and wet and covered in sand. Not knowing the cause of death I knew that I couldn't eat it but I could – in theory – get skin and sinew for cordage. I could even use the bone for making arrow tips or crude fishing hooks or needles. I wondered if it had died because it hadn't been able to drink from the rock seep that I was now drinking from.

I immediately realised that I didn't have a good enough cutting tool to skin the animal so I had no option but drive a small hole into its chest and rip it apart with my fingers. The fur came off easily, rather like a sock, once I'd got going, and I smashed its head open with a rock to get out the brains. Soaking a skin in the animal's brains and water can soften the hide to a more manageable, buckskin-like feel. I left the small, emaciated body on the rocks within sight of the cave to see if it attracted any scavengers. It was already beginning to smell and I was glad I hadn't attempted to eat any of the meat. I could use the bones and sinew from this carcass when I needed them.

It was mid-afternoon now, the sun beginning its slow slide into the water. I sat in the shade of the trees and worked on the fire drill elements with a small shell. Despite not having done any work on increasing the flow of the rock seep I had spent a long time searching for other sources and my fire apparatus was looking good drying in the sun. I was fairly content that I had accomplished what I'd planned to do that day and so, as I knew it would be high tide in the morning, and it would also be dropbox day, I decided that I would head up the hill and, rather than skirting the coast, try and find a route to Lemon Camp over the top of the island.

It was a bit of an excuse if I'm honest. I felt that I'd worked hard doing boring stuff and just wanted to climb and explore. Ten metres into the forest the island floor started to rise sharply. I immediately began using my hands to pull at roots and vegetation to scramble up the muddy bank. With my one shod foot I felt like a staggering drunk in the early hours of the morning who is ill equipped to deal with the exposing light of day. I could stand on sharper thorns and rocks but I slid out of the flip-flop regularly and snagged it on fallen branches. My bare foot needed less attention but slowed my progress as it was still tender and soft and felt every inch of the uneven ground.

For ten minutes I climbed and climbed uncertainly, like some creature evolving from the sea on to land. I'd hardly eaten and was also dehydrated and so my sense of exuberant exploration was somewhat dulled as I slipped and fell and panted hard.

Gradually, however, the ground began to level off and I found myself on the top of a high, forested spur. The waves in the distance could be discerned less clearly; I could hear the birds and the sound of my flip-flop crunching twigs. The size of a golf course fairway, the top of the island felt like another world to the noisy exposed coastline. It was completely covered in forest and the vegetation blocked any view from the top, wrapping this micro world in shimmering leafy paper. The trees were randomly spaced apart like in a mature Scottish forest and I could walk freely between them. Strange ideas went through my head. If people had lived up here they would have been mild, softly spoken, and would have invited me into their little homes in the tree trunks for a cup of tea. Steady, Ed! It seemed a bit early to be going off on nutty daydreams, but the association stuck, and the place became known to me as the Highlands.

In the centre of the Highlands stood the biggest, blackest tree on the island. The mammoth trunk spawned an entire marquee of twisted branches that were further supported along their beams by vertical roots that shot straight down to the forest floor. The structure could have housed a whole gang of merry men and I decided it would be an obvious feature that I could use to keep my bearings. It reminded me of a children's book by Enid Blyton that I vaguely remembered which revolved around a tree that was big enough for many people to live in. In the book the tree was so tall that its topmost branches reached the clouds and it was wide enough to contain small houses carved into its trunk. And so I came to refer to my enchanted tree on top of the island in the centre of the Highlands as the Faraway Tree. Fanciful or not, it was a key landmark.

Between the tree and me was a vague circle of rocks each the size of a large cauldron. The pattern was not perfect enough for me to be sure it was man-made and not random enough to be sure it wasn't. In front of the giant black tree the rocks took on the feel of an ancient ruin or ceremonial site and added to the mystery of this quiet and still space. I walked through the rocks and under the twisted eaves of the tree. My hands brushed aside dusty cobwebs and my shins scraped through small thorny grasses but my mind was as peaceful as if I'd just stepped into a church.

On the far side of the tree the ground seemed to fall away to the front and to the right. My internal compass told me that Lemon Camp would not be straight over this spur – that would bring me out too far north. From my recollections I estimated that I should head diagonally right from the crest of the hill and so I padded barefoot down the gentle slope to the right following nothing but gut instinct. It looked right. It felt right. There was no path and as I left the open Highlands the vegetation grew denser and thicker and I had to pick my way through by pulling aside branches and crawling under fallen trees on my hands and knees.

I felt intensely alive as I scanned the trees, absorbing every detail and fold of the land. My ears pricked up as a faint but distinct bleating rang through the forest. Senses now heightened, I moved as quietly as I could in the direction of the noise. I made sure that my feet didn't snap any twigs and placed each bare foot on the forest floor as if I was portraying 'stealth' in a mime.

The trees drifted past on either side of me as I floated forward on red alert. Before too long a small black and white juvenile goat emerged from the undergrowth only four metres away from me. It cocked its head towards me and paused as it registered what it was witnessing. I froze – adrenaline valves fully open, tunnel vision narrowing down to only the most essential field. Logic overtook instinct, as, although I realised the significance of the find, I also knew that I wasn't yet ready to catch a goat. I had no weapons with which to hunt an animal and I had no method of curing or cooking its meat. It would only go to waste. I gently moved towards the fragile-looking mammal and it started, cried out and ran off into the undergrowth. Two previously unseen larger goats returned the startled bleat and followed it out of sight.

As I write this I now know that there had been a herd of domesticated goats left on the island by the Komo tribe sixty years earlier. They had survived living off coconuts and leaves and had bred successfully, eventually becoming feral wild animals.

I kept the sun behind me and I knew that, as it was now afternoon, I was heading east. The light intensified and the distant waves grew louder, a breeze raising goose bumps on my skin. The slope kept falling away and in my mind the ocean was in front of me about thirty metres below. Gradually the spaces between the branches grew wider and glimpses of blue told me I was almost there. I pulled my way through the last branches and over the fragmented coconut husks and was hit by the blinding sunshine of a rocky beach with a very stiff wind in my face. I recognised the beach from the day before and knew that I was close to Lemon Camp. Black rocks the size of footballs made a giant jagged boulder field. Waves crashed into this rough coast with three times the force of the one that I'd left. Facing the ocean I looked along the beach to my right to see the prominent gap in the rocks running directly from the ocean to an opening in the tree line. A fallen tree that I'd made a mental note of the day before confirmed that I was indeed looking at the entrance to Lemon Camp.

That's remarkable – my inner compass is working! I praised myself. The odds of arriving out of the interior of the island less than ten metres north of the entrance to my intended destination had been stacked against me. Two sets of fresh footprints. Ah, maybe hold the self-congratulation. One set was barefoot and one set wore trainers. I knew immediately that at least one boatman and Steven had been here today. This was most unexpected. Was there something wrong? Had I messed up the days? The dropbox would hopefully tell the story.

In the dropbox was a small Ziploc bag containing a camera cleaning kit! I was so happy – a nice little soft paintbrush for removing dust, a lens cleaning cloth and a tiny bottle of lens cleaning fluid. It felt like Christmas to have this unexpected gift and there were six fresh batteries, too. I wasn't sure why they'd come today and not tomorrow – boredom or intrigue, probably, as the kit that was missing wasn't that urgent. Nonetheless, it was utterly reassuring to have seen signs of other human life and to receive a resupply. I was not being forgotten – there were people assisting from afar. It felt good to be reminded of that.

I stuffed my goodies into the Cinesaddle's marsupial pocket. A Cinesaddle is basically a bean bag the size of a small footstool that you use instead of a camera tripod to put the camera down on to film. It had a shoulder strap, and, handily for me, a large pocket for storing filming ancillaries. As the sun was getting low and the tide wasn't too high, I opted to return home via the shoreline. 'Goodbye, Lemon Camp – and signs of humanity.' I almost wanted to stay and savour the feeling of the presence of other people. It was clear to me I was already very lonely.

Instantly, and increasingly characteristically, I then changed my mind and decided to head back over the top of the island instead. Surely this would be a better use of my time as I could ensure that I could navigate across the interior of the island from both directions.

I scanned the back of the camp for signs of paths into the interior and quickly came across some saplings that had been cut with a machete. One led to another and I slowly crept away from the shore up the hill following a series of old crude markings. As I went I broke branches to show further signs of the path I had taken – I dragged obstructions like fallen branches out of the way. The path was twisting and hard to follow and eventually I just had to use my best guess as to which direction would lead me up to the benevolent Faraway Tree.

Doubt crept in as I started to lose height again. That wasn't meant to happen. Hang on – there is a clearing ahead and a snapped branch here. What?! My confidence tumbled as I real-ised I was back at the rear of Lemon Camp.

I had committed the classic mistake of blindly following signs of a path and believing (because I wanted it to) that it would lead me where I wanted to go. That had taken me another forty minutes or so.

So which way to go? I stared at the path I had taken almost three-quarters of an hour earlier with absolutely no confidence that if I tried again I would get any different outcome. The sun was blocked by the hill in front of me now and there were no shadows to use to navigate in the late afternoon on this eastern side of the island. Bugger. The one thing I did know for sure was that I could get back if I followed the coast. So I bottled a second attempt at finding the Highlands, hit the beach and turned left. On the way home I resolved to draw myself a map in the sand to properly ensure I understood where things were in relation to each other.

When I passed the seep I stopped for an evening slurp of fresh water after my adventure but once again the shallow rock bowl was almost empty. The straw was still there and no sign of goat tracks but I was confused that, once again, the water hadn't continued to fill up the rock bowl during the afternoon.

The low, looping flight of a kingfisher attracted my attention as it settled on a rock about ten metres in front of me. The familiarity of the distinctive black mask and white collar comforted me for a moment before my primal survival instinct came crashing in through the back door. Could I catch it and eat it? I'd heard of people leaving fishing lines with baited hooks on rocks to trap birds. The trouble was I didn't have any hooks or line. I considered improvising hooks with bone or thorns and joining many strands of beach hibiscus together but I knew that if I managed to get something like this constructed I'd want to catch some fish with it! For the moment I let it go.

I turned on the camera and a loud mechanical groaning noise announced the end of its life – never to work again. Day three and one of my two cameras was broken already.

The sun was now very low in the sky and golden light made my beach glow with warmth and tranquillity. Since I'd skinned a dead goat today and smeared sun cream made out of goat shit all over me, and I felt minging, I reckoned I deserved a bath. I unclipped my radio mic from my waist belt, tossed the scratchy sporran up the beach like a dead cat, and turned towards the rows of advancing waves. The sky was shades of pink and orange and the white water sparkled. I'd never considered myself a spiritual person but you do have to marvel at such incredible beauty – billions of years of colliding stars, cosmic dust, gravitational forces all combining to produce something so captivating, so calm and so alive.

Feeling indulgent and childish I ran naked into the waves, allowing them to trip me up and plunge me head first into the cool salty water. As my head went under the peace of being submerged swept up my entire body as if a switch had been turned off in my head. The sensation of being cleansed, not just of sweat and dirt, but of worries and fears, was unmistakable and I surfaced with the most innocent of wide grins on my face. Guilt at the extravagance of giving myself time to wash was carried away by the waves as I soaked up the power of investing some time in myself, of turning the cameras off and just lying in the ocean and splashing about. Of singing U2's 'Beautiful Day' at the top of my voice and finally allowing myself to be joyful and happy.

I knelt in the shallows with the sand under my knees and the water lapping at my back. In this state I was utterly grateful for everything that was happening. Out loud I thanked Amanda for her love, understanding and support – I could feel her still holding my hand; I thanked the kids for their pure, untainted love and their sacrifice of letting me go away; and I thanked my two Aboriginal friends, Jeremy and Harold, whose advice I was leaning upon so heavily at the moment. Not a religious man at all – in fact quite anti-religion in an argument – I also thanked God. Not an old bearded man on a cloud deciding my fate, not a second-hand God from a dusty book, but an all-encompassing energy that ran through me and connected me to everyone and everything. A sum of all the parts – and the spaces in between. A God based on my understanding of how everything seems to fit together and magically work. Whoever – whatever – my smile radiated pure gratitude and love into the water in front of me. I was a part of everything and I had nothing to fear. Crikey, three days in and I'd become a lentil-munching hippy.

Post-wash I examined my thighs and saw that they were chafed by the coarse grass sporran that I'd been using to protect my modesty. I needed to make a proper grass skirt to avoid getting sores on my thighs. With my soul accessed and my brain waiting dutifully silent, this was a clear and easy task that I would do tomorrow without drama.

And then, suddenly, I felt a desperate need to defecate and was concerned by a very runny stream of diarrhoea flowing on to the beach. Communing with the universe was at an end. To put it bluntly, how much water and nutrition was I losing out of my bottom?

Back in the cave I sat and contemplated my situation. My slow progress caused me constantly to question my own abilities, requiring me to soothe my own doubts and coach myself back to a place of calm. 'Little by little, Ed – you're chipping away at a mammoth task. You got through the day by eating thirty snails. That's great!' I told myself approvingly. 'But I have to admit surviving with nothing, caveman-style (says me in my cave!), is hard work. It's really hard work.' I whined a little into the camera, hoping it would offer me sympathy.

The dark new moon announced a new phase. The black nights of the dead moon were over and I was comforted that nights would get lighter from now on.

I dreamed of going for a meal with Amanda on the King's Road in Chelsea, and having a glass of red wine. Then going home and crawling between the sheets and sleeping with the comfort of her warm body close to mine. Then I stopped taunting myself as I knew that this was not going to happen for a very long time, so I just lay on the fast-cooling grit and hoped that sleep would release me from my jail.

||||

The sun lit up the cave, unwelcome as the bright morning light to a chronic drunk. That was a truly bad night's sleep. I had the runs in the night – twice. Because it was so dark, and I had feared slipping on the rocks outside, I had gone in the corner of the cave and wiped my bottom with the grass bedding. The result was that my cave now also smelt of human poo. Is that a step up or a step down from goat? Let me assure you it's a step down, and I chastised myself for such uncivilised behaviour. I lay still under my itchy blanket, not wanting to face the world.

But today was a new day and it looked like it might be a nice one.

I had to do some admin: take a still shot of myself to monitor my weight loss; send my daily 'I'm OK' message via Spot tracking device; mark a fourth white line on the wall of the cave.

The main administrational event today was to visit the dropbox twice, once to drop off dead batteries, used CF cards and a broken camera – then, later in the day, to pick up the replacements. Diarrhoea would not be good news – it could make me very weak if it continued and make everything ten times harder. I crept down the beach and felt the waves of cramp rippling through my intestines. I squatted at the water's edge and had three big bursts. This is the body's equivalent of Scotty on the Starship *Enterprise* telling the captain 'the dilithium crystals cannae take it'. I was cramping up. I groaned at the energy that was leaking out of my body. It's important to be able to distance yourself from your symptoms. Yes, I felt like crap, but I had to decide what kind of crap. Life-threatening? Probably not immediately. Food poisoning? I noted that I had no nausea or vomiting. Could it be too much sun yesterday? It was possible – I knew I sometimes reacted badly to excess sun.

At home I'd have curled up on the sofa feeling sorry for myself. No chance of that here. I had to get on with things.

As predicted, the tide was too high for me to walk around the island so I had no option but to go over the hill to do the drop. I stuffed down some coconut and snails without incident. I'd never before been in a situation where just staying alive was so boring. Coconut tasted like whale blubber, snails like gritty balls of phlegm. 'I think your body knows what it needs and wants and mine is saying stop eating bloody coconut,' I said to the camera for posterity.

The Faraway Tree gave me an opportunity to pause and catch my breath in the still of the celestial Highlands. My feet were starting to get very sore so I was taking it slowly as I walked over the island. I quickly picked up my trail of broken branches again on the descent.

Halfway down the slope I picked up the sound of an outboard motor. Without a watch I didn't know what time it was but I knew I had to be quick if I was to make the drop before they arrived. I hurried down through the last palms to the box.

As I entered the clearing the boat was disappearing into the distance. I'd missed the drop — bugger. Inside the cool box was a new 'InReach' messaging device to replace the apparently faulty Spot. There were fresh batteries, and there was also a note saying, 'Drop missed. We will return mid-afternoon.' I put the broken Spot and the defunct camera in the box with my used CF cards and dead batteries and sealed the whole thing up.

On the fringe of the camp I found a tree with some very slim nuts inside a husk the size of a peach. The flat nuts were very small but I was happy to have some nut fats and proteins complementing my diet – even if there was only a handful of them.

I was underwhelmed to find a spoon amongst the camp's litter as I felt a million miles off eating anything that required cutlery. I took it anyway. 'That'll be good for eating with,' I commented without a trace of a smile.

I took the opportunity to look for tuberous roots among the vines but the ground was very hard and digging using a long stick as a trowel was slow. It was also disconcerting to be expending energy on something that I didn't know would reap any rewards. It was like digging for buried treasure without ever having seen the treasure map. I could be digging for half an hour and there would be no edible root. As indeed was the case. Zilch.

Once more I heard bleating and looked up. The goats had come right down to the camp to eat foliage and were calling to each other. A larger male goat with big horns and a thick black stripe down the centre of its grey back looked me straight in the eye.

I stood up in slow motion without disturbing any of the animals. Black Stripe lost interest, too, and looked away and resumed eating leaves in front of him. As a test I slowly moved as close as I could towards the alpha male. Seven metres, six metres, five, four … His ears pricked up and he shot an annoyed glance at me before sounding the alarm and starting out on to the black rocky beach with his family.

Alone again, I found an old fire pit and some charred bits of wood. I remembered that charcoal could be used to clean teeth so I ground a small brick of it into a fine powder on a smooth rock, licked my finger and dabbed the pad into the black, glittery powder. Even with my blunt finger I could feel how good this was at removing the built-up layers of plaque. It was immediately apparent that the charcoal was abrasive enough to clean properly but soft enough not to do any damage.

The return journey yesterday had been a circular farce but I had to try again in order to rebuild my own navigational self-respect. It would be easier this morning as the sun would still be directly behind me as I walked. Following my own shadow I edged up the hill snapping branches as I went. As the hill flattened out, the Faraway Tree appeared in the distance to my right.

On approaching my multi-rooted cathedral I looked for the exit trail that I'd followed only that morning but couldn't find it. There were no signs of a path going in the direction away from the tree that I'd just come from. This was eerie – I now began to doubt whether it was the same tree at all. I was disoriented; the direct sun had magically vanished. The sky was grey and cast no shadows. The tree seemed more mysterious than ever. Was it a double?

There were stones everywhere but they weren't really in the circle that I'd been so struck by before. This was like something from a nasty dream – or a horror film. These are the thoughts that start going through your head when you're alone. Was this some supernatural weirdness? How was I so confused once again?

I held my finger vertical on one of the lighter coloured rocks and could just make out a faint shadow. 'OK – sun's over there.' I collected myself. 'I need to go this way to camp and keep it behind me.'

I plunged down the hill with no confidence about where I would end up. But the first things I recognised were the plastics that I'd piled up yesterday and I registered that I could see the woodland beside my cave. I had been in the Highlands after all. So why hadn't I been able to pick up my own tracks?

Ever proud of my 'exemplary' pass in navigation on my Mountain Leader Assessment, I was shaken by being disoriented in this way. The cloud cover kept occurring at just the wrong times and I realised that, once again, I was actively destroying my own confidence by being too hard on myself. I had to remember to trust my own judgement and experience and not second-guess myself all the time. Combined with the malnutrition, dehydration, lack of sleep and chronic diarrhoea I was becoming overwhelmed and confused by the entire situation and had to regain control.

I always took pride in my ability to get my bearings quickly and easily, so back up the hill I went so as not to be beaten. At the Faraway Tree I did indeed find the path that I'd marked by breaking twigs and I quickly established that my routes going down to, and back from, Lemon Camp had joined at the tree from completely different directions. That was why I'd been thrown out. That finally sorted, and maintaining my altitude on high ground, I stuck to the coast in an attempt to find the vast rocky headland that was so dominant on my beach. In a world in which I felt out of control in so many areas, getting to grips with the topography of the island seemed vital.

'Wow – that's phenomenal!' I reported to the camera as I broke out of the tree line on to the scorched summit of the rocky outcrop. I was on a spur of rock that crested out from the forest canopy below me like the hump back of a fossilised whale. It was the first time I'd been able to get a decent view of the reef that circled the island and the protected lagoon within. From this new perspective I could see that, at its closest, directly in front of me, the reef's limit was perhaps 900 metres from the beach but as you followed the perimeter fence either way it expanded and penned in a vast expanse of turquoise shallows.

The feature I stood on was about thirty metres high and dropped vertically from its tip to the sea. As I looked out towards the sea I had my beach, Alpha Beach, to my right and what I now decided to call Bravo Beach, the cuter sister beach, on my left. It was absolutely stunning – huge expanses of golden sand and palm trees – and I was reminded how lucky I was to be spending time in such an untouched place.

Back in camp I found another large washed-up flip-flop that fitted. I loved the fact that, like me, Fijians had massive feet. It was a refreshing change after months of walking in the Amazon in South American wellington boots that were one size too small and crushed all my toes. With the repaired one that I'd already been using I would have a wearable pair of shoes

– something that was becoming increasingly necessary as my feet were becoming tender and raw. I used hibiscus but the rubber was so perished that it crumbled at the tension now applied to it, rendering it useless.

I drew a map of the island in the sand on the beach in front of my cave. From where the sun had set the previous night I knew that due west was straight ahead from where I was sitting, through a rock buried in the beach and beyond. I also determined that it must be about midday and, as I was in the southern hemisphere, my shadow should be cast due south. Although it might not be exactly midday I could now draw the four compass points reasonably accurately in the sand.

From this I extrapolated that my beach ran north–south and I also knew I was almost on the northern tip of the island so must be between the ten or eleven o'clock points of the island if it were a clock face. I drew on the landmarks that I knew: the rocky headland, the various beaches, my cave, Snail Rock, Lemon Camp, the Highlands and the Faraway Tree. The interior of the south of the island was still fairly blank but I could improve on the detail as the days went by. It was important for me to log in my brain the aspect (direction of slope) of each side of the island so that I could navigate easier by the sun.

Back in Lemon Camp for the pick-up I found a stick insect on a tree. A stick insect is clearly an animal and so, with only a moment's hesitation, I ate it. It tasted sour. I then washed it down with an unripe fruit that was inedible in its current state of ripeness and tasted like a combination of washing-up liquid and battery acid.

I stayed in Lemon Camp for the lowest tide because I wanted to check for alternative water sources on the beach. My theory was that there might be fresh water at the base of the rocky part of the beach running straight into the sea that would be exposed at low tide. Frustratingly, every flow that I dug out simply filled up with salt water. I became distracted by some washed-up bamboo that I split to use in making a fire. I stayed long enough to find that the tide had turned and the water was rising again. I'd not located anything like a fresh water source and my expectations that I ever would dropped another level.

The boat returned for the pick-up. As this was already my second visit to Lemon Camp today, and I didn't want to go all the way over to the other side of the island, I just tucked myself into the bushes and hid. This was against the rules – I was meant to be well clear of the pick-up area when a boat came in – but I didn't care. I was tired and bored with playing games. I was hungry and this survival scenario was real: I wasn't going to waste my energy when it wasn't absolutely essential. Plus, I was intrigued. I could hear the boatmen laughing and walking up the beach. I felt like Leonardo DiCaprio in *The Beach* as I silently observed the civilised people from my make-believe savage world. I had no desire to go and speak to them, but observing them, knowing that they had no idea I was there, gave me a buzz.

As I heard the motor starting up again I crept out of the bushes and went to examine the dropbox. I unwrapped a new radio microphone kit and the replacement camera and watched the tiny boat disappear through the reef.

In order to have a proper log of the route back to camp I decided to video the whole way home. I had yet to do a journey that didn't involve an element of disorientation and so I was adamant that I would attempt to eliminate any unknowns. The camera was to be my stopwatch and my journal.

As I reached the Faraway Tree I turned around to see the direction that I'd come from and then I took three sticks and made an arrow on the floor pointing backwards so that the guesswork would be removed. Then I did a circuit of the enormous tree and found the arrow that I'd left on the outward journey that denoted the direction of my cave. This was simplification in the extreme but needs must and it appeared that I needed this degree of marking.

It was the first time I'd arrived back into the cave area cleanly, without any mistakes. It felt good to have taken my time to log it and solve the problem. I had left a mini trail of destruction along all routes taken, too – snapped branches and knots tied in palms – so I really could not get lost on that route again. If I removed the messing around at the tree for five minutes the timer on the camera told me I had taken twenty minutes to walk across the island barefoot. That was also good to know. I suppose that the whole procedure was a form of evolution on the island – I now had two signposts and a delineated road.

The evening was unbelievably still and the water, as I broke out on to my beach, was like a vast sheet of polished metal. No waves were crashing on the beach or the reef so the sounds were soft and gentle. I had become increasingly aware, and slightly irritated by, constant earworms in my head. Elgar's 'Land of Hope and Glory' – initially rousing but can get wearing; 'What Doesn't Kill You Makes You Stronger' by Kelly Clarkson – annoying from the outset. But with the stillness that resulted from the lack of wind and waves the tunes obliged and paused their marathon recitals. Thin ragged clouds allowed golden light to filter through, providing calmness and peace.

Home, sweet home. I was back twenty minutes before sunset and so I ate ten snails, smashed open a brown coconut and collected some more bedding so that I would sleep well. I wasn't feeling bad for day four. Maybe it was the fattening up after eating the stick insect. I swallowed the gritty snails without thinking.

From this point onwards I became almost permanently hungry – a hunger that would be relieved only sporadically throughout my stay. This may sound ungrateful but I didn't want only snails and stick insects and spent a lot of time fantasising about proper food.

I thought about food more than anything else. I was constantly battling hunger and food cravings. I wanted stodge – cakes, peanut butter on toast, flapjacks, Cornish pasties, and chips with mushy peas. Basically, if a Greggs Bakery had appeared on the island I'd have demolished it in about ten minutes.

If I let myself think about food before I went to sleep, that was it. I was up all night long salivating over the exact menu I was going to use to bake a carrot cake or what components I was going to build my muesli from once I got home – almonds, coconut, dates ... It would be a bitter-sweet experience.

Ḥ⃥t⃥t⃥

E yes closed. I love sleep. I love lying down. It is my favourite part of the day. Five more minutes – who's here but me to know whether or not I get up?

I had slept well and felt strong and happy as I awoke. I had kept my arms tucked into my body – mittens-style – and I had been considerably warmer. But soon guilt started banging pots and pans in my chest saying that it was time to get up. I blinked and the warm morning light on the ocean constricted my pupils to the size of pinheads. I stood and stretched and pissed down on to the beach. The patch below the cave was starting to smell like a urinal. I clicked my neck right and left and etched the fifth chalky white mark on the wall of the cave to complete my first batch of five days. It was a triumphant bold strike through the first four: IIII. New InReach messaging device powered on. 'All OK' message sending ... Message sent. Power down. Put back in case. Scratch balls like the caveman I have become.

'Good morning, it's day five,' I grunted to the plastic flip-out camera screen while scratching my stubble with my dirty fingernails. 'Only fifty-six days to go!'

Morning poo result: yesterday it had been explosive and I had literally screamed – roared out – across the ocean in carnal release. Today was more solid and settled like a runny cow-pat. For me this was a step in the right direction and I was content with the fond farmyard association. I'd been urinating four or five times a day and it was straw-coloured so, although I wasn't worried about currently being severely dehydrated, I knew that limited fresh water and diarrhoea were a bad combination. The coconut water was obviously filling the gap but for it to be sustainable I had to find a more reliable and plentiful source of water.

Finding another water source would require elements outside my control. It required fortune and I could not bank on luck going my way. I had to make the most of what I could tangibly affect and so I opted to attempt to enhance the flow of water from the rock seep and improve my system of collecting it. I gave myself that task and nothing else for the day so that I could look at it calmly and get something done that was genuinely valuable and would improve my situation long term.

Facing the seep, I reached up for a left-hand grip, then a right, and with my right foot in the water hollow I raised myself off the beach by a metre to examine the top of the crack in the rock. Although the hollow at the bottom could hold four hundred or so millilitres of water I knew what I wanted: and that was to be able to position one of the plastic bottles against the rock so that it would constantly collect water. I was far from certain it would work but I thought that the only way to divert such a slow flow was to use some sort of wick to draw the water from the damp rock face.

I sifted through the assorted junk that I'd so far hoarded in a giant clamshell. One dirty frayed length of cordage was about eight inches long. It looked absorbent – cotton, not nylon – and my hopes ignited that this might just work. Back at the seep I looked at the crack and how it was formed. There were two pools or hollows, one about seven feet above the beach and one about three feet. The one at seven feet filled first and could hold about 500ml of water. The bottom one held about 400ml. The top one filled first and when full would overflow down the rock face and *some* of the overflow would help fill the bottom one. Because the pools were not vertically above one another, the rest would be wasted and flow down the rock face into the sand.

To allow any water to overflow from the top one was therefore a waste. I looked at positioning my bottle above the top pool but there was nothing to wick from – the rock was barely damp – so I knew my bottle had to sit just below the top pool and allow gravity to siphon the water down.

But there was an obvious problem: there was no ledge or surface that I could position the bottle on below the top pool.

The lower pool was four feet lower and the wick was only eight inches long.

The more I looked at it the more I questioned whether this whole formation was natural or had been carved out of the rock by generations of tribal Fijians or Tongans who had visited here and had the same issue. I had a hunch that what I had previously considered to be a natural channel, formed by water, between the two pools was actually chipped out of the rock by man, perhaps many thousands of years ago.

By deduction I came to the conclusion that the rock must indeed be soft enough for me to mould the rock face and so I went to fetch my primitive clamshell hand axe. From the first few strikes I could tell that this might work. It was no hammer and chisel – more like carving a hole in a brick wall with a wooden spoon – but little by little the wall recessed and a ledge for placing my bottle started to form. I worked, with occasional breaks for small raw snails and coconut, for about four hours on the ledge before it was deep enough to allow a 600ml plastic bottle to sit snugly below the top pool. It was held in place by a fist-sized rock to stop the wind blowing it away and it was fed by the eight-inch section of cordage that was in turn held in place at the top by a small pebble that was holding one end in place in the top pool. I tried to ensure that as the wick entered the bottle it did not touch the sides of the lip so as not to lose any water down the outside of the plastic.

I stood back expectantly. This really could work. I had also attempted to open up more of the seep above the top pool to encourage flow by chipping away at all areas that were damp and creating a further gully down into the top pool. The end result looked fantastic. Patience had paid off and I had made alterations to this seep that would last for centuries. And, hopefully, ones that would work. After cleaning out the enormous amounts of brick dust from the whole system with seawater I left the wick-and bottle-siphon system to work its magic.

Fingers crossed.

Feeling lucky, I decided to turn my attention to fire. To have fire would mean so much to me: I would be able to cook snails and mussels – everything that I could find; I would be able to boil water and have a hot drink; I would be able to be warm each night, comforted by a reassuring glow that would fend off cold thoughts.

Why had it taken me so long to get around to attempting fire? I could just put it down to my mind being in a spin, but that would be only half the truth. The other half is that there is an unprecedented amount to do to set yourself up when you start to survive with nothing, and many of these, like water, food and shelter, are higher priorities – you *need* them to survive. Fire was a luxury that no other animal in the world had the ability to master and, as such, it wasn't top of the list as they all seemed to cope perfectly well without it.

And so I acknowledged the progression from crude necessity to aspirational desire. I *wanted* a fire. I needed a wooden stick that I could spin in place on a flat board. The friction between the 'drill' and the 'hearth board' is what would, hopefully, create enough heat for me to form an ember – the very embryo of a fire. I would either spin the drill with my hands or make a simple bow to help me spin it faster, harder, and for longer.

In Australia – about a month before I was dropped on the island – the Aboriginals had mentioned that beach hibiscus would work for a hand drill. I was cocky about my abilities and so, without testing it for myself, I simply logged it as a given and ticked fire off my list of worries.

I returned to the hibiscus sticks that I'd cut and started to dry the day before feeling reasonably confident. I needed a long thin drill, half a metre long and the thickness of my little finger, and a fatter hearth board that I could make from a short section with a two-inch diameter. An hour later I had what I wanted and, exhausted but positive, I carried them back to my cave.

The drill, once the bark was stripped off, just needed to be left in the sun to dry out. The nine-inch hearth section needed to be split longitudinally to produce two long half-moon cylinders. I thrive on simple, practical challenges like this. It's why I ended up doing expeditions in the first place. Everything is tangible and physical and you just have to apply your mind and find a solution. I'd used wooden battens to hammer machetes through logs in the jungle to split them longitudinally and so I decided that I would just swap the machete for a long thin shard of clamshell and see if it worked.

Several demolished clamshells later I stumbled upon a fragment that I thought would work as this chisel-like tool. I rested the white blade on the top of the vertical column of wood and, holding one end, gently tapped at the other with a further section of hardwood. Tap, tap, tap. I created a small trench-like indentation in the cross-section and grew more confident as the shell cut down into the column, splitting the wood apart lengthways.

'Aaargghhhh,' I screamed like a wuss as I hit my finger. But I smiled as I realised that I was making good progress, so the pain was short-lived.

Ever conscious that I wanted two fairly even halves, my focus was on the angle and the force of the tap, and then I could see the perfect result and the two sections of wood gently and uniformly came apart.

'They're actually really good. Oh, I love it when a plan comes together. I could cry – that's so pathetic I could cry.' An unexpected wave of elation rose from within. I started to well up. 'That worked,' I stated – overwhelmed. 'I really *am* on the verge of tears. That fucking *worked*! Yes!!'

Surprised by the happiness that I felt, I allowed the emotion in, but, without realising this, I opened the floodgates to all the other emotions that I'd been repressing. Stowed away was a whole lower deck of other worries and stresses; they all surfaced and I began to sob both with happiness and with the release of the tension of so many days.

Beach hibiscus is a softwood and so I managed to cut an ember notch in the hearth board, using a tiny sharp seashell, in about forty-five minutes. Unprepared and yet excited that now I potentially had a fire kit that would work, I decided to trial my home-made equipment. With the hearth board on the floor and the drill sitting in the notch, the whole set-up looked like an inverted capital T. I held the hearth in place with my bare foot, knelt over the kit and took the drill between my palms. Back and forth I worked my hands – spinning the stick in the hole faster and faster – and gradually the heat created by the friction started to produce powder and smoke rose from the notch. I kept working my hands down the drill until I was exhausted and dripping with sweat. My arms were on fire with the intense short burst of exertion. On examination, the powder that I was producing was light brown; this wasn't good – I knew it should have looked much darker. The hearth, too, was almost worn through after two attempts. Frustrated, I determined that, actually, beach hibiscus must be too soft. I should have known this and so I chastised myself once more for the lack of responsibility in my preparations.

I admitted to the camera that the only trees I could identify were coconut, beach hibiscus, lemon and some sort of pine. As a result I had no option but to use the same tactics I had in navigation – experiment and learn as I went. My old coconut Y-pole was the first thing to be tested but I soon worked out that chopping a section of wood that is not attached to a tree with a clamshell is even harder as the wood bounced on the rock and sent vibrations up my aching arms. Instead I simply fed it through the natural fork in a tree and used all my weight to tension the wood and then snap it. It was brute force over intelligence or skill – but that's never worried me.

After collecting four significantly different types of wood I was covered in sweat and abrasions from the bark and decided that these would do for my first round of trials. I laid the different shades of wood on a rock in the sun so as to dry them out completely. Despite searching intently I couldn't find the mythical tangalito, the one first mentioned to me by Rama, anywhere.

With these new harder woods I suspected that I might need to use a different method of lighting so as to generate more heat with less energy. I would have to make myself a bow.

A fire bow looks like a small bow used by a child to fire toy arrows. I was in search of a curved section of wood that was about two foot long and would not snap. Ideally I wanted a nice Y at one end to assist with tying on the bowstring. I would carve a simple notch in the other end.

This was straightforward – I could do this task. Clutching my clamshell hand axe, I turned left out of the cave and picked my way over the snail-covered rocks that split my beach and were now half submerged by a high tide. On the south section of my beach I turned left again, slipped into the tree line and went in search of a bent stick.

I soon worked out that I wasn't going to find a piece that was strong enough on the floor. If it had been weak enough to fall off the tree then it wasn't even on my shortlist. I soon found a branch that wasn't pretty, more a snapped-in-half octagon than a sweeping crescent, and started the primitive tree surgery. Fifty crude blows, three bloody knuckles and one bellow of frustration later, I used all my weight to snap my ugly fire bow free of its life-long home. I whisked up a small amount of beach hibiscus cordage and trotted back to the cave with my new stuff.

None of the random bits of scavenged man-made cordage that I had amassed seemed of sufficient calibre for use as a string and so, as I was now well aware of the strong yet flexible natural properties of hibiscus bark, I attached a bit of that to my bow.

Glancing at the initial fragile and rather sad-looking water collection frame that I had made on the beach, I decided that it was bad for my morale to keep walking past evidence of my failure and so I ripped it apart and threw it into the tree line. My clamshells had long ago usurped this anyway and were still poised ready to harvest any downpour.

I collected my first load of firewood – all grades, from tiny twigs to big logs; if I ever got an ember I was going to be ready. I placed them in order of size in neat little piles at the side of my cave. I decided upon an area to have my fire and made a fire pit at the side of the cave by building up a flat area of soil and encircling it with substantial rocks. As I was transporting the large stones up into my cave part of the thin goat path crumbled away and my foot followed it down the rock face. My world slowed as I plunged, with nothing stopping me, through the air. In a split second I instinctively I reached out and grabbed the cliff above me to stop my fall and my arm jolted straight under the dead weight of my falling body. The force on my hand was such that it tore the skin off my thumb and forefinger but it stopped the fall. My heart thumping, I looked at my cut-up hand and realised that it was minor compared to what would have happened had I continued falling. Scanning the drop below me I saw that it would have been over two metres on to jagged black rocks. 'That was another warning shot, Ed! You need to be more carful,' I muttered to the camera before placing it down by my feet. I was grateful for such close shaves – they kept me on my toes. Then, as if to further emphasise the danger, the camera wobbled, fell over and rolled right out of the cave.

My final preliminary fire preparations involved collecting bundles of coconut husk and leaving them in the sun to dry thoroughly. These would make the basis of my tinder bundle – a small mass of dry material that I would use to turn an ember into a flame.

I took a thumb-thick section of one of the darker woods and sat down to whittle it into the shape of a fat Cuban cigar. Working with a small shell, I found it cut quite well into the dry wood; and, reflecting on the usefulness of a simple shell, I realised that it might also be the perfect thing to use for cupping the top of the drill to allow it to spin in my palm. A ready-made 'bearing block' – brilliant.

Now I had three parts out of four for my first bow drill attempt. I had made a bow, a drill and a bearing block. All I needed now was a hearth. I took the fatter half of hibiscus that I had split and carved myself a notch for the ember dust to settle in. It was time to trial the new fire set.

The first hibiscus string went back and forth … and snapped. Crap. The second went back and forth, back and forth … then snapped. Bollocks. The third, I pulled back and … snapped again. Bloody hell!

Rethink required.

The obvious flaw was that the hibiscus bark wasn't strong enough to be used in this way. The one positive was that the bow would work if my string was stronger. It's important to stay positive in these situations.

I looked through the small sections of rejected cordage that I'd collected over the past days and decided that two of the longer lengths might work if I tied them together. After assembly and a couple of readjustments for tightness I had the drill spinning nicely in the hearth board. First proper grin of the day. I have a bow that works. Fire is one *large* step closer – all I now need to do is carve an ember notch in the hard wood of the hearth board. But that was for another day as the golden hour was fast approaching.

By late afternoon I needed a break and a drink. I examined the enhanced seep and took a quick sip of water from the top hollow through the straw. The sun seemed too hot for the system to fill and the bottle was empty. Disappointed, I walked back past the kid skin and examined the stiff, unusable, solid mass. It stank and was now covered in flies.

Resorting to coconut water, and having forced the issue by destroying my first Y-pole to make a fire kit, I set about chopping down a really big tall tree. I'd wanted to make a longer pole anyway as I'd outgrown my first one and used up all the low-hanging coconuts. I knew, however, that it was going to take all my energy to cut it down.

I dragged myself up the hill behind the cave in search of a tree with a suitable fork in the trunk to use as a long Y-pole. Once I found one, I sank to the ground beside it to try to summon up the motivation to start cutting it down with my clamshell.

The hand axe I was using now had a dull edge that tore at the wood like a hammer. With feeble mini strikes I worked my way around the tree – ringing the bark and then biting further into the fleshy wood. Every two minutes or so I would collapse on the floor, gasping for breath. I found it hard to decide if the fatigue that was crippling my every movement was due to illness, lack of food, dehydration or even depression. Every movement required a monumental effort. I was incredibly, massively hungry, too, and I conjured smells of baking and roasting in my mind that did nothing but torment me.

To fell a tree with a clamshell you have to bring it to the point at which it is weak enough to snap. There is no front or rear notch to cut meticulously, and the tree will never fall under its own weight. It's incredibly crude and you just have to try to judge the point at which you can put your shoulder to the trunk and snap it over.

When I thought I had reached this point, I put every joule of energy into a scrum-like thrust against the tree. It showed no sign of breaking. Totally spent, I then had to continue nibbling at the ring with the clamshell to further weaken the tree, three strikes out of ten resulting in old sores being reopened on my knuckles and weepy blisters growing larger on my palms.

If I hadn't run out of water I would have given up. My energy levels and my spirits were the lowest that they'd yet been on the island and I still needed the most basic of survival requirements – water. My last Herculean thrust resulted in a tantalising series of splitting cracks and then a satisfying ripping sound as the trunk snapped and the tree was felled.

I sat gasping for a few moments and then rode the tiny positive wave of triumph by snapping off all the smaller branches with my fists, and dragging the mammoth pole down the dense dark hillside and out on to the bright sandy beach.

As I used the pole for the first time I realised immediately that it was heavy — really heavy. I had unwittingly selected a dense wood and, in order to get the length that I wanted, I'd now got a pole with a very thick cross-section at the bottom. But the green coconuts were my lifeline and so I used all my strength to thrust this bloody caber upwards with both arms to dislodge one of them. And then another. The water felt nutritious, sweet, sterile and replenishing and I valued and appreciated each individual priceless fruit.

Then, in the sand, I noticed a dark, shiny nut that looked a bit like a squashed conker. Curious, I stooped to pick it up, and smiled. This wasn't any old bean; this was a burnie bean. Despite their being inedible, Aboriginals say that to carry a burnie bean brings good luck and acts as a connection to Mother Earth. They often decorate them by painting them and they were sometimes hollowed out and used to carry dry tinder for fire lighting. I wasn't sure if they were indigenous to Fiji or whether this one had undergone an epic crossing of the Pacific Ocean; but if there was ever a time to believe in omens this was it.

My survival attempts were gently boosted by this peaceful sign. 'Don't give up, Ed — you're doing just fine, brother,' I could hear Jeremy saying.

The discovery of the nut was a friendly hand on the shoulder reminding me to relax and look after myself. I scanned the beautiful calm evening at low tide. Warm sun tiptoed through the clouds and I knew that a swim would round the day off perfectly. I padded out over the sharp coral and allowed my body to fall beyond into the cool sandy depths. Today I seemed to have composure. It was day five and I felt assertive and good. I had tackled everything with patience and a positive open mind. The inside of my chest was warm and alive.

I felt I'd found my feet today. Rather than a fight to gain control over the island, it felt far more like relaxing into the inevitable. I had cried today. I remembered another wise quote: 'A man's strength is measured in tears not his fears.' I have never been too afraid to cry but I could now see clearer than ever that the ability to release emotion could be a strength rather than a weakness. Anything that produced such clarity – a reset button for my mental health – could not be all bad. Crying had made me honest with myself, allowed me to look at and move through what I was struggling with, and helped clean away stress and madness. Suppressing emotions and keeping a lid on frustrations were more obviously masculine characteristics but I felt I had gone beyond such superficial bravado. This was a time for real internal honesty if I was to get through this intact – and that meant owning my emotions and facing my problems head-on.

The orange glow hit the horizon and cast a burning line across the still water towards my cave. It was the end of day five – a really good day for me. I was carrying the people I loved in my heart but getting on with the practicalities of day-to-day life here, too, without too much of a battle. I felt immensely grateful for everything that I had.

$\bcancel{||||}\ |$

'Morning – day six!' I'd been here almost a week. The number of times last night I'd just thought, 'Will somebody please turn the lights on!' But the nights were black. I had a couple of sores on each foot and so I tiptoed down to the water's edge and bathed them in the sea, rubbing the dirt out. They would be fine, I was sure – they were definitely toughening up.

I approached the enhanced seep and my heart sank: I could not see a level on the plastic bottle. Then I looked closer, I had not seen a level because it was *completely full.* I gently squeezed the bottle to double-check and the water tension over the lip of the bottle broke and water flowed down the sides. The improvements had worked! I had made a wick system using a bit of washed-up cordage, a broken clamshell and a discarded plastic bottle and I had a full 600ml bottle of fresh water to show for it!

I decided to decant the water into a bigger two-litre bottle and then I drank the contents of the two small rock pools before reassembling the wick system. I smiled because I had just drunk fresh water and had a reserve that I could carry with me and drink when I was thirsty. What an amazing step forward! Good fortune, when it came my way, made me happy, but this was better. I had thought through a problem, invested my time and effort into resolving it and it had paid off.

'That's a good start to the day,' I beamed into the camera. 'Yes!!'

For good measure I gulped down the contents of the big green coconut that I had collected the previous night with my new pole. My hands stung as the cuts opened up again with the force of each strike on the rocks. Struggling to swallow it fast enough, I almost choked on the vast quantity of liquid that shot out down my throat.

As I look down at my pitiful grass skirt I suddenly felt ridiculous. That had to change. I needed to get off my bare arse and make myself feel better by making some new clothes. I decided that my grass skirt was so bad it was like walking around with a big sign that told me that I was a laughing stock. 'IDIOT FAILING HERE!' it said to me every time I looked at it.

'There is only one person here, Ed, to alter the state of play. There is only one person who can make you feel better and give you the boost you need.' I physically hauled myself from the floor and decided to do something to make myself feel better. Not something to help me survive, or something to improve the filming, something just for me, to try and make me feel more happy. When people teach survival skills they rightly focus on the needs of the body but, in the case of long-term survival, the needs of the mind cannot be overlooked. And remember: I knew that my ordeal was going to end after sixty days and that, if I had an accident, there would be a boat for me within twenty-four hours. How much more mentally taxing must it be to be marooned with no certainty of rescue?

From the moment I came to the decision I knew that remaking the grass skirt was all I wanted to do. I also knew that this time I was going to make a good one, a good-looking one, one that would last. I sourced some new beach hibiscus and clam-shelled the stems down. I beat them until the bark slipped off like fresh woolly socks off well-talced feet. I strung up my waist band between two trees and I set about attaching the individual strands that would make up the skirt.

As the skirt built in thickness I tested it by trying it on. I wanted it to be below the knee so that the strands were heavy enough for it to hang well. I wanted to pack the strands so closely together that it would not reveal anything and allow me to feel comfortable and civilised. After about three hours of intensely focused and yet calm and constructive time, I had fashioned a skirt I was very happy with.

Like a new haircut, the skirt made me feel irrationally pleased with myself. I had made something that not only worked but looked good, and the process of making it had been very meditative, too. I felt as if I could really start to get on with things now. I had back the armour in which we all live every day and I was glad for that familiar sense of protection.

On inspection, there wasn't much more water in the still. I began to understand the daily pattern. I got the most water in the early morning and the least in the afternoon. I realised that as soon as the sun hit the rock face the seep began to dry up each day, so I needed to take advantage of the first morning drink and the second drink at the end of morning before the sun had come over. I was surprised how long it had taken me to work this out. I must *always* either drink or decant both volumes of water in the morning, otherwise it would evaporate in the afternoon.

Everything I was doing at the moment was on the energy from thirty snails a day and a few mouthfuls of gelatinous coconut flesh. The coconut water had some calories, too, but not many, and with the adaptations to the seep I should now be getting 1.2 litres of fresh water a day as well. It hadn't rained properly, apart from spitting on morning two, and so when it did I would get the opportunity to collect more water.

The afternoon sunlight in the cave was uncomfortably hot and it made me wonder if I could use its heat to light a fire. I'd found a glass jam jar and I held it in the sun over a dry coconut husk and attempted to focus the light passing through it. But the bottom was not conical or smooth enough, and it soon became evident that I could not produce enough heat to make anything combust. It was like trying to light a cigarette with the warmth of your armpit and so I quickly accepted the failure and moved on.

In a day of experiments I also tried the bamboo fire-saw method (a further fire-by-friction technique from Asia that is different to the fire plough method) but eventually concluded that the bamboo was too dry and too old. The sections were too brittle to allow me to apply sufficient force and I gave that up as well.

For some reason I decided to try and make a woven mat out of coconut palms. I'd watched villagers do this on Komo and perhaps I thought that if I sat and applied myself quietly to this task it would calm me and that I would also have a useful covering to sleep and sit on. The trouble was that I couldn't make it. I tried to remember how they did it but the leaves kept unfurling and I got more and more frustrated. All I could do was make the smaller roofing tiles for thatching a shelter. At least that would be useful later on if I built a house.

I'd failed to make the palm leaf mat and that made three failures out of three. As anxieties crept back in, I sought out my stone circle and had to fight hard to stop unravelling. Tears of desperation, bordering on panic, welled up. I felt so sad and so alone. I did the only thing I could in the circumstance: I sat down and reminded myself of what I was doing, why I was doing it and who I was. I hadn't been abandoned here. This was my choice and I had to take that hardship squarely on my shoulders. Slowly I regained control and eventually got myself to a place where I was once again solid enough to stand up, brush the cave dust off my bottom and go and collect some firewood.

At the end of my first week it was time to test my physical fitness by doing a number of exercises that I would repeat every week for the duration of the project. I would do maximum chin-ups and press-ups with no weight. I would take two melon-sized boulders and do squats and shoulder presses. Lastly, I would sprint down the beach, touch the rock at the far end and sprint back. In my heavy-legged state I wasn't looking forward to what seemed a complete waste of energy.

My run was predictably laboured. I had measured it out as forty-five paces there and the same back, and so estimated that the distance was a 140-metre sprint. That was largely arbitrary as it was a record of relative speed in relation to the speed I started at. Would I get slower and slower as the weeks passed?

Balancing the boulders on my bare shoulders and wedging them against my head for balance was the trickiest exercise and as I sank down to do a squat it felt such an alien movement to be attempting in my situation. I managed eighteen.

Dark rain clouds out to sea slowly folded and rose with the thermals and I willed them towards me. I'd not had any rain since I'd laid out the clamshells and I desperately wanted the rains to hit my island.

I collected six more palm leaves to cut out the wind that I predicted would come, and some more grass, too. Nothing could have been more important to me than being warm and snug at night, except perhaps having a plentiful supply of water.

With darkness only about twenty minutes away, the wind picked up and it started to spit with rain. Static noise filled the cave as heavier rain started to fall outside. This was fantastic for me but I had mixed emotions as I noticed that half of the empty fireplace was already wet, as well as the front lip of the cave. Thankfully the rest of the cave was dry.

The rain blew off all too quickly and my field of giant clamshells had hardly started filling. But then the white noise crescendoed again and I could see the levels of my mini swimming pools rising once more from the dry of my cave.

In total it probably rained heavily for only forty seconds before it passed. I gingerly climbed down the now wet rock face and knelt before the clamshells with my straw and an empty two-litre Fiji Water bottle. Not wanting to spill any water when transferring it, by bending over the shells and sucking the water up into my mouth with the straw I could then blow it back into the bottle. Suck – transfer – blow was the routine. In five minutes I had half the bottle full. Considering it had rained for less than a minute I couldn't complain about that. I had my first full litre of fresh rainwater and I was chuffed.

I gulped down ten snails in the dusky light, the bits of shell scraping my throat. I retched on the sixth and it came back up into the sand. I stared blankly at the loss of hydration and nutrition in my vomit on the beach.

There was a magical burnt light that ringed the horizon. It was a distant light, a light full of hope, laden with a heavy ceiling of dark cloud that stretched completely above my head. But out there beyond my own gloomy skies it was beautiful and orange. I could not help but feel the love of Amanda reaching out from afar.

Using that hope and light I tried to hold on to the positives and asked myself what I had done today. Water was now more plentiful and reliable; I had a fantastic new grass skirt; I'd experimented with weaving palm leaves and, although I couldn't make a mat, I could make the tiles to thatch – and in fact that was the important bit. I'd done my exercises (I just had to do chin-ups in Lemon Camp), I'd eaten coconut and snails ... I became distracted by the fact that there was more moonlight tonight. What else had I achieved? I'd experimented with a bamboo fire-saw, and I could do it if I found some better-quality (less dead) bamboo.

'So you've done a lot!' I told myself encouragingly. 'One baby step at a time. I've got so much time, haven't I?' I drifted off and stared into the blackness. 'Don't worry, Ed,' I eventually said. 'It will be all right.'

CHAPTER 3
FIRE

卌 ||

'**M**orning – day seven. Where's my rock?' I grunted as I scraped the seventh mark on the cave wall. 'It's not a system of sleeping that I would recommend. Every time you move it all slips off you and because the cave's at an angle the bedding slips down the hill.' I shivered and it turned into a comical noise that made me smile. I realised I was finding it amusing that I had a very cold, uncomfortable night! Humour – this was a good sign.

I had a new cut under the second toe on my left foot that was not healing well with the sand and cave dirt in it all the time. When I flexed my toes I could feel referred tenderness up the whole tendon that it was attached to, which was slightly disconcerting. There was nothing to dress my various cuts with so I washed them in seawater, left them open and hoped for the best. I wondered whether goat shit and rock powder was bad for wounds. I thought about the diseases you can get from goats. Anthrax? A bit too late to bother about that.

I didn't have a poo yesterday but I could feel one coming on. Let's hope it's not explosive. It was heartening to get up to a fresh water supply in my cave and I had a morning glug.

'Well, you could continue mumbling shit to the camera,' I laughed, 'or you could actually get up and do stuff, Edward. Actually – yes – it's time to evacuate.'

Because of my light-hearted, self-mocking mood I decided to film it. 'Mr Whippy! Excellent,' I spoke into the camera.

'Mr Whippy,' I explained for the international viewers, 'is a type of soft ice cream that comes out of a machine and curls lightly into a wafer cornet. Mr Whippy – I'm relatively firm – and that's good.'

It would be easy to omit endless talk of defecating from this book but for me it offered vital information in a world in which I had none at all. I came to rely on a morning inspection to appraise the state of my physical health. Also, if it hadn't been noted, this wasn't a terribly civilised experiment. Not to discuss the most basic of bodily functions would have allowed a veil to be drawn over something most people don't particularly want to hear about, but it wouldn't have told the full story. Here everything was laid bare – quite literally – and the tribulations of my bowel movements were a significant part of my world.

My lips were starting to crack. 'What a gorgeous pout, eh?' I joked to the camera. The evacuation had taken it out of me and I stood slightly dazed on the beach as my internal organs adjusted themselves into the space left by my now empty colon. 'Right – water.'

The water bottle at the seep had fallen slightly to the side in the night, allowing the wick to touch the side of the bottle. This meant the water had run down the outside rather than the inside. I was left with about 400ml – not disastrous, but I had to be more careful.

I decanted the 400ml into the bigger two-litre water bottle and reset the wick. Although it hadn't rained at all last night my water reserve had now risen. I must not have felt the need to drink all my water yesterday. Over the course of the day I would aim to drink the entire 1.2 litres. I had a big swig. It tasted bizarre – like salty, clammy rock.

Via a note in the dropbox there had been a request for me to do a second drop per week, on a Friday. This was a nuisance as it meant that I lost another couple of hours to logistics every Friday now as well as every Tuesday. The reason for this was that on Komo Steven Ballantyne was struggling to download all of the Tuesday footage on to a hard drive in time for him to send it back to the UK on the Thursday. So this extra drop would even out his weekly workload. I wasn't entirely sure why I was revolving around the requirements of Steven, when he was being fed three enormous meals a day and sleeping in a bed, but, as I actually enjoyed the enforced walk and realised that it would help him out, I agreed. Being on the move seemed to be beneficial for my mental health, and allowing myself to be in a position where I could assist someone else felt good, too. This particular trip served also to turn up some fresh sections of bamboo driftwood and some more of the slim nuts so I felt that just putting myself out there was always a good idea. You never knew what you might find or bump into.

As I mulled this over, as if to prove my point, on the forest floor I noticed a quite sizeable hermit crab scurrying from left to right in front of me. I picked it up by the shell to show it to camera and, to my surprise, it made an emergency evacuation – dropping to the ground, leaving its shell home in my hand. As I hadn't got a fire I wasn't yet in a position to cook it so I left it beside its empty shell hoping it would be able to move back in once it had got over the shock of meeting a clumsy white giant.

As I picked my way back down the western slope from the Faraway Tree I could hear the goats down on the beach near the cave. I yelped as loudly as I could to scare them off. 'Don't eat my bedding!' was my immediate concern. By the time I reached the cave they had gone and the bedding was untouched. I needed to teach these goats about demarcation – this was *my* territory now. In retrospect I might have welcomed them in, making it easier to catch them later.

With my focus very much still on fire I experimented with the three different types of wood that I'd collected from the forest as hearths for a hand drill. I spent all morning carving notches into all the new hearths and the new bamboo saw. None looked that promising but I had to keep trying so that I might eventually stumble upon the right wood. Every piece of wood that I carved was teaching me about wood density, dryness and degree of decomposition. Through my failures I began to get an idea of what I had really been looking for in the first place.

Still keeping my options open, I also wanted to improve my bow drill set. The bearing block (a pretty shell I'd found on the beach) was biting into the top of the drill too much, causing friction where it wasn't wanted and slowing it down. I placed a plastic bottle top inside the shell to act as a smoother inner bearing and the set ran considerably more easily.

One very inconvenient truth was that the snails were running out. It showed that one shouldn't be too dependent on a single source of food but that was an unwelcome lesson as snails were my main protein source and had seemed infinite. Could they be seasonal and now at the end of their season? Had I eaten them all? Would their population re-establish itself? Two steps forward – another step back ...

There are moments in life that you just know are right. Moments that sing through the darkness in a voice of truth and purity and vibrate from within your body so that you know they are significant. I stood and looked at a rather unprepossessing twisted tree with dark gnarled bark and nondescript oval leaves. It was on the edge of my beach and about twenty metres from my cave and I must have walked past it ten times every day since my arrival. I squinted, I smiled, I didn't know whether to put my hopes into words for fear of jinxing what I believed – no, *knew* – to be true.

'Tangalito.' I almost whispered the word. 'I will test it with Rama's fire-plough method to see if it chars. If this is the tree that was identified to me on Komo then I can't express how much this would mean.' My measured words didn't go half way to describing what was going on inside me. I knew this was a game changer. By now I was pretty resigned to the fact that I'd forgotten what tangalito even looked like and I was just trialling any old wood, but something was standing by this tree pointing at it with a green flag. Warmth spread through me as I used all my body weight to snap off a large branch.

I was so confident that I even handled this wood differently – as if it was an antique vase that needed due respect and a light touch. With my bow working well now, I knew that I was going to use that method. There were no sections long or straight enough to make a hand drill anyway. Taking two sections, I braced one against a rock and used the other to work aggressively back and forth as if I was scratching the itchiest of mosquito bites. Sure enough, without too much effort the pieces of wood began to char and a light wisp of smoke floated up. This method of testing could have been applied to every wood that I'd sourced to date and I realised it all too late. I could have saved literally days of carving and whittling if I'd just applied what I already knew.

I skinned a cigar-sized drill and cut it to length, then I carved the two ends into perfect circular domes with such care that I knew I would reap rewards for this diligence. I split the hearth and left both sections in the sun to dry. The wood was live so I guessed it would need a couple of days to dry out. Looking back, having already charred the wood I'm not sure that this was strictly necessary, but I wasn't going to rush this; all my trust was in this wood. If I did this right it would change my existence here permanently.

While my prime candidate was drying, I experimented with bamboo and once more tried the fire-saw method. From the outset I had a far more compassionate and understanding attitude towards the experiment due to the security of having my tangalito in reserve and the reassurance that gave me. I had never tried to use bamboo to light a fire before but I knew the principles and so I decided that I just had to give it a go and see what happened. If it worked – great. If not – I would again have learned more about methods and materials.

In my first attempt the bamboo had been too weak and it had snapped. This new bamboo was better but for some unknown reason I could not create enough heat to get an ember. As a side product what I had found, however, was the best fine-grade tinder I had seen so far on the island, so, at the end of the day, when I decided that the fire-saw was not going to live up to its name, I took the incredibly fine bamboo tinder that I'd made and added it to the centre of my coarser coconut husk tinder ball. I'd learned more about a method and I'd improved my chances of turning an ember into fire by improving my tinder ball. Despite the lack of fire I glanced at the tangalito drying in the sun – I was happy with a productive and positive day's work.

I think working in the shade of the cave with my hands on one single task had been calming for me. I was learning what I found reassuring and what unsettled me. As the sun dropped lower in the sky and filled my cave once more with a golden glow I sat solidly on the Cinesaddle and contemplated my state of affairs on the island to date with camera in hand.

There was a place I could get to where I wasn't in conflict, where everything felt right and things just flowed. At the moment it wasn't consistent but it was reassuring to know that I had the ability to step out of the confusion and the madness and tune into a purer, more peaceful self. I was far from understanding what this all meant but I was happy with how I felt this evening and what I'd achieved. Working with my hands had tuned me in so much that it had opened my eyes to the tangalito that I'd been walking past for days.

I allowed myself to feel out across the ocean to Amanda and the kids. I have the most striking fiancée; she is unique. Half-Japanese, half-British – with the posture of a dancer and the bone structure of a model, her glossy black mane is her strength flowing down her slender back. Her steely will and capacity to face problems head-on had led me to nickname her 'Stands-with-a-fist', after the character in *Dances with Wolves*, as it seemed to fit her inner commitment to what is right so well. Amanda had come into my life about thirteen months ago and I hoped we would always be together. She has two beautiful kids and I missed them now. With all my heart I missed them.

A tear rolled down my cheek in the twilight. I felt the luckiest man alive.

ℋℋ III

y body had tightened up from lying on the dirt floor and I clicked my stiff neck free. Anxiety bit me like a plague of eels as I surfaced to the worries of my situation.

As I pressed 'OK' on the InReach I desperately wanted to say more. To cry out that I was sad and lonely – just to have someone know how desperate I felt. Instead I passively watched the routine message send and powered down my narrow portal to the rest of the world.

My stomach churned and I knew what was coming. Not bothering to put on my grass skirt, I hurried down the jagged rocks and across the sand. Such was my diarrhoea that it started before I reached the water's edge, leaving a humiliating brown trail behind me. Without the strength to squat and keep my balance I went straight down on all fours in the cold wet sand. In this inhuman position I felt pathetic – like a stray, disease-ridden dog. Wave after wave of knotted stomach pain gave way to degrading release as I sank on to my elbows to save energy and increase stability. Head resting in the cold sand I wondered why anyone would volunteer to put themselves through such a challenge. What was wrong with me?

Washing myself in the harsh seawater I felt that the skin between my buttocks was becoming dry and cracked. I walked back up the beach as if both legs were dragging bags of fertiliser through the sand. This, I knew, was a tell-tale sign of malnutrition and dehydration.

I spent an hour trying to repair my grass blanket. My novice construction had been crude and I'd not worked out that the layers of grass that you tie into the strands of bark must overlap, as if you are laying bricks. My blanket had huge lines of weakness where the ends of the clumps all finished together – now gaping holes. It would not survive many more restless nights. It was still keeping me warm but was it worth all this time expended? I put it down to experience – what else could I do but learn from the error?

In the end it took all morning. Crikey. I tried to reassure myself that it was vital to ensure that I slept well. Still, I couldn't help beating myself up for not making it properly in the first place. It's incredible how something so understandable, so easily forgiven in any other situation, starts to feel like a hanging offence when you're on your own and trying to survive. Very crudely salvaged, I stopped work on the blanket. I needed a drink and I needed some food.

Upon inspection of the seep I was confused to see that the second fill of the day had only about 150ml inside the bottle. The seep was now emitting less and the only factor remaining was the uncomfortable reality that I'd not had sustained rainfall (nothing longer than a minute) since I arrived on the island and the groundwater was now drying up.

I saved the precious 150ml into my two-litre bottle and drank the measly 100ml that was in the top pool. The bottom hollow was dry.

I still felt sick as a pig, I'd lost a lot of water and I didn't have the means to replace it. Doctors and survival experts agree that eating raw snails every day would have undoubtedly been one of the causes for my illness. In extreme cases if you lose a lot of water, and that is accompanied by loss of salt, you can fall into a coma and die because your brain starts swelling. But it was the milder symptoms — apathy, irritability, lethargy and poor decision-making — that were wracking me now.

The blazing heat of the sun slapped my bare torso as a reminder that I needed fluids fast. My new Y-pole may have been a good two metres longer than the last one but that meant it was also much heavier. As I struggled along the beach to find a good coconut tree my legs started to set as if I'd just swallowed a bowlful of cement.

I stood below a coconut palm where my Y-trunk now reached the fruit and heaved the cumbersome tool upright like a flagpole. The weight was five times that of my previous pole.

Now I was standing with the base of the pole cupped above my chest in two hands and attempting to thrust upwards like a shot-putter into bunches of green coconuts, hoping to dislodge one of them. Each clumsy shove was feeble as a result of the great weight of my pole and I could not produce enough force to get a single coconut down.

No coconuts ... I am still thirsty ... and now I'm exhausted ... because I've just spent all morning repairing a blanket ... that is still in tatters ... and now I'm panicking ... because I need to drink ... and I've wasted more time and more energy ...

The panic gained momentum, spun around my head in chaos and exploded out of my mouth.

'FUUUUUUCK!'

My verbalisation of despair was long and desperate.

There are times when roaring is a release valve to the mess that is going on inside, and I had no other way of expelling this negative energy.

'FUUUUUUCK!' I screamed again.

I had always said that I would aim to try to ride out any ups and downs in events by staying true to my own sense of self and yet it was day eight and I could not help but cast myself as a useless failure. I was struggling even to find water – let alone concentrate on more advanced survival priorities like making fire. I allowed myself to wallow in self-pity and beat myself up that I was failing miserably. I don't remember ever having felt this low before.

Necessity saw me lying in the sand and kicked me hard in the stomach. I had no option but to continue trying. I had to drink.

I moved slowly down the beach and tried two more trees. From the last tree I got a single green coconut down but it had nothing in it. Letting the pole rest on the sand, I used it to help me to continue to stand. Desperation had levels that I'd previously not known about.

But nothing lasts for ever. My final tree was lower than the ones that I'd been trying and I didn't have to stretch as high to thrust the pole upwards into the nest of green eggs. Pop, one fell down, then another, then a third. Finally, I broke into some healthy full fruits and drank the sweet fluid as if it were life energy itself, liquid love, flooding into my dying body.

But my eventual reward was tinged with dread as I knew that these were the last coconuts that I could get on my side of the island. The pole was at my limit in terms of weight that I could lift – I couldn't make a longer one. I drank the second coconut and carried the third back with me to the cave.

A beautiful Fijian island in the Pacific Ocean. A tropical paradise with sandy beaches and untouched forested interior. An idyllic world with no predators, no poisonous snakes, few mosquitoes and plentiful fish. Why, then, does no one live on it? I'll tell you why.

Because there is NO BLOODY FRESH WATER.

For certain parts of the year the island produces less water than can sustain one adult male. That's why nobody lives, or has ever lived, on Olorua.

I walked back to the cave and looked for something that I could do with little expended energy. I took the tangalito sections up into the cave and decided that the afternoon was a good one to whittle. I used a variety of grades of shells as my cutting tools and I began to carve a hollow in the hearth for the drill to sit in. I had to evolve. I had to make fire.

As the sun approached the horizon I tried to pee. It was a very short burst, dark yellow, and its smell hit my nostrils, causing me to physically jerk my head back from the pungent stench. With that cheery signal of dehydration I flicked off the cameras and packed them away. Bollocks to filming. I walked around the island taking in the last hour of golden sunlight to recharge myself. I couldn't find any water. On Bravo Beach I located one last tree of coconuts that I would still be able to access with my pole.

Although the carpentry and my evening walk had calmed me I couldn't eat supper when I got back. Rationality now slipping, I pulled the leg off a raw crab and tried to force it down. I had always maintained that I wouldn't take the risk with raw crabs. The sharp fishy mass passing through my throat caused me to vomit coconut water on to the beach. Today I had drunk three coconuts, 900ml of fresh water and eaten twenty snails, but due to my rashness much of that consumption was now draining into the wet sand. I felt weak, nauseous and pathetic.

卌 ||||

My short golden stream of urine arced over the rocks and down on to the wet sand below. 'Wee one – day nine,' I scowled at the camera as I commenced a self-imposed pee diary to monitor my dehydration.

The water in the seep was even lower than yesterday. The first check of the day made me wonder if the wick was still working properly. I was desperate for fluids so I gulped down the water in the top pool and decanted the water in the bottle, *just 200ml*, for later. Completely unsatisfied, I longed for a cup of tea or a long, thick banana milkshake, but such thoughts were torture.

I decided to excavate the beach under a big tree that was growing in a prominent crack near my seep. My thoughts were that the crack should allow water to filter through the rock and that the tree must be using this water to survive. Perhaps there would be another seep of sorts below ground level under the sand. Down on all fours with my clamshell, I excavated a hole big enough to bury myself in. I was wrong. The cliff was dry.

I cleaned out my allotment of giant clamshells so that, if I got some rain, they would not be full of leaves and sand. 'Come on, rain!' I coaxed at the benign sky.

The sun had almost completed her ritual daily arc when I opted to excavate some more holes in the beach by Lemon Camp. There were several tiny little streams that were flowing off the beach that I wanted to test for brackishness. I allowed the holes to fill with water and then settle.

Water was the main thing – the only thing – now. Fire seemed like a superfluous luxury in comparison. If I didn't get more water I couldn't survive. I was down to my last few obtainable coconuts. With the extra coconut tree that I found last night on my lap of the island, with a longer stick I reckoned I could survive three more days.

After an hour I tasted the streams and they were still salty – far too salty to drink. I didn't want to call them brackish because I wasn't even sure that there was any fresh water in them at all. The streams must just have been salt water draining from the upper beach as the tide went out. I must have looked very desperate on all fours again, lapping at the pools with my tongue to test for salt, but I'd only had 200ml of fresh water today and that looked like being it. What other option did I have?

'I've checked every crack in every rock. I've tasted every stream coming out of every craggy orifice of this fucking dried-up prune of an island.' It only had to rain and I'd be fine. But it was day nine and I'd had less than a minute of rain in my whole time here. 'I feel like I've been drinking salt water all day. I don't know the solution. I just don't know the solution,' I sighed.

On the way back I found a load of old man's beard – great for fire lighting. This lichen was very handy as I could put it in my tinder bundle. It was super-fine and dry and could help me catch an ember.

More valuable were two taro plants that I spotted in a clearing. It was fantastic news as taro is edible but they were small – about a foot high – and so I decided to allow them to grow some more before I dug them up. Spurred on, I searched the whole of the northern end of the island for further edible plants and roots but found nothing. I was being very aware of the sun and the shadows in order to stay orientated. I walked peacefully – hunger and thirst making my day almost dream-like – exploring the interior.

Staying high from the north tip I worked my way back round the west coast (the left side as you look at the map) to just above the rock headland between my beach and Bravo Beach. I hadn't dipped below about thirty metres above sea level and had had brief glimpses of the neat coral reef that circled the island like the rings of Saturn. I wanted to get to the highest point on the island so from the headland I moved inland and upwards along the spur. As the ground became steeper I had to pull myself up through the bushes to reach the summit, which was just a small patch of uneven rocky ground amidst a tangle of dense spiky plants. Once again – no view at all.

If I'd had the composure I would have laughed at the parallels to my mental state. I was busting a gut to reach a place of perspective and all I could see was the tangled undergrowth around me. The forest seemed to personify *ngan duppurru*. I was based on a beach with the most wonderful view in the world – all I had to do was breathe and open my eyes – and yet I was slogging through the dense jungle interior looking for a better view. I began to think I was addicted to the struggle.

From the summit I headed south. Without looking, I found a green coconut on the floor so I drank the water, ate a little of the flesh and threw the rest away. Then I was hit by the fact that I wasn't as ravenous as I had been. It was day nine – why wasn't I eating everything that I could? Today I'd only had 200ml of water and that green coconut. I hadn't eaten any snails today – I hadn't been able to face them. I looked up into the canopy to see coconut trees all around. The green beacon on the brown forest floor had served to show me that I had only been looking for coconuts around the coast. Of course much of the interior was dotted with the palm trees and I was thumped in the arm by my own stupidity.

The southern tip of the island was a distinct point that jutted out into the sea like the tail of a comma. I could see the reef beyond and hear the waves crashing against it. The shallow water inside the lagoon was a very clear turquoise and even from 300 metres away I knew that I would have been able to see sharks if there had been any. I felt as if I could see every grain of sand beneath the unclouded waters.

As I turned about I contoured around to the east of the island (the right as you're looking at my map), this time to find the third peak, and I spilled out on to a natural amphitheatre and immediately realised that it must be the drainage basin that had Lemon Camp at the bottom. This single view put the whole island in place for me for the first time. I had a mental picture of the topography although I hadn't found any more taro.

I wandered down to Lemon Camp just to verify my guess. In a way I wished that the island had been cleaned up a bit before I arrived. I was finding things that I could not ignore that had been left by the local Fijians on one of their fruit-collecting trips. This time the item that made me deliberate was an old long-sleeved top. The green shirt was half buried at the edge of Lemon Camp and had obviously been discarded as being too old and too full of holes. I gently pulled the item free of the earth and saw that it had hundreds of tiny roots already growing through it. Clearly an item like this was a massive help. I could wear it to go out in the midday sun and fish. I could use it to keep warmer at nights.

But right then, at that moment, I deliberated. This is a Discovery Channel series with the word 'naked' in the title – can I really just get dressed? From a survival perspective it was a no-brainer but I wasn't just thinking from a survival perspective – I was filming and self-directing a television series. Editorially this would change the whole look of the series from this point onwards because I would not be naked from the waist up. Clearly a self-made grass skirt is one thing but a green long-sleeved top? I wasn't sure but I took it as a gift from the island.

On the way home I spotted three of the goats bleating in the sun. I was fairly adamant that the way to kill these goats was to make them tame, lull them into a false sense of security with me and then – bosh – nab one for supper. I decided to speak in a calm voice so that they would know I was there but not relate to me as a predator. My reading-to-the-children voice got me to within three metres of the animals before they fled.

Back at the Faraway Tree I felt like I had a mental map of the entire island for the first time. I knew the three high points, the amphitheatre and gully that led down to Lemon Camp, and the aspect of each of the beaches and slopes above. I was oriented now and the island had lost some of its dark mystery accordingly. Thank goodness.

As I broke through the tree line and my pupils contracted in the bright morning light something was different about the beach. A bit like when you instinctively know a burglar has been in your house, my senses were heightened and I investigated on high alert.

Footprints in the sand. Lots of them. Goats. I registered this and hurried towards my cave. The goats had ventured on to my beach while I'd been out of the camp and I was curious to see if they were in the cave and whether, just maybe, I could trap one.

As I rounded Snail Rock that split my beach in half I could see footprints everywhere but no sign of the goats themselves. I followed the tracks in the soft sand not to the cave but beyond. 'My fresh water!' I unwillingly registered.

The goats had knocked over the collection bottle and it was trodden into the sand alongside the cordage wick. I had decanted 200ml into a larger bottle earlier this morning and screwed a lid on, and that was still there, but every drop that had been collected during my morning walkabout was wasted.

I drank the small gritty slurp of fresh water that was in the hollow and rebuilt the seep. 'I need to lie down. I'm going to the cave.' I threw in my towel to the camera.

It's hard to convey how much I allowed the water situation to stress me. I allowed myself to think that survival on the island might be impossible because of it. On reflection I don't think it was – it was a trick of my mind that I'm only now beginning to understand. I think it gave me an excuse not to be responsible for my situation and to blame something else.

As I write I know that I should have calmly cut a longer, lighter pole, collected more green coconuts peacefully while whistling 'Whistle While You Work' and I would have been just fine. But I was no longer just dealing with the physical requirement to be hydrated – this had become very much a self-created distraction, a battle to become entangled in, a war in my head to avert my attention from the truth. What truth? That I needed to be accountable. That I needed to take responsibility for myself and look after myself. That nothing or no one else should affect my self-belief. That I could trust myself to make it on my own.

Isolation was taking its toll on me and I was running scared instead of facing it head-on. I needed someone or something to get angry with about my situation and so water was currently it. What I should have realised, of course, was that I was the only person who could help myself and I just needed to take full responsibility for my water situation. I didn't – I felt out of control and I spiralled into being a victim of cruel circumstance. I projected bad planning on to the production crew. I felt that the weather was my enemy. Anything to distract me from being present, accepting what was going on, taking my life into my own hands, and dancing through it all. But my anger was all-consuming and blocked the simple lesson I was being taught.

By mid-afternoon I decided – not really sure why – to build a shelter. My mental state was definitely affecting my judgement and I rushed into an attempt at home building. My offering was a sort of Cub Scout bivouac with flimsy poles and a poor attempt at thatching. I spent about four hours cutting poles, making beach hibiscus cordage and lashing a small frame together. By the time the evening was drawing in I had tied on about six woven coconut palm tiles, too, in an attempt to thatch it. The shelter was small, weak, rushed and only half finished.

'Wow – definitely going a bit doolally,' I admitted to the lens in a moment of partial clarity, 'but I am halfway through the shelter and I've invested a huge amount of time into it.' I was freezing cold and the wind was howling in off the beach. There was a storm coming. I was tired, deflated and fucking miserable.

Only a pinch of analysis reveals that I was attempting to be constructive and make something that I could look at and be proud of to make myself feel better. In a flash I saw why I'd needed to walk the Amazon. Hang your hat on that achievement, Ed, and you can forget about growing up and becoming accountable. My expectations of being able to move into my tiny shelter this day were absurd. I abandoned the crappy shelter and returned to the cave deflated.

I was really struggling to get coconuts, and I could have spent the four hours calmly collecting from new sources in the interior. But I hadn't. I'd had twenty snails but I needed to get some carbohydrates in me. I was going to eat snails, felt like retching and I thought if I ate snails again I was going to vomit.

Then it hit me. 'I think I'm actually ill. Fuck.' I feel horrendous and I have fifty days left. I was burping a lot – had trapped air inside me. Illness instantly became the next thing to use for an excuse for my inability. It wasn't *my* fault if I was ill. That was outside my control. Deep down I knew that two months on an island was nothing compared to 860 walking the Amazon but in this isolated, stripped-bare existence it seemed an eternity. I felt very sorry for myself and was scrabbling for a justified escape route from the next fifty days.

'Just absolutely exhausted – at the end of my tether,' I moaned. 'I need to get to a point where I'm eating enough food and drinking enough water.' Projecting the blame on to this one, all-consuming thing kept me in a state of being out of control. 'Without water – you can't have life!' I panicked. I wanted to go to sleep, to shut out the madness and confusion of this world … but it was only lunchtime.

'OK. Take control, Ed – you need to slow down and make something that does actually benefit you.' I acknowledged that I had been wrong to try and build a shelter at this stage as I had my cave. Shelter shouldn't have been high on my list of priorities anyway.

Keep it simple. Small tasks. The green shirt. I hung on to the plan that other achievements would cancel out my frustration with the water. Clearly I was avoiding the one thing I needed to address because I found it easier to blame than to fix. With a sense of purpose I took the dirty green shirt into the shallows and washed it in seawater. I had to be gentle as the worn material was already paper-thin and full of small holes. I carefully picked out every small root, trying not to traumatise further the terminally ill garment. Once rinsed and lightly wrung out, I hung it on a branch in the soft evening sun to dry and was surprised at how comforting it was to have washing hanging out to dry. How utterly, reassuringly normal. But distraction now over, my situation remained the same.

I dragged the giant pole on to Bravo Beach to harvest more green coconuts. With the new view and sitting in the new surroundings I attempted to make a coconut palm hat. I had only ever seen this done on YouTube but it had looked simple enough. I had to split the frond, cut it to just over the circumference of my head, plait it and join the ends into a circular crown.

I managed all this but then there was a bit that involved passing all the ends through the central hole to make a rim for the hat. Try as I might, I could not remember what to do next, or improvise anything that didn't cause the whole palm leaf to unravel. I was too tired to do it properly and I stopped trying after an hour and a half. 'How about I just stick that T-shirt that I found today on my head, eh?' I proposed. 'That'll work.' I looked defeated.

I tried on the green shirt for the first time once it had dried. I did a twirl with my arms extended. 'Clothes!' It felt luxurious and decadent to slip the material over my bare skin. I stared at the camera screen showing me in clothes. The fit was good. 'Thank God Fijians are big bastards.'

With no great expectations, I checked the seep. As predicted, virtually no fresh water in the plastic bottle at the end of the day. The sun, which was now pressing down on the horizon, had cooked and decommissioned the water collection system all afternoon. I tried to bash down ten raw snails before bed and these were slightly different – darker, larger shells with a body that had a green fleshy section on it. I almost gagged after swallowing the first but on number six I started vomiting. And I kept on vomiting. Five coconuts' worth of fluid emptied from my stomach. I'd just lost all my hydration.

Again.

Back in the cave the purging left me feeling reflective. 'Do you know what? I'm never going to take anything for granted again. I have an amazing life. I have an *amazing* life. This isn't amazing, though – this bit of my life,' I chuckled. 'This bit of my life is less than amazing.'

I started to smile and caught myself doing so. 'Why are you smiling, you idiot?' The black humour seemed to work, though, as I became distracted and grinned. 'Eeee – I got a shirt today!'

I was wearing the green long-sleeve top to bed and it felt really good to have some form of proper clothing on. I was a bit warmer, a bit more comfortable, and, most importantly, I felt a bit more normal. I'd said I'd save it for fishing but it was cold at night – really cold – so it became my pyjama top, too.

<del>卌 卌</del>

My triumphant strike through the second block of five on the wall of the cave took me, significantly, into double figures. But I knew ten days was only a fraction of what lay in store.

'Morning, day ten,' I reported to the camera with a clipped matter of factness. I hadn't slept much as it had been a particularly windy night.

At the back of my mind I hung on to a glimmer of hope that digging a well would solve my problems. As a geographer I determined that if there was any fresh water to be found on the island it would be subterranean. The island was too small for rivers but after rainfall water would be concentrated in certain areas. The only obvious drainage basin that I had located was on the east of the island surrounding Lemon Camp. A drainage basin is simply land that is shaped like a bowl or an amphitheatre. Water that falls within the limits of this basin (the watershed) would flow towards the lowest point because of gravity. If my instinct was right, there should be a small gully or natural drainage ditch near Lemon Camp – at the lowest point towards which the water was focused – and finding this was my quest for the morning.

I ambled back into the forest and began to climb. I found it difficult not to sound melodramatic about just how little energy I had in order to complete this journey. My whole body was full of scrap iron, and four times in the (normally now fourteen-minute) journey I had to collapse into the leaf litter so as to recharge my batteries just enough to pick myself up again and start walking. My hunger had returned with a vengeance. The crossing took about fifty minutes.

On the other side of the island in Lemon Camp I found an old basket made from coconut palms that I could use to harvest sea food. I then ate six of the slim wafer-like nuts. I was pretty sure it was the coconut making me sick as I'd just drunk one and immediately felt awful.

Facing Lemon Camp, with the beach behind me, I turned left and followed the land downhill. Within a minute I was standing in an area where, when I was facing the island, the land rose both to my left and to my right. I squinted through the trees looking inland and I was indeed in a very shallow, almost unperceivable, gully full of fallen trees and undergrowth.

I decided to follow the gully inland and to look for an obvious natural point to excavate. I pulled myself through small gaps between trees and climbed over and under fallen boughs. Twenty metres in I found a depression. A large horizontal tree root had created a mini cliff in the gully that had subsequently formed a small dried-up plunge pool below it. The base of this depression was filled with large rocks piled on top of each other. I dropped heavily to my knees in the clay and hauled aside one rock after another. I began to excavate the gully with my bare hands – wiggling the vast rocks from the sucking clay and casting them aside. The sloppier the clay became the more I knew I was excavating the right place. I used a stick and then my bare hands to claw away the soggy lumps of clay and was eventually left with a two-foot-deep hole in the dry riverbed.

I knew that clay is virtually impermeable and therefore that I would not hit a water-table as such, as the soil particles were too densely packed to allow much water to flow through it. This meant my well would not fill from the groundwater seeping in and I would probably have to wait for rainfall. The waterproof characteristics of the clay should, however, ensure it worked as a vast collecting bucket. Rainwater would run down the hillside and concentrate in the gully and flow down to my newly excavated hole and, with a bit of luck, fill it up.

Despite the fact that I'd not been able to hit a water-table, I had more information about the island's hydrology and I had a new method of collecting rainwater on a far bigger scale than I would have imagined possible. Screw giant clamshells – I was now able to harness the rain that fell in an area the size of New York's Central Park.

Should the rain ever fall.

The way back was even slower. Once, when I sank to the floor, I think I allowed myself almost to drift off to sleep. Apathy was overtaking me once more. 'I just don't care.' I reminded myself of the stories I'd been told of Everest climbers who'd given up, sat down and accepted death. Due to the lack of oxygen and fatigue, they just didn't care about death any more – it seemed inviting compared with having to walk any further. The comparison allowed me some perspective and I realised my situation was nothing like as dire. It spurred me on.

I smashed open a brown coconut that had a reasonable amount of milky fluid in it. I forced down a few chunks of the white flesh and then grabbed a fistful of snails from the water's edge. I gulped down the first slippery mollusc and felt nauseous.

The second made me gag violently and once more I vomited forcefully into the sand. I stood, dazed, looking at the familiar sight of my vomit (it represented all my nutrition and hydration for the day) yet again wasted on the beach.

I wasn't learning, was I?

Back in my cave I felt cold and helpless. The vomiting made me despise the sight of the coconuts and I tried to force some of the slippery flesh down but it made me gag again.

'Should I take that first course of antibiotics?'

Long pause for thought.

I needed to get rid of this diarrhoea and vomiting to have any hope of building up my energy levels. 'Maybe I should. I don't care about breaking open the kit any more.' I couldn't have cared less about the project or the Discovery Channel series – both seemed surreal and contrived in my weakened state. Breaking open the medical kit meant that I could not say that I'd only used what was on the island to survive – but I was ill, and desperately weak, and I just didn't care. I took five metronidazole tablets as a one-off, kill-everything-bad-inside-my-gut dose.

In my muddled state, blame still seemed to be my brain's way of coping with my predicament and I projected my frustration outwards. With anger now came a certain degree of paranoia. How could *they* be so stupid as to put me on an island without a reliable water source? Were *they* incompetent or just careless? Were *they* now laughing about this? Wankers. Could I sue them for any illness that resulted from this?

This unconscious behavioural strategy sent me more out of control than ever. I could not change what they had done. I had made myself the victim here and I felt pathetically sorry for myself. I could not make it rain and I got angrier and more indifferent about the survival task itself. It was all so outside my control anyway. In this helpless state I couldn't even entertain the idea of a failure and so, as the afternoon passed, I did no work to help progress my ability to make fire. I lay in the cave and told myself it was a waste of time and wouldn't work anyway.

The sky darkened and mirrored my drab mood. A light grey mist of drizzle blew in from the south-west. But the mood association with bad weather lifted as I watched my prepared clamshells fill with pure fresh rainwater. This was *fresh water* – no amount of depression could suffocate the excitement that stirred inside me as I gazed at the raindrop bombs exploding into my field of ceramic-looking bath tubs. After ten minutes the rain stopped and I used the same sucking and blowing technique with the straw that I'd used for the forty seconds of rain that I'd got on day six. I collected over a litre of fresh rainwater, screwed the lid on the water bottle and took it up to the cave.

I crawled into my patch of dirt and pulled the dry grass over my fragile body. Lying down was bliss. Not having to use any energy felt amazing. There was still half an hour of daylight left but I shut my eyes and told myself that nothing ever stays the same. I had my water. Tomorrow had to be better.

$$\cancel{||||}\ \cancel{||||}\ |$$

I tried to scratch the eleventh mark on the cave wall but, as I'd run out of flat space, they were no longer really recognisable as marks. As I'd got to grips with the cameras I'd decided to set the date and time so the primitive markings were pointless now anyway. Bugger what I *should* do – what *they* wanted me to do. I was going to use everything I had to get through this nightmare.

I took a quick inventory of my physical state and I did feel somewhat less ill – perhaps the antibiotics had worked. I glanced at the two-litre bottle. 'Ooh, that's a nice amount of water to wake up to – I forgot it rained last night.'

I climbed down to the shells. It had indeed rained again in the night so I was able to do my decanting-by-straw palaver again to top up my growing stores. 'That's a pretty special moment,' I beamed at the camera. 'Two FULL litres of fresh rainwater!' I hadn't even checked the rock seep yet. The seep provided another 600ml, including the top pool.

'Drinking freely – drinking freely, Edward! Hee hee hee,' I chuckled.

It was dropbox day and I set out around the coast to Lemon Camp. I was keen to see the results of my newly dug well. 'Water – with renewed vigour,' I stated, already considerably more hydrated and feeling the benefits. 'And hopefully we can put this one to bed as water really bores me.'

I made the drop of used cards and dead batteries and with high hopes went to inspect the nearby well that I'd excavated the day before. I pushed between the bushes feeling as if I had a winning lottery ticket and knew that my numbers were about to come up. Sure enough, as I peered over the circular opening in the forest floor my own reflection stared back at me in a glossy brown mirror of water. 'It works! It bloody works!' I howled through the trees to every living thing that could hear me. Yesterday evening's and last night's rainfall had indeed tracked down from every distant reach of the catchment area to fall at the last hurdle – trapped in my well – rather than flowing out into the ocean.

I had brought five plastic bottles with lids on and one by one I submerged each bottle in order to hear the soft brown bubbles of air escape as they filled with fresh rainwater. If I'd had more bottles on me I could have filled them, too. The resulting liquid consisted of a lot of clay sediment in suspension but I could tell that if left to settle in the cave I could gently pour off cleaner water. From a hydration point of view things were looking much, much brighter.

In the clearing behind the camp were the two taro plants that I'd found earlier. Widespread across South-East Asia, taro is a plant with large arrow-shaped leaves and edible starchy tubers that taste a bit like potatoes. I began to carefully dig down through the damp soil with a sharp stick to unearth my next meal.

I was pleasantly surprised to reveal four potato-like corms and I decided to replant the main stem of the taro in the hope that it might produce again. With two of these corms in each hand I made unusually light work of the return journey to my cave on the beach. Carbohydrate – what a great find! Of course I had coconut, which I had thought was a carb for my time on the island, but for some unfathomable reason it didn't give me much strength or fullness in my muscles. Later, back in the real world of Google, I was to find out that coconut is in fact 89 per cent saturated fat – so it was little surprise that it wasn't the ideal choice for replenishing my depleted glycogen stores. Taro, on the other hand, would do just fine.

In the cave I used a natural ledge at the back to rest the bottles of clay water in a neat row to allow the sediment to settle. I'd found two more flip-flops washed up from the ocean that were wearable and the cushioning under my soles was a real life-saver as sometimes now I woke up in the night for a wee and could hardly stand. The bottoms of my feet were almost beyond soreness. They were a constant reminder that my existence here was still precarious.

The carbohydrate find had been a real boost and, not wanting to spend too long on my bottom in the cave, I took one of the now plentiful plastic bottles into the shade of the woods and decided to make a fish trap. I knew the theory and I could tell it would be simple to implement. But as I explained what I was doing to the camera I found I was stumbling over my words and that even a simple explanation was now a challenge for me. I would benefit from any extra protein and omega oils if this trap worked to get my brain working better again. I had to chop off the tapered end of the bottle to leave two parts: a tall tub and a funnel. My clamshell was too big and blunt to use to cut the plastic and a rusty tin lid I'd found in Lemon Camp days before wasn't sharp enough either. In the end I used my teeth and tore the bottle apart. It wasn't pretty but at least it was now in two pieces – I sighed a half-amused smile at the crude result. I then turned the funnel end around and slid it inside the bottom section, spout first. What resulted was a trap that had a large orifice that tapered down to a small entrance to a contained space. Fish would be able to find their way in, but they are not the brightest of creatures and most of them would never be able to find their way out.

I whistled the tune of A-Ha's 'The Sun Always Shines on TV' as I walked the small plastic lobster-pot-like trap 200 metres further down the beach. The rock pool I selected was cupped by a large expanse of black rock that sat at the south of Alpha Beach like a vast old wooden ship that had run aground. I had observed the pool before and knew it had a good constant stock of two- to three-inch sprats. I smashed two snails, crudely shelled them and stuffed them down the spout into the trap's belly as bait. I then lowered the bottle into the pool, resting it at arm's length on the sandy bottom. The salt water lapped at my armpit hairs and the tiny fish darted in to nibble my cracked fingers. I placed a flat rock on the top of the bottle to keep it in place and, satisfied, walked, quietly expectant, back to the cave.

Even in the sun I realised I was shivering cold. With goose bumps standing my arm hairs on end I tiptoed down to the water's edge to wash the taro corms in the sea. In the state I was in I could have wolfed down all four of these vegetables in one sitting and still been ravenous but they were raw and I knew that I had to attempt to make such valuable food last. I decided I would allow myself one vegetable a day for the next four days and selected the one that would be consumed now. I lay sprawled on the beach to save energy and tried a small mouthful. It was easier to eat than a raw potato. Was that because I'd never tried a raw potato when I was this hungry? The white starch swam around my gums – I could still hardly eat it. 'I feel sick. Anything that goes into my stomach makes me feel sick.' I lay back and let out an exasperated cry: 'Aaaaaarghhhh! What is *wrong* with me? Get out the sun, Stafford. You are embarrassing yourself.'

I dragged myself back up the beach to what I'd now named Shipwreck Pool – for want of a better name – and plunged my arm into the cool water. The plastic broke the surface of the pool and I was elated to see a swirling vortex of brown bodies inside the chamber. I estimated I'd caught seven two-inch sprats. A grin spread across my face as I reaped the emotional rewards of success. That was the easiest fishing trip ever. And I knew I could repeat it at *every* low tide.

Try as I might, I could not ride the wave of elation for long. Back in the cave I lay down on the grass with my eyes shut for about half an hour to recover my energy. I also set the camera down on the back of the large black Peli case (plastic waterproof case that I'd brought all my camera kit in) so that I could film myself cutting into the fish with the rusty tin lid. The cross-section of the fish was perhaps only a centimetre in diameter but I could see that it was indeed real flesh. I removed any gunk from the insides by tenderly squeezing down the body until it popped, like a big zit, out of their rectums. The sprats were in fact more like loach, the fish you buy for your fish tank that swim along the bottom and clean the gravel. 'They're a bit ugly … and they eat shit,' I explained, deadpan. I wiped the black gooey innards on my leg and popped each fish whole into my mouth. They had a nasty sharp twang to them, and they took a bit of crunching into, but they were better than raw snails and they provided me with vitally different nutrients such as omega oils and higher-grade protein.

As the fish fats soaked through my brain, oiling the dry cogs, the innovations department that had been closed due to lack of resources flicked on its lights, rolled up the shutters and put a sign outside declaring it was once more open for business. I held the rusty tin can lid between my dirty blunt fingers. Maybe – just maybe – this could work …

Without a fire I had no chance of cooking the taro corms conventionally but there was more than one way to peel a potato. With visions of large, golden, oven-baked *potato crisps*, I took the metal lid and used it like a knife to slice through the potato. It worked perfectly and a thin, flat, crisp-like sliver was freed from the raw vegetable. Genius.

I padded down my rocky staircase and into the shallows to wash my hair gel tub full of slivers of taro root in seawater. Once washed, and half-intentionally slightly salted, I carried the ingredients over to Snail Rock where I located an ideal flat ledge that was above the high tide and exposed to direct sunlight. I was smiling as I carefully laid out my soon to be Ready Salted Crisps on the black rock – I was having fun today – this was exciting! I stood back and the heat of the intense sun on my bare back told me this would work.

In the dirt of the cave lay the tantalising, almost complete bow drill set. I knew I had to carve a notch in which to build up the ember and I sat down in the afternoon sun and worked the dull shell tool into the wood, initially using the strength of my fingers. Over a couple of hours, as the sun became less intense, the notch deepened and took shape. Fingers and forearms almost cramping up, I glanced over at Snail Rock and decided to check on supper.

They were ready. I felt a *MasterChef* like urge to be über-descriptive so as to make tasting them, not a very televisual experience, actually mean something to the viewer. 'They're crunchy, and edible, and slightly salty' was the best I could muster. I felt thrilled, smug even. Despite having no fire, I'd managed to come out on top and cook a potato using the heat of the sun.

'Do you know what?' I told the camera. 'I needed something like that today. I needed something to go right. It is the difference between having a packet of crisps and eating a potato straight out of the ground. You wouldn't eat a potato straight out of the ground.' I stated the obvious to underline the miracle transition. 'I'm happy with that. *Really* happy with that.'

And I was. I collected up the chips and put them back in the old hair gel container. That was half of supper sorted out.

Having left the fish trap to sit for a few more hours, I returned to Shipwreck Pool. The tide was coming in and I didn't want to lose my new collecting device. I reached down to the bottom of the blue aquarium and retrieved the bottle, which now contained five more fish. The second half of supper was sorted, too.

My main course was simply inserting nutrients. That's how it felt – there was no pleasure in consuming the raw fish and grinding them between my teeth into a consistency that I could swallow with my eyes shut. In contrast, dessert was pure indulgence. I savoured every salty crunchy mouthful of my packet of crisps. The entire meal was probably less than 300 calories but it felt like a feast and I could feel the positive effect of my fish and chip supper filtering through my joints.

Next, I checked the bottles of clay water and found them transformed. The bottom inch of each bottle was pure clay and the water above it was clear. I gingerly lifted each one and siphoned off three litres of clean fresh water. The clay that remained had the consistency of tomato ketchup and I dolloped it out into a giant clamshell for use as sunscreen later. It was smooth and creamy and I knew it would work perfectly.

Water, sunscreen, fish and chips. Not bad for a day's work. I pondered on how much of today's luck was self-created. I hadn't found it easy to keep going but I had done so and was reaping the rewards. I knew I had to learn from this and keep myself positive if I was to thrive on the island. I also knew myself and how hard that would be. I drifted off to sleep with a gurgling belly and full of renewed hope.

░░ ░░ ░░

Hope, and a sated feeling from my fish and chip supper, stayed with me all through the night. I awoke in a light, happy state and spent a pleasant morning pottering in the shadows of my cave. I replaced the fire-bow's grey, knotted cordage with new, tougher black cordage that I had found tied around a section of driftwood on the beach. It was now running much more smoothly and didn't jump. Using the improved bow, I burned in quite a nice black hollow on the tangalito hearth, and the ember notch below was beginning to take shape, too. For the bearing block I was using the plastic bottle top but, as it was still heating up much too much and burning my hand through the plastic, I had begun to carve the top of the drill sharper so as to reduce friction. I also found that adding chewed grass to the bottle top helped; it both lubricated the upper contact point and cooled it down. In short, although you don't really need to understand the details of the above, I was having quite a nice time.

In the afternoon I reviewed the footage and became aware that my reaction to things taking a long time to do was gradually changing. Initially, if a task had taken a long time I would start to panic, to stress and rush decisions. I would accept a low standard of work in order to move on to the next task as quickly as I could. Now I saw myself chuckling at the absurdity of spending a day and a half cutting a one-inch notch in a piece of hard wood with a shell. Each dull scrape with the shell removed only the tiniest fragment of wood and the process was taking for ever, but I smiled, both in acceptance of what was, and at the patience and diligence I was now displaying.

The ember notch on the hearth board (the pie slice that had to be removed to allow space for the hot dust to build up in) had almost reached the centre of the burned-in drill depression. The kit, dare I say it, was pretty much there.

Ⅲ卄 卄Ⅱ Ⅲ

D aylight woke me like a kick in the face, stealing my sleep and leaving me battered and confused in the dirt. In the mornings I always did the simplest things first as they required the least brainpower. Task one: scratch day thirteen's completely unnecessary mark on the cave wall with a chalky stone. My brain yawned and farted – day thirteen: let's hope it's not unlucky for me.

Skirt on, I stepped down the rocks to harvest my morning snails. As I brought the rock down sharply on each shell I longed for the normality of a fridge stocked with fresh groceries, a toaster, a bacon sarnie and a mug of sweet coffee. Picking the tiny splinters of shell from the moist insides I swallowed each slimy body whole – one after the other – until I decided that I'd eaten enough protein. As my brain was now calming down, my newfound composure allowed me to focus on one thing at a time. I allowed myself to consider at what point the snail would actually die. Upon the impact of the rock? In my mouth? As it plunged into my pool of stomach acid? I sipped some clay water and then returned to my dusty workshop in the cliff face.

Today's task was to continue improving the bow drill until I had ironed out every flaw, and then, in theory, I should be able to make fire. To recap, the hearth board was the relatively flat piece of wood about a foot long, an inch or so wide and about a quarter of an inch deep. Yesterday I had been carving an ember notch that was meant to be a 'pie slice' cut into the board. The pie slice needed to be an eighth of a circle, but was mine a bit too small? Would the hot dust collect in a pillar that would eventually reach such a temperature that it would congeal into a single glowing ember? I was pretty sure that it wasn't ready but, because carving took hours with my blunt clamshell fragment as my only tool, I opted to test the bow drill to see how it currently fared.

I went down on one knee in the shade of the cave. My left leg was forward, shin perpendicular to the ground, my right leg tucked behind me under my bum. I coiled the string of the bow around my stubby six-inch drill, ensuring the sharper end was pointing upwards. Wrapping my left arm around my leading left leg I applied downward pressure to the drill through the white plastic bottle top. To reduce friction this 'bearing block' was now lubricated with green leaves as well as spit. To make it sturdier the bottle top sat inside a seashell in the palm of my left hand. All the friction – and therefore the heat – should now be at the bottom of the drill where it sat neatly in the blackened circle on the hearth board. The circle was in turn penetrated by the pie slice collection notch whose dimensions I was intending to test.

Deep breath.

Keeping the pressure on the drill with my left hand, I gingerly drew the bow back and forth with my right arm, causing the drill to spin in place.

So far, so good.

Everything seemed to be working. I increased the frequency of the bowing until small particles of hot wood dust began to fall into the ember notch. As my pace increased wisps of smoke began to emanate from the area where the two pieces of wood touched – a good sign, but it was by no means a foregone conclusion that an ember was being made. But something in my gut was starting to ignite, too. I could tell that the dust was dark and that there was plenty of it and I could see the smoke was thickening and building. Although this was just meant to be a test

– not a serious attempt to create fire – I increased my efforts as my hopes jumped up and down inside me like a hyperactive kid on an overdose of Tartrazine. More smoke, lots more black dust building up. It was looking *very* promising.

The moment of truth comes when you stop bowing. As I did so, a kite line of smoke continued to drift defiantly from the tiny pile of dust in the notch.

I had created an ember.

'Tinder bundle?' I flapped, scanning the cave floor for the melon-sized ball of fine dry lichen, coconut husk and ultra-fine bamboo scrapings. I seized the parcel and gently teased the hearth board away from my nascent ember. To turn the smoking ember into fire I had to transfer it into the heart of this dry fibrous ball very carefully, as if it were a priceless gem. I gently squeezed the husk around it between my fingertips as if I was trying to restrain, but not damage, a butterfly. Holding the entire smoking mass aloft – above head height so as to reduce the effect of the moisture of my breath – I blew softly into the precious bundle.

As the ember started to heat the tinder the sound of my breath was obscured by the tiny roar of materials catching light. My fingers started to get hot and the smoke became thick and white. 'A couple more long, soft breaths – come on, COME ON!' I willed it, and with that – WHOOMF! – an orange flame leapt into life between my palms.

'We have fire! We have fire!' I chanted as I danced around the cave scrabbling for dry wood. I suppose that 'we' meant me and the camera – or was it me and the audience? I'm not really sure – but I did feel as if I was sharing the experience. I laid the pocket of flame in my virgin fireplace and added small twigs, first about the thickness of a match, then of a pencil, until I had a proper fire going and could put wood of any size on it.

'We have fire!' I repeated, on the verge of tears. 'This has to be one of the best days of my life!' All modesty or emotional restraint went up in smoke with the fire and I unleashed a guttural scream at the ocean:

'YEEESSSS!'

This was quite a leap – fire, after all, was one of the greatest discoveries in the evolution of humankind. All I had to do now was invent everything from the wheel, through to the moon landings and the Internet. It felt more important than any of those things. I could cook my food; I could expand my diet to eat shellfish and crabs; I could cure meat in the smoke; I could warm myself throughout the night and sleep better; and – best of all and most immediately – I could have a cup of tea.

On the face of it tea may not appear to be a life-altering factor in the art of survival. But the very ability to do something normal, something everyday, meant that this was becoming less of a survival situation and more of a way of life. The very fact that I could do something that made me smile, that *wasn't* essential, and that reminded me of home, accounted for a huge positive shift in my mental state from this moment onwards.

The entrance of my cave was flagged by a skeletal pine tree that clung to the rock like a desperate limpet. 'Vitamin C!' I thought as I broke off a fistful of the youngest of the soft green pine needles. Pine needle tea has been used for centuries by Native North Americans to prevent coughs and colds and, just as importantly for me, it would make a really nice aromatic tea.

I couldn't believe that I hadn't seen a use for the discarded condensed milk can that I'd picked up a few days before on the beach. It was now so obviously a cooking pot! The top had previously been punctured twice to get at the contents and so, using a shell as a chisel and a rock as a hammer, I excitedly worked around the lip. I folded back half of the top to make a handle, filled the can with my precious fresh water and placed it in the embers of the fire. I added the pine needles and watched the tin can start to turn black as my first cup of tea began to brew.

If coldness, wetness and darkness exacerbate the fear of isolation on an island, fire is the antidote. I sat and watched the red and yellow flames parade around the tin can like loyal soldiers coming to my rescue. The sense of accomplishment – the feeling that I was regaining control – gave me a warm glow of morale-boosting pleasure. It was as if the fire emitted strength, comfort and confidence. As I anticipated my first brew, all the challenges that lay ahead morphed from being frightening and overwhelming obstacles into exhilarating and exciting adventures.

As single bubbles gradually accumulated into a rolling boil I snatched the tin can sharply from the fire fast enough not to burn my London-soft fingers. Watching the steaming can I wondered whether most adult men shared my seemingly permanent doorway into childish happiness. The simple thought of my first sip of tea was making me smile and sing a silly song about having a cuppa: 'I got a brew on. I got a brew on,' I sang delightedly. Why hadn't Afghanistan knocked this excitable kid out of me?

In fact, Afghanistan was at times so mad that I wonder if it made me *more* childish. I had been there as an ex-military consultant, in charge of the operations room in Herat during the run-up to the first presidential elections. Our base was made up of flimsy Portakabins surrounded by barbed wire and sandbags out near the airport. We were out there because our previous base had been burned to the ground by angry rioting mobs.

One day I was sitting in the Portakabin operations room with another former military consultant, Jonny, when there was a thunderous explosion which made the ground shake beneath us. Then another. Then another. We were being mortared by the Taliban and, as we were in a ruddy Portakabin with no overhead protection whatsoever, there was absolutely nothing we could do to get out of the line of fire.

There wasn't a sensible solution to our predicament so we came up with a stupid one to distract ourselves from the threat of impending death. You may as well die with a smile on your face. I wish I'd remembered that during my time on the island. It might have helped put it all in perspective. So what did Jonny and I do? We ran around the room with our hands on our heads, of course, shouting, 'Don't panic, Captain Mainwaring! Don't panic!'

I took the water from the fire and poured my first cup of tea into a salvaged glass jam jar.

The reality was even better than the anticipation. The hot fluid passed my lips and ran down my throat in a wave of pure success. Imagine the best cup of tea you've ever had – perhaps at the end of a mammoth walk in the cold and wind, or made for you by your mum and brought to you in bed on exam day because she wants to get you off to a good start. It had taken nearly two weeks but I had made fire and had an ability that no other animal in the world had – to make a brew.

My stomach grumbled and growled from the wake-up call of the hot fluid. Having been disturbed from a deep hibernation it now demanded to be fed some hot food. I set about making a snail soup. Until now I had been eating my thirty snails a day raw but now I had the means to transform these cold gritty balls into cooked flesh. I delicately removed every flake of shell from the small lumps of meat and popped them into my hair gel tub. Then the ten naked snails went into the pot with rainwater and a splash of seawater for salt.

When it came to tasting, it was not so much amazing as simply reassuring. The snails were cooked now. I could bite into them, I could chew them. There was a soup to drink afterwards that was slightly salty and had a hint of snail oil. My unloved metal spoon at once became one of my most valuable possessions.

Fire was to be the biggest game-changer in my entire time on the island. I was very, *very* happy.

I collected some firewood from the surrounding area and it soon dawned on me that I could not chop hardwood, as the clamshell hand axe was too blunt and the energy and time expended wouldn't be worthwhile. So I needed to collect dead wood that I could snap into pieces. I would clearly have to try to keep the fire as small as possible to conserve fuel.

Early in the afternoon I trod on a couple of terrified crabs and made my first multi-ingredient broth. The crustaceans were fast but I was faster; if I reacted quickly, and they were far enough away from cover, I could bring the flat of my foot down hard and crush them against the flat rock. I emptied 300ml from the seep into the tin, just enough to cover the crabs, and added a splash of seawater for flavour. Lastly, I spotted the remaining taro chips and decided to chuck them in the pot as croûtons.

I could hardly contain my glee.

With the fire going and my crab and taro soup on the boil, I had an overwhelming sense of 'Phew. I can relax now.' I could feel the tension flowing out of me. I took the soup off the heat, drained the broth into the jam jar and picked the legs apart, popping tiny chunks of white meat into my mouth.

The taste was beyond words.

Into a world of functionality and simply existing there arrived pleasure and enjoyment. I half considered whether I needed to avoid certain parts of the crab but threw caution to the wind and ate everything inside the shell. The lunchtime soup was hearty, too, but I noted that I wouldn't add the taro next time, as it was a bit starchy – like drinking boiled potato water.

One thing I was concerned about were the two holes in my feet. One on each foot, to be precise. They were not healing properly and so I hobbled down my beach to Shipwreck Pool and, sitting on the edge, cleaned the wounds as thoroughly as I could. They were now fairly deep into the sole of each foot. I took fistfuls of sand and worked it into the holes to act as an abrasive scrubbing brush. Once clean, they looked better but I knew that I needed to try and keep the cave floor dust out of them to allow them to heal over. They were raw and tender and exposed to everything that I trod on. I submerged my fish trap and rested the rock on top.

An ability to cook was a godsend but as a consequence I needed more fresh water than ever. I realised that I'd left some in the well on day eleven and so decided to travel around the island to collect it now. 'I've had a hot meal!' I smiled as I walked.

In Lemon Camp I picked some of the leaves off a lemon tree for tea. I knew that this would make an excellent alternative tea to pine needles and I could add the leaves to seafood broths, too, to add flavour. The fire had opened up so many more possibilities from which I kept getting further morale boosts every time I realised I could now achieve something new.

I could feel my thoughts accelerating again and my senses coming alive. Hot food had done wonders. I carried all my empty bottles over to the well. A matt-brown surface of dry clay stared back at me in place of my reflection. The bottom was dry.

This was a bit of a blow but I could see why it had happened and it couldn't be helped. The clay probably wasn't 100 per cent watertight and, added to that, the residual water could also have evaporated over the last two days. It would have taken a lot to get me down that day and I took the bad news in my stride. Remembering the fire, I decided to rush back to the cave; if it went out on the first day that *would* be a disaster.

Back at the cave all sorts of things that I hadn't had a use for became invaluable. The hair gel container became a Tupperware soup bowl. It would even keep a meal hot for me if I wanted! I washed it out in the sea below the cave.

'Shit – the fire!' I hadn't even checked it on my return. I looked up at the entrance to the cave and there was no sign of fire. 'Bollocks!' I huffed as I leapt up the stone staircase. There were no flames or smoke but I could tell that it was salvage-able. I slid the charred sticks inwards so that all of the burned ends were touching. They were still warm. I knelt down, took a deep breath and blew gently into the logs. Before the breath was even finished – WHOOMF – the flames jumped back to life. I smiled at the ease of recovery and patted myself on the back. Phew.

It was the end of week two tomorrow and so I did my exer-cises on the beach. The results were unremarkable. Not amazing, as I'd been ill. Not pathetic, as I'd found renewed vigour from the fire. I would build from here, I told myself.

I collected a large bundle of firewood, conscious that I did not want to run out in the night. As I balanced it on my shoulders and looked up at the cave I was reassured to see the orange flames softly warming the entrance and welcoming me home.

I took a cracked bucket I had found that I'd tried to keep crabs alive in and heated the spoon up in the fire. With the hot spoon

I melted off the brittle broken walls, leaving a small plastic camping plate. Simple – but really useful.

As on previous days, as the afternoon came in my energy started diving. My limbs became a burden to haul around and my brain seemed to fill with black tar, blocking any spark of life. I lay down to have a little rest by the fire and sank deep into the dusty floor. Every part of me pressed hard into the ground and cherished the physical support. I groaned at the pleasure of being horizontal and glanced at my new plate. Quiet satisfaction cut through the heaviness and a satisfied grin spread over my face. I closed my eyes.

When the warmth of the fire dropped I sat up to add more wood. The power nap had done me good and I brushed the cave dust from my arms and face. The tide was turning so I collected my trap and a small shoal of unattractive brown loach. Once they'd been disembowelled by squeezing, I washed the tiny fish in seawater and popped them in the tin pot for supper. I wanted to cook again but to save fresh water I opted to cook with seawater. It was an experiment – I knew I would not be able to drink the broth – but the food should be nice and salty and I would then have enough fresh water for a small glass of lemon leaf tea afterwards.

I also experimented with boiling coconut flesh as I was determined to up my energy levels. The meal was seawater, coconut flesh, sprats and crabs.

It was so nice to have fire; in the jungle we called it 'jungle telly': something to sit around and stare at and draw morale and warmth from. Something to focus on. 'There's nothing like a fire, is there? There's just *nothing* like a fire to make you feel comforted and safe. Day thirteen has been a good day,' I told the camera.

The sprats tasted like proper cooked fish for the first time. They had a vague undertaste of sharp fish poo but were relatively good eating. The steaming crabs broke apart in my fingers and gave off oily fats that tasted exquisite. I decided that the answer was to spend more time catching crabs – their flavour was amazing. The coconut flesh was unaffected by the cooking and still tasted raw. That hadn't really worked and didn't add to the dish at all. But lesson learned.

I drank my lemon leaf tea in the dark. What a difference a single day could make to my life. I was sipping hot aromatic tea having eaten my third hot meal of the day and the fire was warming my bare skin and giving my eyes an enchanting sight to focus on. The cave felt so different. The orange glow was guarding me from the dread of the night. The cold blackness could no longer creep in and force me beneath my pile of grass to shiver and wait. My cave had become a warm home from which I could view the outside world with the assurance that I was safe and protected. It was civilised and I could relax. I could not have been happier with what I'd achieved.

HHt HHt IIII

To say that I woke up on day fourteen would suggest that I'd actually slept and I'm not sure that was the case. A night of experimenting with the fire had left me dazed and exhausted.

Initially, the fire had been close to my head – simply because that's where the cooking position was at the side of the cave. But I quickly discovered that to heat my entire body from there I would need a really big fire but that would use up far too much

Above: In all her splendour. Olorua will always be part of my own personal journey.

Right: The fat white giant. Being naked made me feel so much more vulnerable.

Left: Raw snails. To this day the thought makes me gag. Never, ever, ever again.

Above: Feigned happiness. I was actually angry at myself for my pathetic first grass skirt.

Right: My hand-chiseled rock seep with cord wick and plastic reservoir. Water was life itself.

Above: Looking down from the outcrop to my beach and Shipwreck Pool.

Left: Desperation? Eating a raw gecko after squeezing out the poo. Protein was vital.

Below: The rocky outcrop and the reef beyond. Exposed to the entire world I felt so small.

Above: Bush telly. The fire made my cave a home. It was so much more than a cooker.

Above: Orange was Amanda's colour. Sunset was our time to connect to each other.

Above: The cave at night. Fire changed everything and gave me warmth and morale.

Right: An excuse to escape my torture? My illness seemed very real at the time.

Above: The beginnings of happiness. Slowing down to enjoy the simplicity of thatching.

Left: My new home. Putting the finishing touches to my shelter, it was time to move out of the cave.

Above: Shelter, food, fire, and water, but the face said it all. I was desperately lonely.

Left: The big daddy goat was mine. I estimated it must have weighed forty to fifty kilos.

Below: Making goat jerky with my handmade knife and the Peli-case as a chopping board.

Above: Extraordinary. Quite extraordinary. Goat so tender my toothless grandma could have wolfed it down with her lips.

Left: Evolution from animal to man – the use of skins to keep warm and comfortable.

Above: The staple. Crabs, taro corms, taro leaf, and thirty snails. Dinner was one of the best times of the day.

Above: The seedling of sustainable living. This was so much more than a fish, and I knew it.

Above: Escape. Elated and safe once more. Would I do it again?

Would I fuck!

wood and my head would burn! I allowed the fire to die down a little and to grow smaller; I still used the dry grass to help keep my body warm but my torso was still relatively cold. So I decided to make another fire by my waist, by transferring some of the burning logs. This was great for heating my body but I then worried that having two fires was a real extravagance and so I stopped putting wood on the one by my head and let it die down. I built the new waist-level fire in an elongated shape so it would heat more of my body but it soon became apparent that, as I laid wood on the fire longitudinally, it would burn too quickly and too fiercely and was far too hot initially. And then, as I let it die down, I would either run the risk of it going out or add more wood and repeat the erratic cycle. When it was roaring hot I worried that my hay blanket would catch light and I would spontaneously burst into flames in the night and so I put the hay to one side and relied solely on the fire for heat. But the speed with which I went through my enormous pile of wood was frightening. I never fell asleep properly for fear of waking up shivering and without my biggest source of comfort.

Eventually, though, the dark sky softened and the pair of star-lings (that oddly enough I never contemplated eating) began their morning chattering just as I was down to my last few twigs. What a night. I was still happy that I had a fire but I felt that it had created further concerns. How much firewood was I going to have to collect every day? How long was that extra task going to take out of my busy day? Realistically, was I ever going to get a solid night's sleep again? Bloody hell – the stresses of civilisation had arrived only a few hours after I'd lit my first fire.

I wanted to start construction of my new house but there was too much to do. I needed to collect wood immediately, I needed to collect some water, I needed to go out and find some seafood such as crabs and snails as I had nothing in the larder. I needed a new coconut pole as my present one was too heavy, and I needed to collect more coconuts. To cap it all it was dropbox day and I had to visit Lemon Camp twice before nightfall. So much to do – *so much to do!*

For breakfast I smashed into a brown coconut and snapped out some of the white flesh, although I was now sick of the sight and smell of it. I decided that it was the water content and slippery texture of the flesh that was making me gag and so I placed the segments on the rocks around the fire to toast the pure white chunks. The results were exciting and cheered me up: they tasted like burned coconut biscuits and were very edible. They were sweet and much easier to force down and so, as if out of nowhere, I now had a snack I could graze on throughout the day that was both reliable and constant, as these fallen coconuts littered the ground. So my calories did indeed increase a lot, but, as most of my fuel was coming from saturated fats, my legs still felt like lead as I was having to convert my protein from snails and seafood and my fat from coconut into the glucose that my body needed for energy. This was a great way to lose weight but it was an inefficient way of fuelling my body and it caused my energy levels to remain very low.

Foraging now meant that I needed a container in which to collect everything and so I spent the first part of the morning with palm leaves in the cave trying to make my first palm leaf basket. I'd failed in my attempt to make a hat and I had the same difficulties with making a basket. I had to make a circle that looked like a thatched crown and then I had to plait the thorns of the crown together so that they would link and form the underside of the basket. It was easy in theory – but inevitably somewhat harder in practice. I made one – but it was pretty crude and had several large holes in it. I confidently predicted that if I did it again I would be able to make quite a good one.

The fire. 'Shit! Not again!' I turned to look at the flat grey pile of ash. 'Stafford, you are stupid!' I said out loud as I leapt across the cave to examine the crime scene. I held my flat hand over the ash – it was still warm. With my bare hands I flicked the embers together into a small pile and gently blew on them with a slow, sustained breath. The increased oxygen immediately caused the embers to glow and then burst into a small flame. Phew – 'How careless can you get, Ed?!'

I stoked the fire up and headed out to collect wood. The flat, forested area adjacent to the beach had lots of hanging dead wood – perfect for burning as it was off the floor and thus bone dry. I made a number of piles the size of giant Galápagos tortoises and ferried them back to my cave cradled in my outstretched arms.

Once I had a large enough pile of dry wood to last the night I told myself that I needed to decide upon an area for the shelter. I wasn't relaxed – I was storming from one task to the next. Then I caught myself – rushing and rushing and rushing. 'If you were working in England, Ed, you would take breaks,' I smiled to myself. 'Just have yourself a cup of tea, Staffs – yeah?'

As I sat down with the glass jam jar of lemon leaf tea pinched between my forefinger and thumb I let myself breathe. Once more I drew strength from simply gazing into the fire. The warmth reassured me and the dancing flames entranced me.

On my second lap of the island, to complete the day's time-consuming dropbox routine, I saw a couple of quite big fish so I decided to have a bash at making a trident harpoon. Back on the western shore I collected three very straight sections of beach hibiscus. The wood was light and easy to cut and I thought would make a great spear. I bashed the bark off and used it to fill the gaps that were appearing in my grass skirt, as it had dried now and become somewhat revealing.

The dead kid goat had been lying untouched for days and I experimented with the bones to see if they could be worked into a spear tip. I decided to work in the woods as the cave was too hot in the afternoon and I'd been round to the other side of the island twice so far today and had too much sun. The dried-up carcass was too brittle. The bones were soft and snapped easily. It would be like carving a cog out of balsa wood. I wondered if the lemon thorns might work to provide the sharpest point and to make a reverse-facing barb, too. But I still needed to find hard-wood to splice them into – the bones were hopeless.

I tested different woods from local trees but none was hard enough to hold a point and crafting them was virtually impossible. Essentially I resorted to snapping and twisting the wood and to encourage natural sharp, splintered fragments that I could use. The results were low-grade and I knew it – tomorrow I would find stronger wood.

A metallic silver ocean and expansive graphite clouds sandwiched a horizontal band of burned brightness at the horizon as I flipped open the camera screen to record a video diary. 'Everything's OK. I made a trident harpoon,' I began unconvincingly. 'I have decided that if I build a shelter then I have to build something that isn't a thrown-up, temporary affair. It has to be storm-proof, comfortable and able to house me and my amassed items as well as the cave does. The cave is very good in many respects and I can't build anything that's not going to be at least as good. I've decided to build a raised house in the trees.'

It might seem stupid to move out of the cave but this wasn't just a survival experiment. I was seeing if I could thrive here and wanted to see how far I could evolve.

I fought to convince myself that I'd achieved something today and that I had a solid plan. Neither was true and I could see through my self-delusion. I still seemed to be governed by what I was achieving and I couldn't stop planning and worrying. I was basing my sense of self on my achievements rather than a core knowledge of who I was. I realise, looking back, that I was constantly battling to be somewhere else rather than enjoying what I had. That is why, even with a fire and a cave, food and water, my shoulders were still tightly hunched and my forehead furrowed. I still felt no sense of peace.

CHAPTER 4
SHELTER

~~HHH~~ ~~HHHH~~ ~~HHH~~

I'd never had to rely on a fire's warmth for heat in the night before this project. On expeditions I had always had a hammock and a sleeping bag and in the military it would have been out of the question because a fire was not tactical – the enemy would be able to see you. As a result I was still thinking of the child-like drawings in the Ray Mears book after I'd panicked and read it on the plane on the way over. He had this lovely fire that, on paper, looked as if it would be great at night because it was long and thin and kept the entire length of the body warm. As with so many things on this island, though, if I'd stuck to what I knew from experience I'd have fared a lot better.

Having a fire that is long and thin means that it is inherently alight in a lot of places at once over a long thin surface area. Hence the huge amount of heat. But, as the first two nights had so far proved, that meant that you went through a vast amount of wood because when adding wood you have no option but to lay it lengthwise on top and the whole stick burns at once. This may be appropriate in extreme, cold conditions where there is plenty of wood but my nights were just bloody chilly and my firewood situation was somewhat restricted.

My favourite fire has always been a feeder, or star, fire. It's predominantly used for cooking, which is why I'd allowed myself to become distracted by Ray's pretty drawings.

Essentially, though, it's dead simple. As soon as you've got an established heart to the fire you add wood like the spokes of a wheel – with only their tips in the burning heart. This means that each piece of wood burns gradually from the end like a cigarette. It means that after a while the fire will slow down and in order to get it burning you only have to slide the spokes inwards a little and you have a roaring fire again. There is often no requirement to add new logs at all. It is far more efficient with wood and burns far less. It is also great for cooking, as it is adjustable: pull the logs out to turn the gas down, push them in to crank it up. At night if you want the fire to die out you can just pull the logs a bit further out; without other logs to hold the heat they will go out. Conversely, if you stoke it up and have enough wood on when you go to bed, it is often the case that in the morning you can just push the charred ends together and gently blow on them and you can get flames again in a matter of seconds without a lighter. In a nutshell, it's a cracking fire.

So after trialling a method that I didn't like I reverted to what I knew and trusted. My feeder fire was positioned at waist level about a metre from my body. This meant that, in these relatively mild tropical nights, it kept my entire body warm enough to sleep. It also meant that three out of four times when I woke up I had only to feed the spokes into the heart rather than adding new logs. I slept better not only because I was warmer but because my regular interruptions could be done half asleep knowing I wasn't using much wood. I also knew that if the cold woke me up, and I'd overslept my two-hourly fire adjusting, all I needed to do was push the ends together, blow gently on the log tips and I would have flames again in seconds. I began to relax.

I woke up, as usual, without food. On the whole this was the way it was for most of my time on the island. I'd eaten all my toasted coconut flesh in the night and it was time to get out and go foraging.

The tide was low and still going out and so I set the inverted plastic bottle trap in the rock pool. On the way back I saw a small dark shape disappear into a hole in the sand. A crab! So far my crabs had come from the rocks, and this sand variety was new. I leapt towards the hole and forced my hand in like a vet assisting a cow to give birth. The crab was not in the main tunnel shaft so I dug sideways trying to locate it. My fingers touched something harder and I felt the tips burn as the claws clamped into my skin. I grabbed the entire crab, still attached to my fingertip, yanked it free of the sand and instinctively pressed my thumb through the shell on its back into its head. The pincers relaxed their grip. I carried the crab in one hand and looked along the beach that revealed a short row of similar holes with small sand mounds beside them. I ran to the next and my knees sunk into the sand as, like a ravenous JCB, I excavated the primitive burrow system. After twenty seconds there was a hole the size of a space hopper but no crab. Bugger. I rose and sank by the next hole and repeated the exercise. Again, I couldn't find the homeowner.

In the next six holes I only caught one more crab, which I despatched again smartly with my big blunt thumb through its brain. But two crabs *was* exciting. Two crabs was breakfast. Back in the cave I put the new species of crab in my tin can to keep them out of the dust and I returned to the rocks to collect snails with my hair gel container. Because of the crabs I only picked five small snails and screwed the lid tight. The rock pool yielded two more sprats and so I had the makings of a decent meal.

I could see from the foam that was bubbling on the top of the can that I was in for something a bit special. There was colour to this brunch – and it was green. The first mouthful of the hot broth was remarkable. The addition of these different, green, sand crabs had transformed snail soup into a wonderful rich concoction. They were only about the size of a fried egg – legs included – and so I simply bit them in half, the exoskeleton being soft enough to crunch and swallow, and that became the way I ate crabs for the whole trip. No shelling, fiddling or waste – I devoured them like whole logs fed into a wood chipper.

It's next to impossible to convey how good food can be when you are almost starving. It's also interesting why it is so necessary to explain just how incredible it tasted. Food itself becomes all-consuming because your taste buds are so awakened that every mouthful is quite extraordinary The crab had real meat on it and I could feel the nutrients seeping into my muscles and into my brain. The sprats, too, were wonderfully different with their more fishy texture and flavour and the whole dish just kept me searching for superlatives. I savoured the last slurps of the broth from the plastic bowl and then I refilled the tin with clay water for a morning brew.

It was the beginning of week three. There still wasn't quite enough water to do what I wanted to do and to be comfortable and, as a result, I was always slightly uneasy. My well was still dry and in fifteen days I reflected that I had received less than fifteen minutes of steady rain. So, in order to focus on something that I could indeed control and influence, I started to plan.

With fire now achieved, I decided I would build a shelter fairly close to the cave, about 150 metres south and tucked into the tree line above the highest tide. This meant I was still on the protected side of the island and that the trees would further reduce the cooling effects of the wind at night.

Remembering the farce of my previous attempt at construction I tried to talk to myself calmly: 'I'm not going to panic about it, I'm just going to build a little bit each day.'

To further emphasise my control I broke down the day into sections.

'Today I'm going to start the construction of a house – I'm going to do:

four hours' construction work,
two hours of fishing,
one hour cooking,
one hour collecting water,
half an hour collecting firewood,
I'm going to take two fifteen-minute breaks,

and I like to have the first hour and the last hour to myself.'

I suppose I was just searching for down time rather than the constant responsibility of survival. I had every waking moment to myself. If the list seems ridiculously regimented and overly structured now, there was necessity in this carving up of time. I knew from experience that in long-drawn-out tasks where there may not be perceivable regular goals it can feel as if you are treading water and achieving absolutely nothing. But by setting mini goals and allocating these periods of time I could congratulate myself on having applied myself for a certain period of time whether or not I had actually achieved any goal, such as catching a fish. It was a technique I had employed when revising for my A-levels – I set myself the goal of doing ten hours' revision a day. Revision, by its very nature, has no obvious tangible goals at the end of each day – so it was vital to create some artificial goals to keep me motivated and to reassure me that I was working hard and not wasting my time.

Those were my tactics anyway. In fact, I think that the obsessive planning and thinking put undue pressure on me. I was so out of control that I was trying to build a set of rules and schedules to stick to in order to give myself a sense of mastery. In fact none of it mattered – but I managed to create pressure and drama out of a situation in which there was none.

I went out to look for hardwood for the trident spear – my softwood splinters wouldn't penetrate a jellyfish. On the steep bank behind my beach I picked up a hermit crab that was inhabiting what looked like a blue plastic shotgun cartridge. I wondered if it was the same one that I'd terrified out of its gastropod shell and that had then found a new, more modern abode. It didn't matter – with my fire burning he was now reclassified as food. Not wanting to kill the crab, and therefore start the decomposition phase, which would mean I had to cook him quickly before he went off, I simply broke his legs to disable him and popped him in my basket alive. This sounds pretty brutal, and it's normally something I would never even contemplate. But in a survival situation, with no fridge to keep things fresh, keeping something alive is the best way to keep it fresh.

Through the undergrowth I then ran into the goats and, even though I didn't yet have a weapon, I decided to stalk them to see how close I could get. Frustratingly, they skipped up to the north of the island, moving too fast for me to keep up, so I gave up my pursuit and wandered down to my cave via the Faraway Tree.

The nylon cord on my flip-flops was now cutting into my skin and leaving raw sores on the tops of both feet. I took some ragged blue material that I'd found attached to another flip-flop and I wound it around the nylon string to make it less harsh.

Despite not having hardwood barbs, I managed to assemble my first trident spear. I simply bound three six-inch softwood splinters around the end of my straightest beach hibiscus pole with bark and there it was — my first hunting tool. It was pretty crude but it would do for practice and I wanted to get out there and fish. Despite the day being overcast, I covered myself in clay to protect my skin from the reflection of the sun in the sea. The soft brown creamy clay went on thick and smooth and I could tell it would work well in protecting me from exposure when fishing in the shallows.

Covered in clay with my grass skirt, basket and new spear, I walked towards the water's edge feeling and looking the part for the first time. Two weeks in and I was no longer the awkward chubby white man desperately throwing rocks up into coconut trees. I was clothed and protected from the sun. And, for the first time, I was armed.

Spear held aloft, I glided into the calm water with a look of intent on my face. I felt that I was doing what I was meant to be doing. I wasn't sitting in the dust of my cave moaning — I was thigh-deep in crystal-clear waters poised to strike and kill my prey.

Sadly, my feel-good factor didn't translate into food. The wind picked up and the water became choppy so that I couldn't see below the surface. My spear felt wrong — the head felt impotent and the weight was at the other end. Naively I'd tied the barbs to the thinner end of the pole, thinking that the spear would fly better with the streamlined narrow end cutting through the air. Holding the weapon aloft it was at once obvious that the weighty end — the blunt end — had to be at the front so that the thin, tapered end would act as the flight. I twisted the spear around in my fingers and it at once felt balanced with the fat end at the head. I threw it on to the water and it did indeed fly better. But I still couldn't see what I was doing so I gave up and waded back to the beach. I'd not seen a single fish.

By late morning I decanted another third of a litre from the seep. I was content with the end product but still needed more water so I brought a large palm leaf around to this beach to try to shade the seep from the merciless rays of the afternoon sun. Hopefully this would now allow the seep to continue working outside its normal office hours of dusk to midday.

Enjoying my wanderings, I travelled round to the other side of the island to collect lemon thorns and to try and scavenge crabs and snails en route. The thorns were long and strong and if used intelligently would be a fantastic addition to the point of a spear. While I was there I stocked up on lemon leaves for tea and, as I picked the young soft foliage from the branches, it was then that I realised that the smaller thorns on the younger branches were more like large rose thorns and could make great fishing barbs.

On leaving the camp I noticed a pile of very old coconut husks littering an area the Fijian clan had obviously used to break them open. In the middle of the area there protruded the stump of a sapling that had been felled with a machete to a sharp point. The locals must have used this hardwood sapling to open the coconuts and I immediately saw this as a gift: I'd identified at least one proper type of hardwood. With my clam-shell axe I split off a section that I could later whittle into spear tips in the cave.

I headed back to the cave to tend the fire. I really was just inching forward every day. I'd told myself that today I would do four hours' construction but by the time I had foraged and fished it was early afternoon and I'd not even started work on the house. Every day there was so much to do just to survive. I saw no crabs as I walked around the shore, and that deflated me. Another two paces forward, another one step back.

Back in the cave, the fire was still alight so I decided to break for a late lunch of the blue-housed hermit crab. This was a different grade of crab from the green skinny beach crabs or the standard brown rock crabs – a higher class altogether. The strong legs were hairy and the abdomen was plump and fleshy. In the pot it turned bright red and I devoured the body and savoured the juices that flowed from the abdomen. 'It's full of something fatty – is it shit?' I mused. 'Perhaps.' But I was drawn curiously to the odd oily flavour. I munched each leg whole as if they were Twiglets as they contained vital protein. Sipping lemon leaf tea I felt recharged by the meal and ready to start work again.

I spent several hours in the afternoon walking around the flat land just inside the island's forest. If I was going to build a house I wanted it to be a good one. I didn't want to waste several days on a house that would fall down or one that was temporary and would need replacing after a couple of weeks.

I had proposed this whole adventure to Discovery Channel. I had sold the idea of the programme on the premise that from scratch I would evolve from a primitive beast into someone who tamed the island and was living a sustainable life in comfort. I even claimed I would be in a tree house by the end – Tarzan-style – with pulleys to haul up water and a veranda to sit on in the evenings surveying my territory. I knew therefore that I had planted seeds in the commissioning editors' heads and that expectations were very high.

By now I was only too aware how long things really took when you had no tools. Cutting down a three-inch-diameter tree took the best part of two hours using a blunt piece of clamshell as a hand axe. So when I began surveying the location of the impressive tree house I intended to build, I naturally looked for existing tree formations that would demand the least possible work. Perhaps I could find three trees positioned in a triangle that I could use as the main pillars of my raised home and, hopefully, I could find ones that had boughs coming off at the right height so that I could slot in beams for the floor.

I searched and searched but I could not find the right configuration of trees to help me convert my dreams of a home in the sky into reality. I began to realise that such a building would be ridiculously over-optimistic. Even getting to the stage where I had a raised triangular platform could be three days of hard work and then I didn't know if it would be strong or stable enough. Constructing a roof over this raised platform meant that I would be working at quite some height above the ground with no ladders, no ropes and no safety equipment. I started to fear that this pipe dream in the sky was never going to work.

Time out.

I returned to the cave, sat in my stone circle and breathed in deeply. Crikey, why was I piling so much pressure on myself? I looked out to sea and said a big thank you for the fact that I now had fire. I *was* winning. I then turned to the construction project and asked myself why I was really moving out of this cave. It was, after all, warm, dry and serving me perfectly well.

The answer was that I could have slept in the shit on the floor of a cave eating raw snails for sixty days if I'd wanted to, but my aim wasn't to just survive; it was, as I have said, to evolve and eventually to thrive. Building my own house had to be a significant part of that evolution. I accepted that but then asked myself why was I building a tree house and not a simple but practical shelter on the ground. The answer was that I wanted to live up to my naïve promises to Discovery Channel. I wanted to show off, to prove how I could not just get by, but I could live in *style*. I laughed at myself and the place that I'd got to. I could not have predicted how difficult this project would be – no one could – without actually attempting it and finding out how all of the different factors would come together to make it exceptionally hard. So why then did I not just allow the project to unfold naturally and build what was an appropriate shelter considering what I now knew?

I concluded that my shelter did not need to be off the ground. I had an area that was dry and flat, and to ignore this very amenable forest floor was daft. I would build a simple double lean-to shelter – like a thatched ridge tent – and it would be waterproof, windproof and, most importantly, realistic to build in the circumstances.

I wasn't elated by the realisation that I'd have to redefine my goals because it meant that I probably wasn't going to evolve as far as a tree house with built-in hot tub, but I consoled myself with the fact that I would at least be able to move into a home that I had built myself rather than adapted – and that I was doing the very best I could.

More composed now, I walked back into the forest interior and looked at three different sites that had relatively flat ground and that were flanked by two large trees that would be the end supports for my shelter. I calmly walked between the three sites, assessing the pros and cons, and eventually decided upon a site that was a couple of feet above the line of coconuts that demarcated the highest of high tides and that had two great solid trees with handy Y-forks in their trunks just above head height that I could slot a ridge pole into. I walked back to the cave reassured that I had made the right decision and that I now had an achievable plan.

In the evening I cooked in seawater again to save fresh water. It meant I couldn't drink the snail broth with its vital nutrients but I had to be careful with my fresh water supply. I allowed myself a half-glass of lemon leaf tea and while its warmth was still in my belly I curled up beside my star fire and closed my eyes.

〜 HHT HHT HHT I

'Morning. It's day sixteen.'

I smashed a brown coconut open on a rock and arranged the randomly shaped tiles of flesh around the fire. My baking technique was evolving, too, and now I particularly loved the blackened edge where the fire had burned and carbonised the sweet fragments. Each bite caused a mini explosion of hot sweet juices from beneath a caramelised shell.

I replaced the softwood barbs with the hardwood that I found yesterday, this time lashing them to the fat end of the spear. 'I'm no fisherman – I really am not – but looking at the ocean I can't harpoon fish in this. It's too rough,' I said, gazing over the white waves of the lagoon. I told myself that there would be considerable periods of time when this method of fishing would not be possible. Should I turn to hunting? Rats? Birds? Goats? I berated myself for not spending enough time with the Fijian clan prior to the experiment. I didn't know how they fished, where they fished, when they fished, or with what they fished. The whole fishing thing was a daunting prospect, not because it was scary but because I was loath to risk wasting time getting nothing.

I therefore switched my attention to shelter as it would give me a more certain result. The first thing to erect was a ridge pole – the heart of my construction upon which everything else would depend, so it needed to be solid. I paced out the distance between the trees and quickly realised that I could not fell one tree that would be long enough and strong enough to span the gap.

Confidence in my own ability brimming now, I opted for a tried and tested method that I'd used in construction projects in Belize – albeit with sawn lumber and nails. I would splice two poles together and lash them tight with hibiscus bark. This would make the pole long enough without my having to cut down a big tree, thus expending far too much energy.

I decided that my heavy coconut pole was too heavy for its current use and that it would function perfectly as half of this ridge pole. The second tree that I selected came down relatively easily after about an hour's work. I dragged it down the steep slope to a point ten metres directly above my construction site, where the cliff became almost vertical. From there I simply propelled the pole off the cliff into my camp below and I then took an easier route to the bottom to collect it. With the branches trimmed off, I laid the two poles with their fattest ends outwards and overlapped the inner, narrow ends by four feet. I then tightly bound the joint together with bark to produce a very strong, very long ridge pole.

By now, although I was still feeling very positive, all of the energy supplied by my breakfast had long since been used up. I just had to slot the pole into the natural nooks that were created by the support trees. 'I think this is going to work – this is starting to be fun,' I said as I could see the project coming to fruition. I eased one end up into the cradle of the branch and then brought the pole parallel to the ground by raising the opposite end and slotting that in place.

I stood back to admire my handiwork.

The effect was immediate. I had the beginnings of a decent shelter with a very solid ridge pole standing about eight foot off the ground between two trees. It had taken about three hours. But I was so chronically malnourished that everything I did drained me completely. 'It's like building a house on an overdose of Valium,' I told the camera. 'That there ridge pole means quite a lot to me – that's the start of my new home.'

I realised I had been admiring my fledgling timber frame for a good ten minutes in silence. One of the great things about the area was the bank of immature palms that separated me from the beach. The band of foliage was about five metres thick and completely cut out the wind blowing in from the Pacific. The more I thought about it, the more this site made sense. 'I'm very dehydrated now – I can hardly speak.'

As I wandered back to the cave I mulled over my day's work and also considered the extent to which my most productive times had all been when I focused on one single task. I could already tell that it was going to take about a week to construct the frame and thatch the shelter – and that was if I focused solely on construction. To avoid starting something that would drag on and on, I would give all my working day to construction. That meant I would clearly have to do the daily admin to keep me afloat, such as collecting firewood and foraging for snails and crabs, but I would have to put more adventurous activities such as hunting and fishing on the back burner for now.

I had become a little bit casual about the length of time I was leaving the fire unattended in the cave and I came back to the smallest of embers in a pool of light grey ash. I wasn't worried, though; I was now so comfortable with my fire and how to keep it going that I knew a couple of sticks and some gentle blowing would raise flames again in seconds. That practical competence gave me confidence in myself.

I bit some chunks of taro and spat them into the pot for supper. 'It's been a funny old day, Granville,' I confided to my best friend, the camera, referring to the closing scene in the British television comedy series *Open All Hours* that somehow reflected my daily struggles and the acceptance of the repetitiveness of life. 'I could feel panic rising this morning because I hadn't achieved anything since lighting a fire. So I committed to the shelter and announced to myself that there would be no fishing or hunting until I'd made a good home. Once I'd committed to the one project – rather than flitting from one thing to another – I immediately relaxed and the work became easier.'

Eating the toasted coconut 'biscuits' from the rocks around the fire had given me more energy throughout the day. I hung my coarse grass skirt up on a hook-like protrusion in the back of the cave and sat down naked on the Cinesaddle.

A ten-minute walk earlier in the day had turned up a handful of sprats from Shipwreck Pool and I went in search of more edible marine life. My pot of thirty snails was now a given – why eat ten when you can eat thirty? I spotted a crab darting for cover under a rock and hurled myself towards it to catch my swiftly departing supper.

'Got 'im!' I sang triumphantly.

On the lowest rock that formed the precarious ramp up to my cave I smashed, peeled and washed the snails and with the lone crab made myself up a half-decent dinner.

With hot food inside me and a brew on the go I sat in my rock circle, the sun about ten minutes from kissing the blue horizon and disappearing.

'Thank you, Amanda. Thank you, Jeremy. Thank you, Harold. Thank you …' the list was endless and I felt a deep gratitude for everything that had happened over recent days. My appreciation of small comforts was enormous and I felt that I was being looked after again. I allowed the successes to bask in their glory and to feel the warmth of the fire on my side as the evening cooled. It had taken a long time to get here but I was definitely on track.

As the sun hit the horizon I connected mentally with Amanda. 'Hi, my love!' I began. We had talked about how we would handle the zero contact for sixty days, we decided to set aside a part of the day when we would both take time out and do nothing but think about each other. The knowledge that we were doing this at precisely the same time, on other sides of the world, was comforting and it helped to keep us connected despite the vast distance between us. It felt a bit like sitting on the phone without speaking to each other, just knowing that Amanda was taking time out of her morning in the UK to think of me meant that we were still together despite the odds.

Anyone who has ever felt the presence of a loved one after their death will, I'm sure, understand my desire to keep that connection open at all times. It didn't have to be a case of out of sight, out of mind; that was the last thing I wanted. We'd opted for my sunset, as I didn't know whether I'd be able to stick to any other time accurately. All Amanda had to do was Google 'sunset time in Fiji' and she would know exactly when to tune in for a bit of time to ourselves.

I'm past caring whether this brands me as a sissy or an alternative hippy freak. This was for Amanda and me and no one else. It was an acknowledgement that the separation would be tough on both of us and it was a way of improving difficult circumstances. So why mention it? Because it is the coping tactics and the unexpected stresses and worries that make this real-life story interesting. Of course I could stick to writing about coconuts and snails but the truth of the matter is if you are stranded on an island, you are taken to far deeper places and faced with far greater demands than eating and drinking. What really matters in life is made utterly clear to you by what you miss and what you think about. Private or not, macho or otherwise, my attempt to maintain a real connection with the woman I love played a big part in keeping me positive enough to complete the ordeal.

'Goodnight, my love. I love you with all my heart,' I said out loud. Another tear rolled down my cheek in the darkness.

卌 卌 卌 ‖

'It's day seventeen. Good morning. Very roughly forty-three days to go.' I scratched the chalk mark on the wall all too aware of precisely how long that was.

I walked up the beach, taking the inverted plastic bottle sprat trap to keep my omega oils up. A coconut tree had fallen in the night and this provided me with a bountiful gift of green coconuts that I could simply collect from where they lay on the sand.

Bizarrely convenient considering that I'd used my old coconut pole in the construction of the ridge pole only yesterday. I was being looked after again.

I caught a hermit crab opportunistically munching on the fallen coconuts and scooped it up for lunch, automatically twisting the claws to snap them and render the creature defenceless. I collected brown coconuts, too, for grazing on – these were by now far and away my main source of calories.

The goats were in the woods when I went in to start work. They slowly walked up the hill away from me. I contemplated having a bow and arrow or a spear. Hunting surely had to be my next project, rather than fishing. But for now I had to concentrate on construction.

The first thing I did, after necking a full green coconut, was to clear away all the small vines and foliage in my build area so that my construction site was clean. On my hands and knees I used the clamshell to tidy the sixteen square metres of turf. There was also a big branch in the way where the roof was going to be. I hacked at the bendy limb for ages – it moved every time I struck it – but eventually the build site was clear. Lunchtime.

From downing tools to having lunch on the fire took forty minutes. I collected sprats, snails and crabs and added them to fresh water and my now usual splash of seawater. 'It will take ten minutes to boil so by the time I've eaten it will be an hour lunch break,' I fretted. Then I caught myself. I was thinking like a berk. 'You've not been resting – you've been working collecting food! You've only just sat down. Don't worry! Relax!'

Sitting and waiting for the pot to boil, I realised that the sea was always so much calmer at low tide. I quickly worked out that it must be because the reef adds more protection at low tide,

as it is relatively higher, thus protecting the lagoon. I extrapolated from this that I should therefore try to fish at low tide
when the water would be less choppy and I would be able to see
the fish more easily.

I wiped my plastic bowl clean from breakfast with my fingers
and banged out the remains on my knee. A crack had developed
in the bottom of the bowl so I had to tilt it when eating so as not
to lose any of the nutritious broth that I loved so much. 'Nectar,'
I said as I swallowed it. My diet wasn't so different from the time
I was ill but the fact that I was now cooking it before eating
made so much difference. 'I think I'm going to appreciate fine
food and nice things for the rest of my life. I now salivate at the
thought of the juices of sea snails. They are amazing.' They say
hunger is the sweetest of sauces and clearly I wouldn't touch
these at home, but in a world stripped of luxury joy comes from
far smaller, simpler pleasures. I now loved finding food, cooking
food and eating food. I appreciated every step of the process.
And this from a man happy to eat pasta and gravy for dinner if
that's all that is left in the kitchen cupboard.

More profoundly, I was even, on occasions, beginning to
enjoy my own company: the quiet and the calm. This was a
million miles from the man whose days were normally crammed
with meetings, training, phone calls, tweets and emails. Once
I'd adjusted to the solitude, and had scrambled through that
feeling of being totally overwhelmed by everything for which I
now had to be responsible, the resultant freedom was clear
and light.

Thankfully, day two of construction was always going to be
quite straightforward. I knew I wanted twelve trees to act as
rafters that would effectively lean up against the ridge pole and
provide the bones for one side of the construction. These rafters

would be the skeleton upon which the thatching would be lashed and so they needed to be relatively straight but, more importantly, they needed to be strong enough to support the weight of hundreds of palm leaves.

I scrambled up the jungle wall behind the campsite towards the Highlands in search of suitable poles. The interior behind my camp was open forest and there were many mature saplings to choose from. Ever conscious of expending energy, I wanted ones that would do the job but that weren't overkill. I used my fingers to gauge the circumference of some possibles, and could tell at a glance the trees that would work best.

At each selected tree I knelt down and commenced the lengthy process of gnawing round the trunks with my clamshell hand axe. Each tree took the best part of forty minutes to fell. Every short, intense burst of chopping was interspersed with exhausted, panting breathers to recover.

By mid-afternoon I had three trees down and dragged to the shelter. After a quick stop to set the loach trap and eat some burned coconut, I felled a further three trees in the late afternoon, then the day had gone. I began readjusting my estimation of how long this build was going to take.

I was still leaving the palm leaf shield over the seep in an attempt to increase the afternoon flow but it didn't help much. The heat radiating from the rock was still strong and I swilled a mouthful of warm plastic-tasting water around my mouth. I decided to forgo my lemon tea in lieu of snails and loach soup. This could be a much bigger meal if cooked with fresh water and I didn't want to lose the oils from the tiny fish.

I reassured myself that the morning spent clearing up the site had been vital and that cutting trees down is something that just takes time. I had hoped to cut all the rafters today but six would have to do. It was progress – physical, tangible progress – but I still wasn't quite satisfied.

A fter three back-breaking trees I was exhausted and decided to stop for lunch. I was feeling down because I was facing snails and coconuts again. I mean, I like snails and coconuts but I like other things, too – variety being the spice of life and all that.

'But I haven't got enough time in the day to eat better if I want to get this shelter built,' I told myself. 'I can survive on coconuts and snails – but I don't want to live off them for the rest of the time here – I really don't.' I acknowledged to myself that eating simply for a while was the sacrifice I was prepared to make to build a new home.

During the afternoon the sound of crashing waves proved too much for my inactive brain to process and listen to quietly. It seemed that my coping strategy was to overlay the relentless white noise with annoying songs. I recalled how in the film *Touching the Void* the song 'Brown Girl in the Ring' had got stuck in Joe Simpson's head for several days as he dragged his injured body from the depths of a crevasse to safety. 'Bloody hell – I'm going to die to Boney M,' he thought. My song for the afternoon was 'Grandfather Clock', a perversely inane song that focused on a clock ticking as if to twist the knife by making me ever more conscious of time:

My grandfather's clock was too large for the shelf,
So it stood ninety years on the floor;

It was taller by half than the old man himself,
Though it weighed not a pennyweight more.
It was bought on the morn of the day that he was born,
And was always his treasure and pride;
But it stopped – short – never to go again
When the old man died.

Ninety years without slumbering (tick, tock, tick, tock),
His life's seconds numbering (tick, tock, tick, tock),
It stopped – short – never to go again when the old man died.

After a few hours I was starting to envy Joe's playlist. I tried to sing other songs in my head but as soon as I paused – *tick, tock, tick, tock* would resume.

At one point I just had to stop everything and sit down. My brain had been going berserk and I had to calm down and listen to my mind. As I stopped identifying with the voices and neurotic thoughts they faded away and I managed to relax a little. But the songs kept on playing and playing. If this seems trivial I can assure you it did not feel so at all. I was faced with the unsettling truth that I could not control my own mind, not great when you are alone on a tropical island for sixty days. Does that mean I'm mad? If I want it to stop and it's not stopping, then who is bloody well playing the songs against my wishes? Another bit of me? Am I schizophrenic? Who are these two voices? Which one is real?

Three more trees felled, I laid the final six rafters up against the structure. I decided I would do one side of the shelter at a time. The side that backed on to the prevailing wind was obviously the most important so I would construct and thatch that side before I worried about the other. It made sense as I could live in half a shelter and, being half the size, it would be twice as fast to build. For the first time my lean-to started to take shape properly in my eyes and I reflected on why I was building this type of shelter.

It was a vast surface area to thatch and I was concerned that the thatching would take days. There were several factors in play here. If I built a shelter that was big enough just to house me when I was sleeping then I would immediately need another one for a fire, another to store the huge pile of firewood in a dry place and yet another to house my camera equipment and accumulated stores. This didn't make any sense as, presently, I was living in a cave that was perfectly big enough for all of these things under one rock-solid roof. So it was clear that if I was moving out I needed space equivalent to what the cave was providing.

The next factor was that I would hardly be evolving (Discovery's and my mission in all this) if the shelter leaked – I would be regressing – so the thatch had to have a steep enough pitch to allow proper run-off and to minimise pooling. Pooling equals leaks. This steep pitch meant that, to get the floor space that I needed, I had to build high. Significantly more than head height, actually – so about eight feet tall. This meant that the shelter was about twelve feet long, eight feet high, but therefore that the diagonal rafters were about ten or eleven feet from the ground to the pole. So the surface area to be thatched was eleven feet multiplied by twelve feet – 132 square feet of thatch! A lot when you consider that it would only cover sixty square feet of earth floor space. I was now predicting that the entire build, including thatching, would take ten days. If I was devoting six hours of my working day to construction, that meant that the cost of my real estate was one man-hour per square foot. Actually, that didn't sound too expensive.

Including the time spent on reflection it was still only mid-afternoon and so I made a journey to the other side of the island in search of water. The sun was scorching hot and, as I wanted to travel along the coast, I again used the clay residue from the water that I'd collected as sunscreen. This was one of those things that I'd heard about, then had its efficacy confirmed by the Aboriginals, but it was only when spreading this viscous mud on my body that I could appreciate how remarkable it was. The clay spread smoothly on my skin; it did not harden, feel itchy or crack and fall off – rather, it felt as if it was feeding my skin and remained supple and protective all afternoon.

Sadly, my search for water was fruitless. The hole, despite some light rain, was dry once more and I realised that I needed to be pretty sharp if I was to make use of this collection method. Directly after a storm it would be full to the brim – but it was not the perfect solution that I had first thought it might be.

Behind Lemon Camp I dug up various plants to determine if they had edible roots. I dug for over an hour in the hard clay soil using a stone and a long pole as a digging stick. By now I had shed my flabby excess City weight and was leaner and darker skinned with a green T-shirt wrapped like a turban around my head. My digging, however, produced nothing.

I pulled up the taro that I'd replanted. There were no more taro corms but I decided that the core root of the taro was starchy, too, and therefore I would eat it. It was the size of a large turnip and a not insignificant addition to my carbohydrate. I duly chucked the hairy root into my woven basket.

Ever on the lookout for alternative foodstuff, I decided to eat a leaf of the vegetable; they were large and green and looked as if they should be edible. They were, after all, sprouting from an edible root.

Immediately I did so, my gums and tongue started stinging. I knew straight away that I was having an adverse reaction as pins and needles attacked my mouth and my lips and tongue swelled alarmingly. 'Stafford, you are stupid,' I said to camera. 'My tongue is on fire.' I knew all too well about the process of testing new foods when you haven't positively identified them as edible. Even if I skipped the rubbing on my gums I should at the very least have limited my testing to a very small portion. But I'd just screwed up the whole leaf and chomped through it like a fat lad with a kebab at closing time.

The effects of malnutrition and dehydration, compounded over time, were taking their toll and I had become complacent as my body was eating itself up from the inside. I spat out every scrap that was in my mouth and gargled with some fresh water to strip out any last remnants. I could still breathe – check – I could still speak – check. As the reaction subsided I took solace in the fact that it must not have been a severe reaction. But if it had been worse and required hospitalisation I could well have died.

On the way back I scooped up items that might come in handy and shoved them in my basket, like an old bag lady: ropes attached to discarded fishing floats, several more water bottles (I wanted to be ready for that first proper downfall), even a toothbrush wedged between the rocks. The latter find meant that with ground-up charcoal I now had a means of ensuring I got right into the gaps my blunt fingers couldn't reach. 'Brilliant – absolutely brilliant,' I grinned. Then – almost too ridiculous to be true and only on a Fijian island – I found a rugby ball.

I was smiling but, realistically, what on earth was I going to do with it? It wasn't fully inflated and my chances of finding a bike pump and a needle valve were slim. But I slung it in the basket anyway and it made me feel happy to have such a familiar item, one that reminded me of my love of the sport, the weekly battle alongside lifelong friends that legitimately allowed me to give vent to the pressures of everyday life. I had made a point of not watching Tom Hanks's *Castaway* for fear of being tempted to copy certain scenes from it but I knew the gist of it. I had my own Wilson – a volleyball Hanks finds in the film. Or in my case 'Gilbert', a leading brand of rugby ball.

Now in full scavenging mode I noted that there were also various long, smooth poles that had washed up from surrounding islands. They had all been cut with machetes and must have been old boating poles used by clans to get their crafts over the reefs. I decided I would drag one back every time I returned to my cave as they could make the base for a very flat, comfortable bed.

As I placed my spear into the sand it snapped. I immediately reassured myself that it didn't matter because much of the length of the spear *behind* the hand must be superfluous to my needs. Then I tested it and, of course, the spear was now unbalanced; it required the weight behind the hand to hold it level. I chuckled at the cogs grinding in my brain working things out that I'd never even contemplated before. My primordial survival knowledge and experience were growing.

Back in the cave I smashed the taro root on the wall and I could see that the inside was indeed potato-like and starchy. I could eat it! This had doubled the productivity of the single plant and I didn't care if you weren't meant to eat that bit. I would. I picked the tentacled bean-sprout-like roots off it, too, and went for a bean-sprout broth from the menu for tonight's meal.

The evening was calm. A silver mackerel sky blanketed the peaceful lagoon at low tide. I had done what I wanted to do on the third day of construction. Tomorrow I would lash the rafters on. It was only possible to work about three and a half hours a day on it; the rest of the time had to be spent just surviving: collecting wood, collecting food and fresh water, and on administrative tasks.

I reckoned the taro root would last me over a week if carefully rationed. Before I arrived here I would have said it would last a couple of meals. Life was different here and many of my preconceptions were changing, too. 'All good then,' I concluded. 'I'm getting three hot meals a day and I'm progressing with the construction each day. Nice one, Staffs. Nice one.'

I found that I could now use the semi-inflated Gilbert as a pillow when lying on my side. 'But I'm not going to start talking to it, though – it's just a pillow – well, it's actually a rugby ball – but it's my pillow,' I muttered to the camera, clearly toying with my own madness. 'Do you know what?' I further confided, 'I have to really rein my brain in every day. I think if left to just race it would have bizarre conversations and stuff.' I felt I couldn't have prepared myself for being cut off from every other human being on the planet. You just had to experience it to understand the weird effects of isolation.

'A very big part of surviving on this island is holding it together and staying sane and not going nutty bonkers. And it just needs a bit of checking in.'

I powered down the camera and lay down beside the fire to rest.

HHT HHH HHH IIII

The new toothbrush worked a treat. I ground the charcoal into the finest particles possible on a relatively flat rock and then dabbed the end of the wet toothbrush into the sooty powder. I relaxed into the civilised rhythmical action of brushing my teeth. 'There is no other animal on the planet that does this!' I said to the camera, exhibiting a marked lack of knowledge about the habits of the macaque monkey.

Despite the absence of minty white froth, the charcoal worked even better with the brush than with my finger and as I ran my tongue over my teeth they felt smooth and truly clean again. My image in the camera screen showed Persil-white teeth shining out of my weary, weathered face.

The morning's scout around the shore for food revealed that no banquet had washed up overnight. My basket had been empty and so I decided to start hauling up large rocks and looking under them. My first find was an eel. It moved like lightning and it was only through pure primal hunger that I managed to stamp on its head and then eventually stun it enough to kill it. I thought I recognised the next find − a sea cucumber as I recollected from a summer holiday in Greece. It was emitting sticky white mucous from its anus.

'I'm going to take it and put it in the fire and ... see if it's edible,' I said. It was a lesson to me: on days when you didn't have much to eat, just turn over some rocks. 'Two things under that rock, an eel and a bizarre-looking animal that looks a bit like a massive shit.' As ever, when luck was on my side it didn't rain − it poured − and I found a further six crabs, which meant that for the first time ever I had collected enough for two meals − lunch and supper.

I laid the eel on the fire in one piece, as you might a snake, and allowed it to cook in its skin to retain moisture. The result was better than expected: large chunks of sticky white meat that fell away from the spine. I held it in both hands and ate it like a corn on the cob.

With a belly full of eel I collected a lot of beach hibiscus. In the end I had perhaps 150 metres' worth of cordage hanging over a stubby branch, all of which would be used over the course of the following days' thatching. I lashed on the rafter poles from the day before and collected twelve coconut palms with which to start thatching tomorrow. As I dragged the huge palms down the beach I remembered the days of palm leaf collection that I'd taken part in with groups of volunteers to thatch houses in Central America. Now I was on my own and I winced at the scale of the project I was embarking upon solo. It would take hundreds of palm fronds. As I mused on this, large raindrops began to patter onto my shoulders as the skies darkened and growled.

By mid-afternoon it had started to rain steadily. Exciting news for my water collection, but this new climate brought its own overlooked issues. I ventured out and collected a nice amount of firewood from the forest – my wet skin was covered in dirt from the wood as I hauled it all back. Coated in mud, bark and general shite, I quickly dived into the sea to wash myself down and hurried back up the beach shivering in the damp air.

I popped some caramelised coconut into my mouth and shut my eyes as the hot sweetness burst between my teeth. I was eating a coconut a day now that I'd found a way of making it not slimy and my body appreciated every fatty calorie.

It wouldn't be dark for a few hours but, due to the rain, I hung my grass skirt up for the day. I had decided to have an afternoon off. I sat by the fire and thought about life. About my real life, that is. About Amanda and the kids. I decided that I couldn't be bothered to go back out into the rain, that I was going to treat myself to just sitting by the fire and thinking of home.

There was something beautifully simple about boiling water in an old tin can on a fire, when it was raining outside and I was dry and warm in my cave. I think it was because I felt that I was winning and had made my life comfortable enough even in bad weather. The contrast between outside and inside made me happy.

By early evening water was streaming off the front of the cave and I filled my bowl and chain-drank cups of pine-needle tea one after the other. Not wanting to leave my warm den in the storm, I put my faith in the clamshells and knew that I would have plenty of water in the morning. I promised myself two more cups of tea when I woke up as a treat, too.

Firewood was my next concern as the wood that I'd collected was wet and I worried that I might not be able to keep the fire going all night. I positioned the damp wood close enough to the fire for it to dry without catching light. It was a warning to collect enough firewood on dry days to last me when it rained. One more lesson learned. I would make it a priority to build up a huge stockpile of dry wood in the morning. My fire was never going to go out – I was adamant about that.

With less than an hour until nightfall my niggling worries started to get the better of me and I ventured back out into the rain to collect more firewood. I couldn't chance it. I slipped into the vast wet gloom with just the GoPro (head-mounted point-of-view HD video camera) on my head. The short mission calmed my fears and I began the process of drying out this second batch of soggy wood.

Just as it was about to get really dark I remembered that the sprat catcher was still set in the rock pool. I reprimanded myself for allowing myself to relax too much this afternoon and for letting things slip. And so I had no option but to run up the beach in the fading light in the now torrential rain.

'Run, Stafford! Run!'

The run in the rain was utterly invigorating. Just breaking into a stride was exciting and I had done it naked as I wasn't filming. 'Got it!' I grabbed the plastic bottle from the shallows and was surprised also to find I had a small catch.

I now needed a bigger fire and one that would be hot enough to dry out the wood. The theory was sound but I was burning through the wood at a pace. It would last – I told myself – and it had the pleasant side effect of keeping the cave warm.

My cave had fared excellently in the wind and rain. I would get a light spray of water in a big gust but on the whole I was dry and protected. The night outside was angry and tormented but I observed the natural chaos from my warm pouch in the belly of the island.

||||/ ||||/ ||||/ ||||/

In the morning, much to my surprise, the rain was still cutting down into the beach. Hmm, hadn't banked on that.

'Morning – really not the greatest night's sleep.' I had been constantly putting wood on and never really relaxed about the fire. I consoled myself that I wouldn't have had enough firewood if I hadn't fetched more. It had been a wise last move. Right, out on to the beach.

I shivered as the wind and rain stripped away my night-time warmth. Crouching naked on the beach, undeterred I sucked all the water in the clamshells up and gently blew it into my bottles. Six and a half litres of water – the most I'd collected in one go to date. I felt genuine elation at such a simple thing.

I now had seven litres of emergency water stored at the back of the cave, water that I was never going to touch. With my other four litres' worth of bottles my plan was to fill up regularly, safe in the knowledge that I would always have a week's worth of water – one litre a day – at the back of the cave plus whatever I could get each day from the seep.

'That feels like in my mind I'm in control of the water now. Which is good because the water actually, surprisingly, is quite stressful.'

'Blowing a hooley out there. Unbelievable.' I had to raise my voice to be heard by the camera's recorder.

I collected firewood for the first hour of the day and then – when I'd stacked up the same amount as I had the day before – I went to collect more. I had also brought back a load more plastic bottles. I couldn't miss this amazing opportunity to collect a massive reservoir. Water might be abundant today but I didn't know when it would rain next. I was determined to stockpile water and wood in case I got caught out. That way I could begin to relax.

I do see that it seems as though I could never relax – no matter how much I tried to – but I think that's quite a lesson in itself about living hand to mouth. When there is no energy provider to supply you with electricity or gas, no water company to deliver fresh water on tap and nothing to take away sewage, and no supermarkets selling groceries, you have to do it all yourself. It is striking how the progress of civilisation has taken the provision of these entirely essential needs out of our hands and how we now take them for granted. The only way for me to get to a stage where I could relax like the proverbial man with a beer and his feet up in front of the telly on a Saturday afternoon was to put in the hard yards. Preparation and menial, laborious tasks were the payment for such services in my island world – and if I got lazy all my amenities would be cut off without a word of warning.

I cleaned out the fire. The ashes had built up and spread over the rocks and so the roasted coconut was getting increasingly dirty and grey. I scraped it all out with clamshell and then re-arranged the rocks so that they had flat upper surfaces that would accommodate more coconuts for toasting. Nice.

I didn't want to let the weather slow progress on my first day of thatching, especially after such a productive run. Sitting around idly was a bad plan, too. On top of this, if I left the coconut palm leaves lying on the floor too long the individual leaves would curl up. I'd witnessed it on those that I'd used to lay over my grass blanket to stop the wind penetrating at night. They had worked OK the first two nights but then the once flat leaves began to close like a venus fly trap, leaving large gaps between them and allowing the wind to breeze straight through. So plait them into flat tiles in the rain I must.

I thought back to my first jungle expedition to Belize in Mayflower National Park when we had had almost six solid weeks of rain. The base camp was knee-deep in mud and the mosquitoes relentless. I had been a mere assistant leader at the time, fresh out of the army, and I saw it as my job to motivate the rest of the group into believing that they could not be held back by the weather. There was no option but to work – we had twenty-nine kilometres of trail to cut and days off were not an option. What was an option, I soon realised, was that you could let the conditions affect you. Frustration and annoyance are almost always born out of maintaining resistance to something that is going on. In the case of the weather such frustration is pointless – it will never make conditions better and only make you feel worse. So every day we would go out and smile and sing and work hard in the rain. Soon we didn't notice the rain any more – we were wet, dirty and happy. I suppose it's no different from the famous serenity prayer of which I quote the first part:

God, give me grace to accept with serenity
the things that cannot be changed,
courage to change the things
which should be changed,
and the wisdom to distinguish

Omit the word 'God' if you need to in order to hear what I'm trying to get across. There is nothing serene about being frustrated by the weather, your age or the passing of time. It is utterly pointless and a bloody waste of energy. So you relax about the things outside your control quite simply *because* they are outside your control. No-brainer The things that you *can* influence, you should; and in my experience it is this little internal check as to whether it is one or the other (*the wisdom*) that can save a lot of unnecessary angst.

After a lifetime of whining, it took me a while to adjust to living by such simple rules. It's disconcerting – there's nothing and no one else to blame. But isolation forces you to the point of addressing negative behavioural patterns that you could probably get away with in normal life because you have to deal with the direct results of your own thinking. No one else would pick me up.

I sat down on a rock in front of my pile of coconut palms and attempted to plait the first one in the rain. I'd never done this before but I'd seen it done in Fiji on my arrival and knew that it was the only way to stop the leaves curling. Not surprisingly my initial attempts were pretty amateur and I had to slow my wet fingers down and just ensure that I did each leaf properly. Having reminded myself that it was only me who could make myself happy or miserable, I started to sing songs to myself. Robbie Williams's 'Angels', of course, and a few other songs that were played repeatedly on the radio when I had been a painter and decorator and so I knew all the words. Eventually, as ever, when you have been educated at an English boarding school with chapel every day, you resort to hymns. By the time I'd belted out 'Bread of Heaven' to the treetops I found I was loving my manual labour in the rain. Once mastered, plaiting is simple; it just requires some basic knowledge to produce a large shiny green tile that is watertight and will last for years. It's actually very satisfying when you get it right, and I continued to sing while I deftly manipulated leaves into roofing tiles.

In my cave on a tea break late morning I realised that I had enough space to plait in there and so I dragged the palm fronds back to the cave and sat watching the storm play out. 'Any fool can be uncomfortable,' I reminded myself as I sipped lemon leaf tea in the warmth of my cavern.

Keen for some visible (and successful) evidence of my work, I decided that each day I should add the completed palm tiles to my roof. I had thatched the roofs of many primitive structures before in Belize and knew that the theory was simple. I would start at the bottom and tie on a full row. Then, the next row would be tied just above the first so that there was significant overlap and so that the rain running off the second row would flow on to the first. It was important to keep the rows close together; the more densely packed, the stronger and more watertight the thatch would be.

My first effort produced two and a half rows of thatching. Although the expanse still to be filled looked bigger than ever the rows looked professional and tidy.

'What a difference a day makes.' I stood back and admired the new thatch. 'Yesterday when it was blowing a hooley I was feeling quite alone and vulnerable. And when the sun didn't come out this morning it took me a long time to pick myself up. I had to really actively work at jollying myself along, I started singing songs out loud to raise my morale.' I paused to savour the scent of victory that had altered my mood for the better. 'Then I got better at the plaiting and the last few ones were really good. Tied on to the house and they look fantastic!'

At first it really did feel as if this simplest of achievements had lifted me once more. 'Not a bad day. This thatching is not going to leak,' I boasted. Then I realised that this was more than just satisfaction at my own handicraft. I'd lifted myself *before* I'd finished the task. At the time when I would normally have been getting stressed about the time I was taking and beating myself up, I had dragged myself up by the bootlaces and changed my mood for the better by singing. This childishly simple ability to jolly myself along shouldn't warrant the credit that I'm giving it but in this case it *was* significant, because it was an indication that I was beginning to have more control but also because I was being kind to myself. Before I would have seen singing as an irrelevant waste of time that wouldn't achieve anything. Now I was recognising my own need to be happy. I had started to look after myself.

ℍℍ ℍℍ ℍℍ ℍℍ |

My end-of-week-three exercises were conducted in the morning on a shaded beach with the tide almost too high to run my route to the rock. Salty foam licked my heels as I panted towards the camera.

'Not bad – although I felt weak on the shoulder press,' I droned. I managed sixteen chin-ups in Lemon Camp, however. 'Sixteen! Yeeesss!' and was elated to find my strength actually *increasing*. I put it down to the crabs that I'd been eating.

Clearly I didn't need to get stronger – I had the physical ability to do everything that was necessary on the island. But the improvement did wonders for my morale. It was proof that I wasn't degrading. It was proof that I was moving beyond survival and into the territory of a sustainable existence.

~~HH~~ ~~HH~~ ~~HH~~ ~~HH~~ II

P ad – pad – pad. Buff! I bounced down the rocks and landed softly in the sand on two bare feet. There were fresh crab hills on the beach and I ran to see if any of the occupants were at home.

After a two-crab breakfast I did another hour of wood collecting. It was an hour that I wanted to spend in construction, and predictably – despite the inherently relaxing nature of this simple task – I stressed.

To complete the previous day's health tests, I measured my resting heart rate and got an average of sixty. 'Bollocks! It's getting higher! That's not actually that comforting.'

Then, before work, I had monumental diarrhoea that could have been easily passed through the eye of a needle. The brown puddles on the beach were bigger than cow-pats. 'Is it too much sun?' No – it had been raining. 'Is it food poisoning?' I didn't think so as I'd not vomited. 'Is my water contaminated?' Only if the bottles were dirty, I postulated. Either way, I needed to up my intake of water to avoid severe dehydration.

Collecting palm leaves is the most boring of preparatory jobs. It offers little satisfaction and yet you just can't skip it. If I'd been in a village on an island, I would have paid some kids to do this dullest of tasks and then I would have sat in my house doing the far more rewarding work of thatching. But in my primordial world I had no such options. I had to be everyone, from architect to labourer's mate. So I collected and plaited palm leaves. It's not that hard to chop down a palm frond with a machete with a half-decent edge on it. The fronds are fairly pulpy and the blade slips through the stalks as if they were soft fruit. With a broken clam-shell in my hand it was altogether tougher. The soft stems actually have sharp edges and when your knuckles hit these edges as often as the clamshell, it becomes about as enjoyable as hammering in nails wearing a blindfold. I would tension and hang off the fronds to increase their likelihood of splitting cleanly and then I would twist, snap and smash the remaining fibres until the palm frond was free. Usually there was a pinkish tint to the exposed palm flesh caused by my blood. Once down, the palm leaves would have to be dragged out on to the beach, stacked up and dragged back to the shelter with about four under each arm.

Once back at my building site I would collapse in exhaustion. There was no satisfaction in the collection – I could not stand back and admire my work – I'd simply brought the raw mate-rials to the workshop and the crafting now had to begin.

At lunch I made a soup of crabs that I had caught the day before. They smelled a bit and, as I had had the runs all day, I reminded myself to eat everything that I caught that same day.

By day three of thatching the weight of the magnificent-looking roof was already significant. The problem now was that the ridge pole bowed noticeably and I saw it wouldn't support the weight of the remaining thatch. I needed a much fatter Y-pole to support the weight and prop up the sagging ridge pole.

At the end of a hard day's work I had nothing for supper. Heavy-legged, I wandered round the coast in the evening glow and apathetically looked for snails and crabs. There is a state you can reach where energy levels hit a certain low and then you can't be bothered. I would prefer to sit by the fire and conserve energy than go out on the hunt for food. This apparent laziness is, I am sure, a valid way of conserving energy but it's not good for morale to sit and not do anything, so drag myself out I did.

A larger crab with a solid exoskeleton withdrew into a crack in a rock. It wasn't the usual sand crab that you could bite through and swallow in one. It was a proper crab – a tough little number – and so I put down my Cinesaddle and camera and went to look for a stabber stick. 'Dead or alive, you're coming with me,' I told the crab, quoting from *RoboCop*. After quite a bit of stabbing it ended up being levered out of the small crack pretty dead.

My feet were taking a pounding, despite my all-terrain flip-flops. They were tired and bruised and still covered in sores. They ached, too, as if I'd been jumping up and down in a field of nails and scrap iron.

I estimated that I'd eaten 600 calories in the whole day and I was having to battle with self-pity at my situation. Minor illness had clearly dampened my mood and sapped my energies. I clasped my open palm over my face and rubbed my smoke-irritated eyes. Bugger me, this was hard. Still, only thirty-eight days to go. My God, I really doubted that I could make it.

‖‖‖ ‖‖‖ ‖‖‖ ‖‖‖ |||

Firewood was taking longer and longer to collect. By now I'd had a fire burning constantly for about ten days and every scrap of decent dry wood in my immediate vicinity was gone. To combat this I made a point of always trying to bring a large piece of standing deadwood with me if I was out in the island's interior, or driftwood if I'd returned via the coast. The hand-to-mouth existence was unsettling – I yearned for a gas cylinder and a reliable hob. It was like bailing out a sinking ship – even when you had bucketed like mad and emptied the hull, you knew that you would have to do it again very soon and that there was no opting out.

The lack of opportunity to be lazy had now begun to annoy me. I wanted a day off. I wanted just to eat and recuperate. But the truth was, if I wasn't collecting water or looking for food or firewood then I would not eat or drink and I'd lose my most precious fire. I couldn't afford to let that happen. Even if I took a day off from thatching I would just feel guilty that I was being idle and so there was no genuine relaxation. Interestingly, the times that began to be the most relaxing were the repetitive tasks that gave me a sense of satisfaction. I may still have been working but they allowed my mind to calm, and there was no quibbling with the results. I was being productive.

My one opportunity to add some form of variety to my diet was to be extra alert while out catching crabs and snails in case I stumbled across a rare, unusual treat. 'Stop biting me!' I complained as my latest catch had swung its head back and clamped its teeth into the flesh between my thumb and fore-finger. Eventually, its head pummelled with a rock, it lay limp in my basket. Eels, it has to be said, put up a fight. I washed my hands in the sea and wondered, with no antiseptic, whether catching eels was worth the risk of infection.

卌 卌 卌 卌 IIII

By my calculations, using hand spans and guestimates, I was adding about fourteen inches to the thatch each day. Today was the fifth day of thatching and I now predicted that I would finish in nine days. These calculations came with the sense of resignation that this was only *one side* of the shelter – a basic lean-to and no more. I had to step in to beat the converging depression off with a large stick.

'Unless you can have a thatch that is watertight, what's the point? It's got to be better than the cave, hasn't it?' I coached. 'And with one person this is how long it takes.'

卌 卌 卌 卌 卌

On the sixth day of thatching I did no thatching at all. It was dropbox day and was raining so I split the morning between trips to Lemon Camp and time in the cave. I collected some fresh lemon leaves and two and a half litres of water from the clam-shells. But I wanted more.

I gave in to my desire for laziness and allocated the day solely to my own comfort. For consolidation. For relaxing. I contemplated burning the old coconut shells in place of firewood because of my concern about running out of wood but they burned too fast and hot and so I decided that I would revert to driftwood and just increase the distances I had to carry it. I collected loads more bottles and realised that potentially I could now have a huge reservoir of water.

Coming back down the steep slope into my camp I spotted two goats, a mother and a kid, *in* my shelter eating coconut. From twenty metres I looked on incredulously at the audacity of these stupid animals and realised that my frustration was at myself. 'Why haven't I got a means of killing these goats yet? It's just madness.' It was more than three weeks in and I hadn't even fashioned a basic club. 'I've got to get some tools to kill goats.'

I felt so much better for giving myself the time to consolidate. In a good place mentally in the cave, I contemplated baiting a spiked deadfall trap with coconut to kill the goats.

 ᚼᚼᚼ ᚼᚼᚼ ᚼᚼᚼ ᚼᚼᚼ ᚼᚼᚼ I

For lunch I had my snails and taro root staple supplemented with a fairly big hermit crab. The abdomen of the hermits was full of fats and delicious. I still wasn't sure whether that bit was actually edible or whether it was waste but as it tasted bizarrely fantastic and greasy I ate it all.

I now had six litres of water above and beyond my emergency seven litres and, thanks to the preceding day's foraging, I had a further sixteen litres of bottles to fill. I wove my roofing tiles in the comfort and dryness of the cave and then ventured out in the afternoon to attach them to my new home.

I stood back and surveyed the lean-to. The thatch was above head height and I decided that, with a good day's thatching tomorrow, it would be ready to move into. I hadn't gone quite as high as I'd planned but I was bored with thatching and one more day would have to do.

It was the highest of high tides – and no beach meant no beach crabs. The feeder fire was smouldering and I pushed together the logs to reignite the flames. One long blow. Easy. Snails and taro root again for supper – a great day and a good amount of work done.

The tide was the highest I'd yet seen. There was no beach under the cave and the sea cleaned my doorstep of piss and palm scraps.

'Last night in the cave,' I reflected. 'Am I going to miss it? Am I fuck.' It felt good to swear. It felt like a deliberately edgy form of expression in a tortuously muted bland bubble. In truth, the cave had been amazing for me and I'd felt safe even in the strongest of tropical storms. My outburst might have been directed at anything. That said, I think the cave did now represent how long everything was taking; it was time to remove my training nappies and step out into the real world where I would provide my own protection. Bored with the walls around me, too, I also wanted a simple change of scenery.

⫴⫴⫴ ⫴⫴⫴ ⫴⫴⫴ ⫴⫴⫴ ⫴⫴⫴ ||

Having noted on day four of thatching that my Y-pole brace was too feeble, it was now a fairly immediate concern. The weight of the thatch was already colossal. To understand how thick it was you have to appreciate the basics of thatching. Thatching isn't like using roofing tiles for one simple reason: the materials are not waterproof. So, rather than putting something impermeable on your roof you are putting something vaguely weatherproof on it. This imperfection is factored in and you acknowledge that each layer of thatch will deflect only a bit more of the water. To construct a watertight thatch from coconut palms the thatch had to be layered so that it was about a *foot* thick. The result looked bomb-proof and yet, despite the meticulous construction, the whole lot would collapse if I didn't prop up the sagging ridge pole with a stout brace.

Yesterday I had attempted to cut down a fat Y-pole brace but the difficulty of chopping such a tree down with a clamshell had meant that it was a job that had to take two days so as to ease the physical exertion. There was no point in doing any more thatching until I had braced the whole roof and so I set off up the hillside to finish the job I'd started.

The 'huge' tree had a trunk between four and five inches in diameter. It was a relatively hard wood and I inspected my previous efforts. The tree was already well ringed but required further 'nibbling' with the clamshell hand axe to get it to the point where it would snap.

Tired by the mere thought of the task, I sank to my knees next to the tree to save energy and so as to be at the right height to work. I hugged the tree with my left arm for stability and swung my forearm like the handle of an axe with the axe head being the clamshell fragment.

I felt I was becoming work-shy by using the excuse that energy conservation was key. But that wasn't conducive to getting things done and so, rather than conserving energy and resting more, I had to tell myself that working hard was great exercise and that I needed to stay fit, so that every tree felled, every bundle of firewood collected, had the positive side effect of keeping me in good physical condition. This also helped me deal with the worries of wasting too much energy. I was killing two birds with one stone.

Here at my chosen tree I was alternating between nibbling away at the tree on my knees, hugging it for support and weakening the shaft, and trying to snap it. The latter demanded monumental thrusts to the trunk from the shoulder with my body in a horizontal scrummaging position. The thrusting in fact came from my legs and, for the most part, the tree did not even notice my efforts.

But plug away at the cycle I did until one thrust produced a faint crack and then a snapping in the internal fibres of the trunk. Then, gradually, with every scrap of my strength, I amplified these noises until the splitting sound tore through the forest.

Big tree down. 'Yes – thank you.' I expressed my appreciation to whatever forces were responsible for deciding that I'd put in enough effort and the tree should now fall. Thank goodness, indeed.

I snapped off the tree's branches and hauled it down the hillside fat end first. Above my shelter I then launched it through the air over the last ten metres of very steep ground to watch it come to rest just inches from the precious thatch. In one thoughtless throw I had nearly taken out my shelter. 'Think it through next time, Stafford!' Tiredness and not thinking could have undone days of hard work in seconds.

Then, as if ignoring the lesson I had just learned, I decided to throw down some firewood, too, and forgot about the taro plants that were planted near the shelter. Both suffered broken stems as a direct result of my clumsiness and so I had to splint them with sticks and some very thin vine. Once supported they stood up again OK but it remained to be seen if they would survive. 'Slow down,' I told myself, rubbing my sweaty forehead with my dirty fingers.

Having used my coconut pole to make the ridge pole of my shelter, and having drunk the contents of all the fruits from the conveniently fallen coconut tree, I had to admit that I now needed to make coconut pole mark three. Even though my frustration at using the second, heavy pole was etched on my mind as one of the most desperate times on the island, it had forced me to re-evaluate and evolve my tools. Clearly my next pole couldn't be so heavy – if anything it needed to be longer – and the two requirements seemed contradictory. On examining the longest of the smooth, sun-dried boat poles I'd scavenged from the high-water line I found that one was long enough and yet light enough to work. But being a boating pole, it had no natural 'Y' on it with which to thrust upwards into the coconuts. 'No problem,' I decided. I could just lash one on with beach hibiscus.

That is when I had my epiphany. If I was tying on a Y-shaped section of wood, why not attach it upside down? A hook would be many times more efficient as I could just place it over the stem of the coconut and tug down rather than jerking up. It was one of those ideas you have that you know will work the moment you think of it. Once I'd lashed on the sturdy hook I found that the pole was so light and versatile that I could even climb small trees to a height of about three metres and use the pole in the air! This opened up the potential for a vast coconut mountain, and collection became fun rather than a frustrating and exhausting chore. I felt as if I could just reach up and casually pick the coconuts that I wanted as if from the top shelf of a pantry. 'That's what I call evolution!' I grinned, as proud as a child who's just ridden without stabilisers on his bicycle for the first time.

I slotted my mammoth Y-pole into place and even banged in a stake at its foot to ensure that it didn't move. The result was reassuringly solid and I had no doubt that the structure was now inherently strong enough to support the weight of the thatch. The rest of the morning was spent plaiting and tying on more palm leaves.

By mid-afternoon – I had now been thatching for eight solid days – I collected firewood for the big move. On the northern-most beach I found a huge piece of driftwood. It was about seven feet long and I hauled it upon my back and across my shoulders like a vast crucifix and trudged contentedly back to camp under its enormous weight. It was bone dry, incredibly heavy and would last for days.

I loved the challenge of getting these enormous pieces of wood around to my side of the beach. Once the pile was big enough to last me the night, I lay down under the thatch and contemplated my sleeping position. The lack of space worried me and if it rained the fire would be close to the edge and could easily be extinguished. After a long pause and an admission that things had slipped more than I was comfortable with, I acknowl-edged to the camera: 'Do you know what? I'm moving in too early – there's not enough space. If the rains come in this isn't big enough – really. I'm so exhausted. Back to the cave.'

The admission hit me hard and I was really low in the cave. 'I can't believe how little energy I've got. Now, the truth is that I'm dehydrated, malnourished, umm, all of my time goes into repetitive tasks that aren't interesting – and so I've just had a bit of a struggle getting out of quite a negative thought pattern.'

The negative thought pattern was me seeing myself as a victim: 'I keep thinking like I've just been left here and nobody cares. I'm really craving company – I'm really, really lonely. Every bit of me wants company. Every bit of me wants to have a chat with somebody.'

But who had left me here? I had, of course. The whole project had been *my* brainchild, *my* challenge to myself. Despite this, in these darkest moments I still failed to accept responsibility for my own situation. The projection of blame and self-pity only made things seem further outside my control but for now I didn't care – I just wanted to feel sorry for myself and hope everyone else would feel sorry for me, too. 'One person doing this with nothing is extraordinarily hard.' Despite having seen this trait in myself early on I was still succumbing to my debilitating self-torture. A lifetime's habits, it seems, are hard to change.

Then, like a cloud passing and a bright ray of sun piercing down to light the way, I could see my way through. My core self-belief still stood there, ragged and wretched but alive and prepared to fight another battle in my name.

'But I'm not going to give up. And I'm not going to go mad.' My eyes showed renewed resilience. 'It's just tough.'

卌 卌 卌 卌 卌 |||

Thoroughly whipped by the wind ripping through the cave, I didn't get much sleep. But the tin can kettle was on and I was about to have a lemon leaf tea – surely the solution to everything in life.

The previous evening's desperation now contained, I felt much more able to take control of my own time on the island and write my own story. Being present in the moment was the key, I was sure, and so I focused on what I was doing now rather that allowing my mind to run around and play silly games.

As I sat and plaited a coconut palm I concentrated on what my hands were doing. I relaxed my shoulders and watched my fingers now quite nimbly weave the leaves through each other and create a small, simple work of art on my lap. I breathed in deeply and looked around. I was sitting in a patch of forest from where I could see out on to the beach through the trees. The coolness of the shade made for pleasant working conditions and the bright sky reflected on the vines and branches above me. I could hear the ever-present crashing of the waves and accepted them, perhaps for the first time, as a reassuring soundtrack to an experience I would never forget.

I felt I had turned a corner.

I found I was grinning to myself. Just completely and utterly absorbing the moment, really, and enjoying being on a Pacific island – and doing a very Pacific island type of activity such as plaiting palm leaves. There is a peace that comes from a space in thinking. There is an energy that is freed inside that can make you feel euphoric and makes me wonder why I don't put more into meditation, and more often. You can regard it as airy-fairy rubbish if you like but to me it's just another tool and, importantly, one you can carry with you naked.

For the moment it was true. As I sat in the trees I was truly happy.

I attached the ten palm tiles I'd been plaiting and had to sit on a branch that ran parallel to the ridge pole to do the last ones as they were well above my reach. The thatch crossed the crossbar and there was now a truly massive space below me. There was just a little to complete on the right and then it would be done.

By now it was mid-afternoon and I needed to go back to the other side of the island and do the dropbox pick-up. While there I managed eighteen chin-ups in the strong breeze that tormented Lemon Camp. It was late in the day and the sun had gone from the camp and the beach on that side of the island. It was the end of week four and I was ecstatic about my strength. 'Quite pleased with that bad boy,' I said as I flexed my biceps and winked at the camera.

My afternoon walk uncovered another taro plant that I'd previously passed but not seen. Fingers as diggers, I excavated the carbohydrate with a smile on my face. 'One potato (well, taro actually), two potato, three potato, four; five potato, six potato, seven potato …' I heaved out the entire root bulb of the plant and placed it in front of the rolling camera, '… more.'

A hermit crab scuttled in front of me, its sudden movement giving it away, and it was scooped up without further ado as my main course for the evening.

'It's funny how things come to you when you are calmer.' Without the usual cacophony of deliberation and worry in my head I found that I had had my most productive outing in several days. I was more aware now and so I'd seen things that had always been there but that I'd been too occupied to notice before.

I knew that I needed simply to go with the flow, to relax and accept what was. If I didn't accept it, and wished for something that I didn't have, it was a waste of time and energy. What was – quite simply – was. I revived my forgotten lesson in serenity. Stop resisting Ed – let go.

'Works very well in theory!' I grunted to the camera. 'I'm working on it.' I knew I was still a long way from mastering true surrender to life's ups and downs.

On the way back I spotted a fishing boat out at sea. It was white, with a roofed area to the fore and aft and a raised cockpit in the middle. The whole vessel was covered in masts and what looked like antennae. I estimated that it must have been at least a mile outside the reef. It was weird to think of people being on there with proper food and drink and wearing clothes. I felt odd seeing a boat and I wondered whether I would see any more.

In those last couple of hours of the day I completed the thatching and took it well over the bar.

'It's complete.' The sun was low in the sky and the soft glow shone through the trees on to the inside of the thatch. I was very pleased with myself and proud of the thatch on closer inspection around the back.

'That is one monster thatch! I am so happy with that!'

The thatch was indeed something to behold. It was almost a foot thick and had so many layers of leaves that it looked both padded and insulated. It was vast, considering it had been made entirely without tools, and I was elated that I'd not cut corners and that I'd stuck to my original plan and kept going.

It was too late to move in tonight – and I was too tired anyway – but it no longer mattered. I had completed the most ambitious of construction projects and I would never have to plait another palm leaf as long as I lived.

It was time to go and eat some snails, a hermit crab and some taro root, and to sleep well with a smile on my face.

'I have four and a half weeks ahead of me to live in the shelter. Eleven days of construction. Happier than I have been.' I emitted short sound bites as my brain clocked out for the day. 'More periods of being positive and strong. Having water and being hydrated. I have twenty-eight litres stored now. With water nothing bothers me. I'm hungry all the time but at least I've got water, so all good. Right – cup of lemon leaf tea. Then sleep.'

CHAPTER 5
HUNTING

|||| |||| |||| |||| |||| ||||

It was moving-in day. I slotted the camera equipment into the case, added my green top and toothbrush and clicked the plastic catches firmly shut.

On the beach collecting snails for breakfast I found five and a half metres of nylon cordage. The quality was poor, though, and I suspected if I put any real tension on it that it might snap. But it made me think I should make a bow and arrow. A plan was hatched. Today I was going to move into the shelter after brekky, get organised. Then this afternoon I was going to start to make a bow and arrow. I fantasised about barbecued goat meat and decided that I needed to shift up a gear and become a hunter.

I left the seven litres of emergency water in the cave. I also left a night's worth of dry firewood with the fire-lighting kit and a brand new tinder bundle. In the event of an emergency withdrawal to the cave, in hurricane or tropical storm, I wouldn't have to take anything with me. I felt like a doomsday prepper ever ready for the worst-case scenario but it was reassuring to have a fall-back base that I knew I could rely upon to be dry.

'I feel a bit weird moving out of here – I'm somehow apprehensive. I think this cave represents warmth and dryness and security, actually – and I'm moving out into something that's a bit more unknown.'

It was the right thing to do – I knew that – it just felt odd, different. The move took three trips: one for the camera case, one for my palm leaf basket with pots and clamshells in it, and the final trip was to transfer the fire, and as I held the glowing logs away from my bare legs the smoke trailed behind me down the beach. Under the shelter I put the hot ends together, added some fresh dry wood, and gently blew – a long slow resuscitation. I had life and flames again in under a minute.

Today of all days was indeed one on which I could relax a little. I decided that, being an Englishman, the only true way of christening my new abode was to … have a cup of tea. Still riding what I hoped was now a permanent wave of positivity, I described the excitement and energy that was circling around me. It meant a huge amount to me that I wasn't in a cave full of goat dung any more. I was sitting in a house I had built myself. I relaxed and allowed myself to ramble about my dreams.

I lay down in my sleeping position for the first time and realised I needed to move the fire – I was cooking my head again. While in the horizontal position, and feeling as if I was on a little holiday of sorts, I gave way to my heavy limbs. 'I might just stay here for five minutes,' I yawned.

I then spent the next hour and a half on my knees hacking the tangled roots away from the forest floor with a clamshell. But if I struck a root with my shell it would just bend the root into the ground – it would not break. So I quickly adapted and realised that I needed a mobile work surface (to slide under each root in turn) to act as a backstop to the strike; a flat stone worked well for this. By the time the floor was clean, and fresh flat earth all exposed, I was quite exhausted.

For lunch I found a new rock to smash snails on, as returning to the cave for every meal would waste valuable travel time. My new preparation surface was a ledge on Snail Rock, the rocky outcrop that split my beach, which was now conveniently on my doorstep in my new home in the trees. The ledge was at waist height and allowed me to crack my snails in the early afternoon sun. By now I wasn't looking in bad shape. My love handles were long gone and my body fat must have been much lower but I wasn't feeling strong, just leaner. The huge green snails that I'd collected on the outgoing morning tide had a white cap or trap-door at the entrance to their shell. 'This is a huge amount of protein – huge for me anyway!' It was lunchtime.

To kill a goat I needed to propel something sharp with enough force to penetrate its skin. I could have tried to trap one with some sort of deadfall device but I decided a goat was too big to kill with deadfall. It would have required a similar falling object to that which would kill a man. That seemed a bit over the top for now. So I would make a bow and arrow – a short four-foot bow that I could carry through the forest without it snagging on everything.

The first bit of wood that I picked up to use as a prop (so as to be able to explain to the camera what type of wood I'm looking for) worked so well that I selected it and sat down to tie on the new blue cordage.

On the first, wary drawing of the bow the blue nylon rope snapped and so I doubled it up to make it twice as strong. I sat under my new roof rolling the improvised cordage on my knee. Once finished, I tied it on to the shaft and inspected my handi-work. It was as crude as they came but at least I'd got a bow. There was so much tension in the string that I could hardly pull it back. This was a good thing and would create more power. I needed to have another lie-down – I was exhausted.

By the fire I ate termites off a rotten log as they tried to escape the fire. This wasn't because I needed the calories – they were insignificant – it was out of boredom, a distraction. When you find yourself eating termites for entertainment – that's boredom.

It was late afternoon, golden hour, by the time I tied my spoon on to a hibiscus stick and walked down to the beach to test the flight of the impromptu arrow. I held the bow in my left hand, elbow locked out in front of me. With my right hand I rested the weight of the crude arrow on the fingers of my left hand and clamped the end against the nylon string. As I drew my right arm back the force made the string slip off the side and the arrow twanged rather pathetically on to the floor. I reloaded and tried to clamp more strongly with my right hand but each time I released my grip on the end of the arrow the string just slid to the side. The bow was potentially powerful, I could tell that, but for the moment I could not transfer that power into the flight of the arrow. I was done with bows and arrows for the day but I mentally began to craft the end of the arrow to try to solve the slipping and loss of control and energy.

Coconut chunks spat, hissed and caramelised as they roasted round the fire. It was the end of day twenty-nine and my video diary tells me that I really struggled today. I'd made a bow but that hadn't lifted me as I'd thought it would.

'I just don't know why I've found today so difficult. I have no energy, ate twice my ration of coconut, and even had a brace of crabs for lunch.'

It seemed that even when I made progress I still needed to keep myself positive and motivated. I had simply allowed today to happen and as a result I got low. I needed to go through the process of keeping myself positive and light-hearted and humorous. This had to be an adventure to be embraced. I reminded myself it was not life or death. If I didn't catch a goat

I was still going to be alive at the end. I had thirty-one days to go and I needed to stay on top mentally. Tomorrow was halfway – a milestone. It was a good time to take stock.

'Even if the bow doesn't work, Ed, everything that you do is learning. Today I used bad cordage to make good workable (if somewhat ugly) cordage. There are lots of positives – you're in your new house. It's nice weather, the sun is shining. Tomorrow is day thirty and you are going to enjoy it a lot more than today – OK?'

Despite the fact that my inner coach seemed to be saying all the right things I wasn't convinced. I had to take myself back to the cave to sit in my stone circle. Where was this unsettled feeling coming from? Why wasn't I more at peace? What the fuck was wrong with me?

I stepped into the circle and into safety. I kissed the dusty floor of the cave with my bare bottom and rested my arms over my hunched knees. I gazed at the fading light over the horizon.

'Breathe, Ed,' I told myself. So I did and a sense of calm did indeed return. The circle shut out the rest of the island. In the circle there was just me and yet, somehow, I was connected to everything and everyone that mattered to me. I smiled in a knowing way that rarely came outside the circle. In here I had perspective, humour, peace.

As the black blanket of the night came down I brushed the dust from my bum and looked up at the sprinkled dust of stars. The nights on the island were incredible, mind-blowing. I could easily see how isolation gives people spiritual experiences. You couldn't feel anything other than humble under that sky.

My stiff knees clicked as I stood up and made my way back for my first night in my new home in the woods. Adding more wood to the fire, I stretched out on the floor and could sense in the orange flickering that something was moving. *Lots* of things were moving, in fact, on the forest floor right in front of me.

I flicked the camera on to night vision to reveal an army of hermit crabs going about their nocturnal business. They were tiny – the size of small snails. I fumbled for my tin pot and from my reclining position I half filled it and stuck it on the fire to boil. It was suppertime.

Ht Htt Htt Htt Htt Htt

I woke up this morning and immediately went for a massive poo. I had eaten two whole coconuts yesterday and it was apparent. The night's sleep wasn't as pleasant as I'd anticipated, largely due to the presence of some small rats that kept running over me. Luckily I'm not particularly bothered by that sort of thing but neither do I welcome it.

While collecting little snails I also picked up a couple of flat rocks so that I could smash the shells in camp around the fire rather than out on the beach in the direct sun. One of the rocks had a very flat face similar to the sharpening stones that I'd seen Amerindians use in the Amazon to sharpen their machetes.

I had a circle of metal, a bit of an old outboard motor that I'd been using to crudely chop up taro. It was blunt and about as effective as chopping tomatoes with a plastic ruler. But I suddenly had no idea why I'd not considered sharpening it before. Not only had I been in possession of a piece of metal for some days now but I'd even been using it as a crude knife. Yet for some reason the penny had not dropped until now.

I spat on the flat stone, held the metal disc in my right hand and started tracing a figure-of-eight pattern, ensuring that the angle between the disc and the stone surface was about thirty degrees. I could see the lighter metallic shine coming through on the metal and it indeed started to sharpen. This meant I could add a handle and make a knife that I could carry around with me and use for all sorts of tasks. A knife! A knife, I quickly established (after a mere thirty days), was essential – so this morning I made my knife.

I had to grind away enough metal on each side of the disc so that the two sloping surfaces joined and formed a sharp edge. I tested the edge by running my finger across the blade. It felt sharp. I shut one eye and looked down the blade, point on, to see if there was any surface that was still reflecting light at me. I ground out an edge that covered about two inches of the circumference, about a third of the pie.

I made the handle from hardwood, using my now sharpened disc to strip the bark away and make it smooth and clean. I then used the disc itself to tap down into the end of the handle to create a split in the wood just long enough to hold the blade in place. A knot in the wood threw it off line a touch but not enough to matter. I left the hand grip end solid. I removed the disc again, twisted it so that the blade was facing outwards and reinserted it.

Fine strands of wetted beach hibiscus bark tightly bound the wood shut. My teeth made a good vice, clamping the split shut as I wound the strands of hibiscus in front of my face to hold the blade firmly in place. As the strands passed my chin they trapped parts of my beard in the lashing and yanked out several hairs. I couldn't help but be happy with how incredibly effective it was, though. I lashed the handle end first, so that it didn't split, then I lashed the top end as tight as my teeth could bite.

The quantity of taro root that I had rationed for two meals was the size of a matchbox. I used my new knife to chop it up for lunch and peeled off the skin. 'Jamie Oliver, eat your heart out,' I chuckled, using a square bit of plywood that I'd found on the beach as a chopping board. The knife felt good in my hand and opened up so many possibilities; as well as snapping, ripping and abrading I could now cut and slice. The tool was as clear an indicator of evolution as my fire or my shelter.

After lunch I needed to make arrows. I had already collected several straight sticks of hibiscus from when I'd been making natural cordage for the shelter. The spoon was too valuable to me to sacrifice on an arrow and slightly too cumbersome, too. I had one nail and so I selected the straightest of the sticks and, again using fine saliva-wet hibiscus bark, I bound on the nail to the front of the arrow. It looked good.

While I was working away with my hands, I mulled over the fact that because a goat is considered a domesticated animal you'd naturally think you could just run after it, as if it were a farmyard animal, and catch it. Once caught you could, of course, just tether it, milk it and make cheese. What could be simpler? I considered then how 'feral' was the operative word here. These weren't domesticated goats, they were *feral* goats, and getting close to these wild animals was far harder than you might think. These goats were naturally wary – they didn't want to be caught and had a natural tendency not to want to provide cheese for anyone.

Arrows taking shape in my hands, I declared, 'There's going to be a goat dead within the week.'

I then used my new knife to cut a notch at the end of the arrow shaft just big enough for the bowstring to sit in. I determined that this little groove was essential to stop the slipping that had been occurring last night. The notch would keep the bowstring aligned with the arrow throughout its release and would ensure that the power released would be transmitted to the arrow's flight. In theory. I stood outside my shelter in the woods and, with vegetation all around me, the only space for testing was above my head. I pointed the arrow up into the canopy and drew back the string that was cupped in the new groove on the end of the arrow. Gently, I released the string and the arrow flew straight as a die up through the canopy and beyond. Only as it slowed in flight did the arrow drift slightly sideways in the air. 'It works!' I grinned, quite surprised at the success. It was actually really encouraging. Maybe this was why I was down last night as I doubted whether the bow would really work. But now I had a rear notch system to use the full force of the bowstring. Now the arrow just needed a flight to stop the back end drifting out at longer ranges.

Turning my attention to a second arrow, I had a couple more nails from driftwood but they had large flat heads that I couldn't remove. Next I tried the rusty tin lid that I used to cut the taro chips but it wasn't heavy enough or strong enough to make into an arrow tip. Leaving the camera running there were long pauses as I struggled to find a solution to making arrow tips that would be suitable for the job.

In examining what I had at my disposal, however, I became somewhat distracted by the decision to make a spear. This was probably because I had come to a dead end with the second arrow tip. I tested several long poles simply by holding them aloft and launching them at a spot on the ground. In the end I opted for a nice seven-foot spear and mused over fire-hardening the tip.

It was the end of day thirty – my second night in the shelter. I'd completed half of my time on the island and I celebrated by boiling some water in the tin can and making myself some lemon leaf tea. I congratulated myself on my progress so far. I felt I'd come a very long way. I was eating well, had enough water and had built myself a home. I was sitting by a warm fire and making myself a brew. I had hunting tools: a knife, a bow and arrow and a spear in the making. Aside from the tangible signs of progress I knew I was in a far better mental state, too. Far more of my time was spent composed and at peace. I'd settled into the whole experience and felt constructive and positive about the next thirty days.

More immediately I then thought about the night to come and remembered the rats running over me last night. They had kept me awake but I wasn't too bothered by them. The other minor irritant was the termites that crawled over me after they evacuated the burning wood. They were completely harmless, of course, but enough of a distraction to stop me from resting soundly.

But I was learning more and more that pretending on this island never worked. After all it was just me here and I would soon see through the pretence. Being positive was only beneficial when I wasn't avoiding or hiding from the things that actually *were* disappointing. Honesty with myself was key. In this instance the slight regret I had about the shelter was that now I could no longer see the sunset each evening. Darkness fell faster now, and without the evening light show my end-of-day connection to a wider world seemed to have been cut out and replaced by rats and termites. 'I'm not moving back, it took eleven days to build!' I joked without seeing anything funny in the situation at all.

Ж₭ ₭₭ ₭₭ ₭₭ ₭₭ ₭₭ I

'_ve got to make a bed!' More rats had been nibbling at me all night. I would hear a rustle, then a scurry, then one would pluck up the courage either to run over a part of my body or nibble at me as if to see whether I was edible.

I carved the end of my spear with the new knife. It meant continuously sharpening the blade but that wasn't a problem as I positioned the whetstone on the floor between my legs. Once it was sharp enough I wrapped the spear tip with the tin to reinforce the wood and add a slightly sharper point and lashed that in place with hibiscus.

While I was working, the goats trotted past the camp on the beach side, blissfully unaware that I was crafting weapons designed to kill them. They scampered up Snail Rock and along the spur on to the top of the island before disappearing into the tree line. I didn't want to stop this sort of close encounter by making the goats more skittish than they already were and so, as my weapons weren't yet finished or tested, I just observed and noted their movement pattern.

A journey around the coast produced a bumper crop of food. One eel, the biggest so far, was now killed by cutting into the back of its head with my knife. The biggest sea cucumber that I'd yet seen, too. A giant clam. I had no idea whether you could eat the clam but it seemed likely and it was definitely alive as I had witnessed it snap shut when I poked it. Add to that four crabs, several mussels and two full pots of snails and I had a seafood banquet fit for a king.

'Crikey, I'm going to eat well this lunchtime, tonight and tomorrow for breakfast. You're still alive – so you're supper,' I notified a crab that was trying to escape.

I wore my green T-shirt on my head as the direct sun was fiercely hot and chatted away to the camera as I organised my bumper crop of food. I ran out of container space and had to use giant clamshells to carry the plentiful food in. I washed and shelled everything. Good fortune seemed to be magnetic – it attracted more good fortune. Things were going well.

As I only had a small pot I cooked the clam and the crabs in the embers. Not wanting to eat it now, I left the eel hanging from the rafters in the smoke for supper to stop it getting attacked by flies. The seafood squeaked as the moisture escaped. Once the clam was dead the shell was easy to pry open. It looked like a giant muscle inside. It had muscular flaps that I ate cautiously. It was chewy – but at least it was meat. The novelty factor soon wore off and my taste buds became more honest with themselves. 'That was rubber. Do you know what? I would not serve that to a dog.'

The mussels that I'd collected were great. A taste of sophistication that felt like real food. Importantly, the meal was different and hit my senses and brought me to life. All very welcome. A meal I wouldn't think about twice if I ate it in a restaurant was now taking on the aspect of life-changing importance.

It was mid-afternoon by the time I'd both eaten and filmed everything and, as ever, I stressed about how the daily administration of looking after myself and just eating dominated my time. I went out on to the beach and practised with my spear and my new bow and arrows. I set up a plastic bottle, half filled with sand, as a target and fired all my ammunition at it. The arrows needed flights, of that there was little doubt, but the spear flew well, although it needed a stronger and sharper tip. It was all good constructive feedback and I was satisfied that my hunting tools were improving. Tomorrow I would add coconut palm leaf flights to the arrows and improve the spear's tip.

It was the end of day thirty-one. 'Just add flights tomorrow, Ed, and you can start hunting,' I told myself, wondering why I was referring to myself in the second person. Talking to myself had almost become a self-reflecting parody of my own dual voices. I knew it sounded odd but it seemed to convey the conversations that I was genuinely having to have with myself. Perhaps if you don't have company, you just invent it, but I certainly had two voices and the conversations and debates seemed real enough.

'It's going to be fun. I've eaten really well today.' I self-consciously reverted to the first person. 'I've eaten well just foraging. I'm full. I haven't been able to say that very often recently.' But I wasn't content to settle for foraging. 'Tomorrow I'm on the hunt – and goat is on the menu.'

||||| ||||| ||||| ||||| ||||| ||||| ||

I walked up and over the other side of the island to do a drop off of dead batteries and used CF cards. It was the first time walking with my new spear and I felt alive and bold, like a caveman ready to strike if the opportunity arose.

On my way past the splinted taro plants I noted they had recovered. They had both shot new leaves out the centre, which I decided was very cool. I was now a plant doctor, too.

On my return the goats were standing idly in my camp. For some reason they reminded me of tracksuited youths smoking at a bus shelter. Maybe it was distain – or jealously of their simple existence. As I approached, the group, now rumbled, scattered, and for the first time I followed at pace, trying to run them down. I was surprised that they could outrun me easily and my hopes faded as they disappeared into the thicker undergrowth where I couldn't follow them. Left standing holding my unused spear, I saw that it would be necessary to lull them into a false sense of security. I didn't want them to be nervous of me – I had to get closer to them to make a fatal strike.

As I sat down in the shelter I heard a lone goat bleating in the distance. It must have become separated from the others after my hunt and I could hear the fear in its cry. As I didn't think I could get close enough to the animals to launch my basic spear, I refocused on improving the arrows.

While I had been thatching, I'd had to remove single leaves from the palm fronds so that the number of leaves was even. A requirement for plaiting. This meant that I would repeatedly throw away the odd wasted leaf, and it had struck me, while watching the leaf after it had been launched through the air, that it flew rather like a paper aeroplane.

The leaves therefore became the obvious natural material to use as flights for my arrows. I used the strength of the spine of the leaf to lash on the flight and the flat leaves were easily cut into shape using my new knife and chopping board. As I worked intently with my hands I realised I was smiling again. In less than half an hour I had a respectable three-flight arrow.

Arrow placed carefully in the rafters of the shelter so that I didn't accidentally stand on it, I deconstructed the spear as it was now clear it would just bounce off a goat. I took off the tin, created a recess for the nail with the massive head, and lashed both the nail, and then the tin, back on. It was another two hours' work but I would not have wanted to get hit by this spear coming through the air towards me. It looked bloody lethal.

On the beach I was firing the arrows at a plastic bottle when the entire herd of seven goats distracted me further up the beach. I immediately saw the opportunity, bow and arrow in hand, to hunt them. Having sprinted up the beach I was close to the herd by the time they noticed me. I got to perhaps five metres from them but when Black Stripe, the big old male, spotted me he bleated a warning to the others and they turned and fled. I loosed my arrow at the centre of the group but it disappeared into the undergrowth and they all vanished up the hill.

Annoyed, I then spent half an hour looking for the arrow. After I had scoured the ground several times I gave up looking. It was soul-destroying – it had taken half a day to make and I had used the only straight nail on the entire island that did not have a massive head and it was gone after the first release in anger! I was dependent on that arrow. If *only* I'd waited a little while longer. The goats had been too far away. 'That's gutting – really gutting.' I stared at the camera forlornly.

卌 卌 卌 卌 卌 卌 III

' just found my arrow.' I had woken up, walked around the back of the shelter and through the forest with the steep slope of the island rising to my left and the shaded beach to my right. I walked straight to it. It wasn't hidden or buried in leaf litter. It must have deflected off something. Who cared? I had found it and it was a very good omen for the rest of the day.

The early morning find had boosted my morale massively. I reflected on how I had lost the arrow and came to the conclusion that it was best to wait for opportune moments rather than stalk the goats. On reflection, this seems madness – crazy that I would so easily give up a proactive hunt of the one animal that I really wanted to catch, that I would wait until the goats came to me. I stated to the camera that I thought stalking would not pay off; I reckoned the goats would just learn to be nervous of me so I decided that when they came close I would have my hunting tools to hand and take my opportunities. I can see how I came to the decision – it is logical and requires zero energy to wait for the goats. It gave me a valid excuse not to go hunting. I shouldn't – it would be counterproductive, I told myself.

But the real fears were deeper and it is only on reflection that I can point them out. I was scared of wasting my time. I was scared of wasting my energy. I was scared of failing. I was scared of being made to look stupid. Construction, both of the shelter and the making of the tools, had been a sure thing. I knew that there would be a tangible outcome, something I could touch and feel, something concrete to prove that I'd achieved success. But hunting wasn't such a safe bet. I was unskilled and ungainly. I was tired and slow. My mind panicked at the thought of days and days lost to hunting the animals and still getting nowhere. So as to keep myself positive I needed to do something whose outcome was more predictable.

I started work on my second arrow but I had used my only suitable nail on the first. The other nails, such as the one I used on the spear, had such large immovable heads that they could not be attached to the slim arrow shafts. Scanning the numerous items that I'd hoarded, I took a section of U-shaped metal that had been riveted to the circular metal disc knife blade. I hammered the strip flat with a stone, leaving a rectangle of metal six inches long and half an inch wide. Half an inch was still too wide and the metal wasn't rigid enough so, with a flat-head nail for a chisel and a stone for a hammer, I created a V cross-section by gently tapping it into the right-angled edge on the camera case. This worked and allowed me to fold the metal lengthways on itself to make it just a quarter of an inch wide and, more importantly, twice as strong.

I sharpened it on my whetstone into a long fine point. On the shaft I duplicated the notch and the flights. By the time I'd finished, arrow number two looked great – a masterpiece replica of the original. Perhaps better, as it had a longer, heavier arrowhead. I had doubled my ammunition.

$$\text{卌 卌 卌 卌 卌 卌 IIII}$$

Under the cover of my shelter in the spitting rain I spun the new arrow back and forth between my stained, cracked fingers. I decided I would make a trap for the goats. I felt that I needed to tackle this mission from all angles. I would increase the likelihood of catching the goats. Unlike hunting, a trap would be an extra soldier on the ground, ever-present, doing the work for me while I slept. It would be energy efficient and ever-patient.

After lunch, having collected firewood and water, the first part of the trap I would make was the gate, the door that would be triggered to entrap the goat. So I spent the afternoon selecting a good site and began to make a wooden pen large enough to contain the biggest goat. The design was no different from one of the small mammal traps that are designed to catch mice and voles without killing them. A simple enclosed area, with a door at one end that was hinged at the top that would slam shut if the goat entered. I buried myself in thinking through the mechanics and in the physical labour. 'This would be simple. Time well spent,' I told myself.

〷〷 〷〷 〷〷 〷〷 〷〷 〷〷 〷〷

As I continued working on the gate for the goat trap I began to realise that I was tending towards building things that would take a long time. It was a self-inflicted torture that I had no one to blame for but myself. As I stripped the hibiscus, cut down the wood and lashed it all on I was constantly and uneasily aware that it was all taking too much time. How did I get to this place of having two months to fill and yet always feeling under time pressure? Of committing to huge construction projects when perhaps they were not the best use of my time? My apparent need to be immersed in something constructive in its literal sense meant that I could never relax and I seemed to be for ever chasing a tangible goal that would put my mind at ease. But that goal just kept slipping further and further away.

As it was Friday it was time for my end-of-week exercises. I'd been on the island for five weeks now and I'd eaten really well recently but I had no energy at all. I think I was beginning to get depressed. I didn't feel grounded and my emotions were erratic, causing huge mood swings. Often I had to drag myself up from feeling extraordinarily low. Having eaten so well, I felt as if I was putting weight back – the lack of energy must be down to my mental state.

I could only manage ten chin-ups. As I released my grip on the branch and allowed myself to drop to the ground I felt pathetic. I had managed fewer repeats of every exercise than I had done at the end of week one.

I dragged my bow and arrows to the beach for some target practice. I had to become proficient with the new weapon if it was to be of any use at all.

Late that afternoon I left on a search for crabs and snails and didn't get back until five minutes before it was dark. Apathy had meant that I hadn't even worked out timings and I cooked in the dark. My harvest was twelve crabs, which was now quite normal and nothing to complain about, and so I ate eight of them for supper in two successive pots and saved four for breakfast. I now needed it to rain again as I was close to having to dip into my seven litres of emergency water in the cave. My most basic fears about water came flooding back again and once more I felt as out of control as I had on day one.

My depression then led me to panic and look at other options for food like fish. I talked to the camera about the reef having an abundance of fish and that I was wasting my time trying to catch a goat. They were too fast and too wily to catch. I made a drama out of the dangers of building a raft and became overwhelmed by a sense of being out of control.

Retrospectively, I can see that I had become reliant on successes to bolster my confidence but I was therefore riding a very turbulent journey of ups and downs as I was swept along on the tide. I wasn't really supporting myself – I was torturing myself about how I was managing my time and myself, and the only person who could come in and stop my mental torment was me. But I didn't seem to be able to snap out of the never-ending drama of my predicament. I was driving myself mad.

I scolded myself, too, for not making a start on a bed to get me off the floor and away from the rats but I had been so busy with the goat trap, the archery practice and feeding myself that I hadn't been able to fit it all in. As the rats began moving around me I felt more dismal than I can remember and fell into a half-sleep, worrying that I didn't even know how to build a rat trap.

𝗛𝗛𝗛 𝗛𝗛𝗛 𝗛𝗛𝗛 𝗛𝗛𝗛 𝗛𝗛𝗛 𝗛𝗛𝗛 𝗛𝗛𝗛 𝟣

I awoke clear with the certainty that there was no point in doing a little bit of everything and never getting anything done. My aim for the day was to get the gate on the goat trap functioning.

As I plodded up the hill I dreamed again of peanut butter with loads of real butter on crappy processed white toast. Since arriving on the island I'd not once had indigestion – usually a constant irritant for me – so I could come off the island and stick to a diet without caffeine, sugar, wheat, nicotine, dairy and alcohol to retain the new digestive state of calm. But all I could think now was just to indulge and binge and treat myself to all the cheap processed food I could eat when I finally got off. I didn't care if I got indigestion again – it would be worth it.

By midday I'd finished my thirteen-bar gate on the goat trap. I was exhausted – this trap had better work. Midway through the afternoon it rained and so I halted construction to fill up with water, as I desperately needed more.

Half an hour's rain produced fourteen and a half litres of water. 'Got to be happy with that!' I grinned, staring at the dark sky and hoping the rain would return. If it rained in the night it would test the shelter but I was fairly relaxed that it was watertight. The beach was chilly and so I sat by the warm fire. I could hear the wind picking up on the beach and causing coconuts to fall from the canopy. As I plopped a fistful of massive snails in the pot I took comfort from my shelter and my fire. It felt like one area where I had indeed taken control and I enjoyed watching the wet storm grow around me from my dry warm space.

Before it finally got dark the last thing I did after the rain passed was to test-slam the goat gate. This mechanism needed to be fast and strong to ensure the goat was trapped securely. I allowed the heavy gate to swing shut from horizontal and the right-hand post promptly snapped as if it was made of brittle toffee. I felt the sadness and loneliness enter me with the failure but told the camera that I wasn't bothered. 'I'll just replace it,' I fronted up. But I wanted to cry. I wanted to be saved. I wanted to be looked after. I said none of this to the camera — things were getting too desperate now and no one but me needed to know how I felt. I felt that by now I should have been beyond such self-pity.

With nothing else to make me happy I took solace in food. The coconut that I was roasting by the fire provided little sweet bursts of comfort. I tried to think positively but I was still very worried about the time I was wasting on the goat trap.

~~~~ ~~~~ ~~~~ ~~~~ ~~~~ ~~~~ ~~~~ ||

On day thirty-seven I woke up early and walked round the island. Nineteen crabs and two full pots of snails were my reward for my diligence. It would be a good day's eating once more.

Then fortune decided to twist my nipple and spit in my face by allowing my cooking tin can to develop a leak. 'That really is a disaster,' I announced, stating the bleak truth. I now only had a tiny tin to cook in — less than half the size of my now leaky one — more like a metal shot glass than a cauldron. Maybe a clamshell would work — it would take longer to heat up but it was worth a try. I was pretty sure I remembered being told that they had a tendency to crack when placed in a fire. My trusty pot had lasted two full weeks on the fire — not bad, I suppose, considering how many cups of tea I'd drunk. Probably over sixty, I calculated, and forty-two meals, too.

I drank a half-glass of lemon leaf tea boiled in my inconveniently small tin. Only twenty-three days to go, I told myself. I had long ago started counting days remaining rather than days completed.

For lunch I tried to use a clamshell but, as I feared, it cracked before the water started to boil, which didn't surprise me. 'I didn't need that pot to die today. I didn't need that.' I glared at the flip-out screen, exasperated at my misfortune.

My hands were still covered in sores and my tongue traced a rough filling that seemed to have been partially dislodged. 'Brilliant — just what I needed.' I shook my head in resignation.

By the afternoon I had replaced a broken vertical bar on the rustic gate and wedged the top-hinged door open with a six-foot Y-pole. The heavy gate looked strong now and capable of entrapping a goat by slamming securely shut. I then needed to create a mechanism whereby the door would be connected to a trigger. I tied together several thick strands of beach hibiscus and threaded the line from the bottom bar of the gate up and over a high, smooth branch, and then down to a release mechanism at the back of the proposed enclosure. My plan was to connect this line to a pressure plate trigger at the back of the enclosure on the inside. This would then be baited with coconut. To do this I had to climb the tree, an activity that evoked childhood memories of grazed knees and elbows and the thrill of being high enough to know that one slip could result in a nasty fall. I was enjoying myself once more.

Once in place, I armed the trap and walked around to the trigger plate and gently pressed down on the wooden plate. The wooden toggle was freed and shot into the air as the weight of the gate came crashing down to slam shut against the gate posts. It worked: the gate was still in one piece and it had a working trigger! Now I just needed to build some walls to enclose the trap like a sheep pen.

The childish thrill of setting the trap kept me going but my energy was still rock-bottom. Walking up the hill and even back down to my camp left me feeing like there was zero glycogen in my muscles and that I was eating my own body up to provide energy. But the effort was worth it; at last I had a mechanically functioning trapdoor.

As an experiment I decided to attempt to boil water in a plastic bottle suspended just over the flames of the fire on a line of hibiscus bark. It took an age to heat up to a temperature vaguely suitable for tea but I didn't risk it actually boiling as I didn't want to melt the plastic. It was a method that I'd read about somewhere in a book, but, like most such survival advice, it seemed fiddly and inefficient, created more for effect than anything else I suspect. I knew it wasn't my long-term solution.

Sipping the lukewarm lemony tea, I decided that I would make three clay pots. I knew that if I hardened them in the fire some might break so I decided I would have to make more than one to allow for this natural wastage. I set down the unsatisfying tepid drink, gathered my hunting and filming equipment together, and set out to find food for supper. Having worked in the forest all day it was refreshing to be able to see distances on the beach and my eyes blinked in the brightness. The light evening wind was soothing on my skin and it was calming to be walking my familiar paths on the alert for seafood. I returned with seventeen crabs and two full pots of snails — another abundance of food — and decided to sacrifice another clamshell to cook them in even with the knowledge that it would crack. It performed a temporary service and, again, I ate well as the light faded.

卌 卌 卌 卌 卌 卌 卌 III

To make a trap that contains but doesn't kill an animal requires that trap to be strong and without any weaknesses that the beast can exploit. Building these stick walls required large quantities of saplings and, less obviously, huge quantities of cordage to lash them all together. It was late morning by the time I had converted a further four large beach hibiscus trees into a pile of strong crude rope.

By the time I'd carried the cordage up the hill and stripped it to finer, more usable strands it was well beyond lunchtime and time to go looking for some food. On my outing I found an intact plastic jerrycan and thought that it would make an amazing reservoir under bamboo guttering on my shelter. I already had one bucket but it was cracked and leaked — this new one was pristine. I would be able to utilise the 132 square feet of thatch and direct the runaway water into a single container. I could then dispense with clamshells and straw sucking, and this heralded an advance in my striving towards a comfortable, sustainable lifestyle on the island. But it wasn't a priority and so, for the moment, I let it sit on the back burner in my mind.

In the afternoon I collected twenty-two trees to make the goat enclosure. *Twenty-two trees.* 'Crikey, I'm shagged,' I eloquently expressed my fatigue as I picked skin off my new knuckle sores and walked back down the hill to my camp.

In front of my shelter, about twenty feet from where I slept, was a huge hanging dead tree caught up in the vines. This dead-fall was tangled and unsightly, and as I'd now made a very smart shelter I didn't like my one and only view being so obscured. The wood that was hanging there would also make excellent dry fuel for the fire and so, despite my weariness, I attempted to bring the whole lot down.

As I stood beneath the *ngan duppurru* (a timely reminder: it means fucked or tangled) mess, it made me think of my Aboriginal friends. What would they make of me now? I knew immediately that they would be all smiles congratulating me on how far I'd come. It was good to remind myself that I was actually my harshest critic and to realise that they would probably be full of praise.

I could make out the strong cable-like vines that suspended everything from the rafters of the canopy. I tugged from the ground but that was about as effective as a tick on a cow. I then pulled myself up into the mass of dead wood, hoping that my body weight would help to snap some of the main vines, and I bounced and shook the whole mass like an angry baboon trying to make a fierce display in the treetops. My heart raced as I knew I was taking quite big risks. I was standing on, and being supported by, the very thing I was trying to dislodge and bring crashing to the jungle floor. Luckily for me nothing moved. I was totally spent and for ever stuck with my fucked-up view of the world. Adrenaline coursing through me, I laughed out loud at my inadvertent play on words.

I'd had quite a hard job staying positive today but I had managed to do so – which was reassuring. With all the crabs, I was pooing for Britain, too, so I couldn't really work out why my energy was still so low. 'I was hanging,' I noted, referencing 'hanging from my chinstrap', an army expression whose meaning is pretty obvious. You are so tired that you can only stand up because you are hanging from the chinstrap of your helmet. 'Chin-strapped' is another expression.

The whole experience was still so much harder than I'd expected it to be.

𝖧𝖧𝖳 𝖨𝖧𝖧 𝖨𝖧𝖧 𝖧𝖧𝖳 𝖧𝖧𝖳 𝖧𝖧𝖳 𝖧𝖧𝖳 𝖨𝖨𝖨𝖨

The warmth of the fire had kept me snug all night. Lying in a foetal position I faced the shelter and allowed the radiated heat to blanket my bare back. Apart from the necessity of waking to stoke the fire, my sleep had been deep and replenishing. I became aware of the bleating of the goats close to where I slept. I blinked open my eyes and craned my neck round, keeping my body still, to try to catch a glimpse of the herd. They were scattered over the hillside and slowly making their way across my front porch to the beach. I lay still for a while, observing the relaxed grazing and ambling of the close-knit family. The patterns of their movements seemed to be based around edible vegetation and they were on a morning breakfast walk. As the main group exited on to the beach I silently rose from my patch of dirt, lifted my bow and arrow from its home in the thatch, and crept after the group with killing on my mind.

The beach was bright and exposed and the goats spotted me as I stepped into the open. The herd, which by this point was grazing on the grasses on top of Snail Rock, became alert, and moved purposefully up the headland and back towards the high tree line. They weren't frightened, just wary, and they continued to graze as they moved off, heading northerly along the tree line until they were out of sight and out of range.

As my eyes once more adjusted to the morning gloom under the canopy I could see two remaining goats in my camp. 'Come on, Ed,' I urged myself, 'observation is sensible but you are now armed and have to take your opportunities.' When I was as close as I thought I could get before being noticed, I drew the bowstring back, notched an arrow and took aim at the breast of the nearest animal. With a silent release the arrow shot through the air and hit a goat. Less encouragingly, it simply bounced off the tough hide. I had fired from twelve metres away and it was clearly too far as the arrow was decelerating by the time it struck. The flight was like that of a table tennis smash – initially fast but soon slowing to a floating harmlessness. My internal computer fed me the results of the experiment in real time. The arrows needed more weight and I had to get closer to my objective before firing. At that distance with my arrows I would be lucky to pop a water-filled balloon.

The sleep had done me good and I extrapolated the positive feedback from the hunting experience to thrust me into the new day with vigour. It had been a buzz. I had actually struck a goat! That was a big step in the right direction.

While collecting breakfast I found a washed-up Japanese soybean oil can of about ten litres and immediately recognised it as an amazing, huge cooking pot. It was so good in fact that it made me laugh to myself about having settled for such a small rusty tin for so long. Under my shelter I used the big-headed nails to perforate a line around the centre of the can to remove the top half. I was left with a square about the size of one of those luxury tins of assortment English biscuits and it was in pristine condition. I even saved the last dregs of soybean oil to fry with. Oil-fried snails! I could not wait for the luxury of fried food. In my glee I lost concentration and badly gashed my palm on the razor-sharp serrated edges of the can and had to bandage it quickly with the material salvaged from my flip-flops. It wouldn't get me down, though – not today – but it was a lesson and I was grateful for the wake-up call.

After frying about five snails in oil and indulging myself in the sheer pleasure of chewing each fried morsel slowly – my God, they tasted terrific, vaguely like bacon – I spent the afternoon lashing the poles that I had cut yesterday on to the back of the goat trap to form the enclosure. After eleven trees the day was gone. I hadn't come as far as I would have liked and raised my eyebrows in acknowledgement of the familiar length of time that everything was taking. I stepped back and appraised the trap. I had built two-thirds of one rear wall and had another two to go. Exasperated, I flopped down the hillside into camp.

I was happy to ignore the discomfort from my gashed palm because I was so happy with my new cooking pot. I ate crab soup for supper for the first time in a few days and was grateful for the return of fatty broth. There was more of it than ever now, of course, as I had no restriction on how much water to add and the discovery made me wonder again whether someone was indeed looking after me. Perhaps I'd not been abandoned after all.

The rats, too, decided to remind me that constructing a bed might not be a bad idea at some point. At least they were some sort of company.

$$\text{卅 卅 卅 卅 卅 卅 卅 卅}$$

nce again the morning drizzle nagged at me to add guttering and a collection bucket to the shelter. It was now approaching the rainy season and with a few simple additions I could have a far superior system with water virtually on tap in my home. I worked through the rain and added the other side to the goat trap, but as I worked it became evident that I also needed to add a back and a roof to the construction.

'Get this goat trap finished, Ed. Today is day *seven* working on it! That is almost as long as the eleven-day shelter!'

And so I worked like a bastard. I didn't stop for lunch and all afternoon I lashed and snapped and cut until I had completed the back and the roof. I stretched my stiff back and arms to the sky as the sun was already close to the horizon. It was done. I didn't want to set it, though, as I needed to ensure that when the door shut it would stay shut. I couldn't risk the goat getting out when triggered – or, even worse, smashing the trap up in a panic. Tomorrow I could tweak it and set it, but for now I was proud of my commitment. Also completely knackered. Down the hill I went.

I was satisfied enough, though, and rewarded with a beautiful orange and pink twilight. I could feel the support of Amanda in the light. I can't really explain it but I could still feel her holding my hand loyally through all my struggles.

╫╫ ╫╫ ╫╫ ╫╫ ╫╫ ╫╫ ╫╫ ╫╫
|

On day forty-one I felt I was on the home stretch, that the end was in sight. I cleared the soil away from the two fully recovered taro plants that were close to my camp and made what looked like a little vegetable garden. Aesthetics then gave way to hunger and I decided to dig one up as I'd run out of carbohydrate and, as ever, energy was low.

My sore, weathered fingers moved away the soft soil and gently freed the stout root. I placed the main plant down and excavated the rich supporting earth to harvest all of the nutritious corms. As I dug, the inescapable bad news stared me in the face. There was only one potato-like vegetable on the whole plant. I glanced over to the second plant. Driven now more by shock than hunger I had to know whether it would be more fruitful. I scraped and pulled but, unbelievably, it too had just one small potato.

'I don't know what to say – I feel robbed,' I stammered. 'That's bad. The only other carb I have is coconut. These two tiny vegetables are all I have to last me the next nineteen days!'

The sneering, bullying prefect had kicked me out of the dinner queue again. Once more I was the helpless victim of bad luck. 'I didn't need this this morning.' Try as I might, I couldn't help but feel hurt by the sheer bad fortune.

I sliced off five small slivers of taro and made a snail and taro broth. It was meagre at best but the warm liquid filled my stomach.

I was now sick of wasting time making things elaborately and so I threw a basic fishing spear together in ten minutes with my disc knife. It might snap or get blunted but it just needed to be functional and get me out fishing. As I approached a famously plentiful rock pool an eel darted through the shallows towards the open water. Instinctively I used the crude spear like a riding whip and slapped it down hard on the creature's neck, stunning it. I then picked up the eel and chucked it in the basket for lunch.

I let out a half-amused sigh in recognition of how simple that had been. Because my new spear wasn't precious I had just whacked it on the ground and the greater reach of the pole had meant that it had been very easy to strike the eel.

Despite the catch I couldn't throw off this morning's garden tragedy and I was struggling mentally. I felt really bloated, demotivated and distinctly off my best. I had to make up some more cordage and finish that trap. Steeped in apathy, I started to do all the things that I said I would this morning.

By day forty-one I knew that I didn't want to be taken in any more by the ups and downs of everyday life. I knew that the best way was simply to surrender to the natural flow of life on the island and to accept what was. Some days things would go well, others wouldn't be as easy. Yet my very sense of being mirrored each and every incidental peak and trough as if I had no roots of depth at all. It was as if I had no inherent sense of confidence in myself that could carry me through the tougher times without being affected by them. It was giddyingly unstable but every time something went wrong I felt tragic.

As the negativity crept in I recognised the familiar catalyst. I began to realise that I felt distinctly unwell — something that was guaranteed to bring me down. The goat trap only needed setting but I became too ill to go up the hill. My stomach became bloated and gradually began to get worse, and I started to develop abdominal cramps and pains. Remembering my mum's medicine cabinet and the charcoal tablets that she had taken for trapped wind, I munched down some cool charred remains from the fire.

Before long I gave in and lay down by the fire. The stomach cramps caused me to writhe in pain and I began to move about restlessly in order to get comfortable but the discomfort kept chasing me to roll over again and again in the dirt.

With a project like this, designed to demonstrate that I can survive on my own, it is pretty clear that I have to deal with all eventualities on my own. But as the pain worsened I allowed the possibility of reaching out for help to enter my mind. How did I know that what I was experiencing wasn't serious? What on earth was going on inside me? I considered the options. I had a satellite phone that could connect me to a doctor in the UK. Perhaps he might be able to ease my concerns if I talked him through my symptoms. But any such intervention was a tacit admission that I couldn't fend for myself. That the island had got the better of me. That I had failed. I must not be so weak. I can't justify the use of the satellite phone.

The waves of pain increased and coursed through me more intensely. I was now in serious pain, of that there was no doubt. My fears multiplied accordingly and I began to be genuinely worried about my health. What could it be? A parasite? Maybe I had ingested something that was growing in my belly? Perhaps it had reached the size where I was now feeling it inside me. Could it have been from the raw snails? That would explain my low energy if I was eating for two life forms. Perhaps it was a virus or an internal infection. I cursed myself for not being more knowledgeable and being able to self-diagnose. I cursed myself for not being more cautious about eating raw meat.

I made the snap decision that I was being bloody-minded and that I shouldn't risk my health for the sake of a TV programme.

I'm sure that I often undermine myself because of my inherent honesty but I was aware that there was also a clear understanding that intervention meant contact with somebody who was actually there to help. Now that I think about it, the idea of that must have been so appealing because I had been isolated for so long. I would be speaking to someone who could listen to my problems, someone who might just be able to provide some solutions. And someone whose job it was to care.

I fumbled with the bubble wrap that was gaffer-taped around the satellite phone and held down the power key to turn on the electronic device with my grubby digits. It all looked alien and unfamiliar. My first point of contact was always to be to Steven on Komo and so I entered the bizarre digital world of the phone's menu and contacts and found his number.

'Steven, it's Ed.'

'Is everything OK, Ed?' answered Steven, despite clearly knowing that I'd only break out the phone in an emergency.

'Yes, mate – I'm sure it is,' I found myself answering, immediately feeling more in control, 'but I've got some quite severe abdominal pain and I'd like to speak to a doctor in the UK just so that he can put me in the clear.'

'OK, I'm on it. Leave your phone on, Ed, and I'll get Dr Sundeep to call you.'

Having hung up, I virtually crawled down on to the beach to get a clear view of the sky. My Iridium phone worked through low orbiting satellites that required a very clear view of the sky to receive incoming calls and I couldn't afford the hit and miss of being under the canopy.

I do not know how long I lay on the beach but by the time the phone rang it was dark. I had my green top on to keep me warm but no grass skirt as it was awkward and uncomfortable and I was in no mood for the silly costume. I spoke to Dr Sundeep Dhillon, a leading expedition doctor, during the occasional lapses in my pain and was able to talk him through my condition as I lay in the sand, waves of pain coming and going. It began to spit with rain.

'I would say eight out of ten,' I told him in reply to how bad I thought the pain was.

Sundeep didn't pull any punches.

'There is no reason why you couldn't have developed appendicitis or indeed an obstructed bowel.' Fantastic news, I thought sarcastically, but I was incredibly relieved to have someone thinking about me. 'If you were in England I'd admit you to hospital, put you on a drip and run some blood tests. But I understand the position you are in and it is only you who can make the call as to whether you need to be evacuated.'

I didn't have the answer. I wanted him to make the call but he wouldn't. I knew that if I pushed him he would have to err on the side of caution and take me off the island. I didn't want that. Did I? I needed time to think and so asked the doctor if we could speak again in half an hour. He promised to call me back.

I was now probably suffering an equal amount of mental torment as I was physical pain. The temptation of a hot cup of tea, a bed in a hospital with crisp white sheets and professionals to ensure that I was comfortable was alluring. But that would be the end of my experiment – and ultimately I would have failed.

The cramps rose and crashed through me anew. I knew deep down that I had to do something about this.

After forty very long minutes in the rain, with wet sand now coating my lower body, the damp phone vibrated.

'Ed, any progress?' asked Sundeep.

'None. It's the same, Sundeep.'

'I've tasked Steven with bringing you out three courses of generic antibiotics so that you can be treated on the island without having to physically break your experience. They will be with you soon.' We got cut off but that was enough.

I was on my own again but they were coming. It felt amazing to know that I was going to see someone very soon. I gingerly lifted myself to my feet and walked through the darkness and the coconut husks towards the flicker of orange under my shelter. I wearily unstrung my grass skirt from the rafters, wrapped it around my waist and sat down by the warmth of the fire to await the boat. I felt better already.

Crikey – I felt better: that's not good! Maybe I could catch Steven in time to tell him not to come. I rang Komo but I couldn't get through. This wouldn't be surprising if they were already at sea, crossing this part of the Pacific with its vast waves in the dead of night. He was coming and I'd instigated it. I could not stop it now.

I thought I could hear the boat's motor half an hour before it arrived. Every sense was tuned into the forthcoming meeting and my mind warped the wind and waves into mechanical sounds that didn't exist. At last, a real motor could be heard in the distance and it was immediately followed by torchlight and voices.

'Ed? Are you there?'

It was Steven.

The worst of the pain now past, this was actually the last thing I wanted. Nothing against Steven, he's a lovely guy, but I didn't want to see him. I could make this on my own. I started to boil with frustration at the decision I had made.

The torchlight advanced up the beach and entered the forest. 'Ed?' he repeated, 'I'm coming in.'

'I'm here, mate,' I sighed. Steven approached the shelter, filming as he went. This annoyed me as I didn't want this indiscretion to be recorded. 'You say it started yesterday,' he began, pointing the camera in my face.

'Can you switch that off?' I snapped. 'I'm over the worst. But an hour ago I'd have been leaving with you on the boat.'

Steven dispensed the three courses of antibiotics that I was to take and asked me whether I needed to come off the island. The contact, far from refreshing me, frustrated me and I just wanted him to leave.

'No – I'm sorry.' I was grateful for the antibiotics, and for the boat coming out in the dark, but I wanted to stay put. 'They will kick in and I'll be fine. I don't want to come off the island.'

Steven was slightly confused. He had expected me to be in a worse state and I have to admit I was feeling a touch stupid as I wasn't nearly as bad as I'd felt earlier.

'Let's speak tomorrow,' I suggested, 'and if, as I suspect, I'm fine, then we continue as normal.'

Steven agreed, spoke to his companions from the boat and they withdrew to the vessel. I could hear voices for a while before the motor coughed into life and the lights faded into the distance.

'You cock, Stafford,' I berated myself as I lay down again to rest. It was good to have the antibiotics, but could I have managed without them? Well, perhaps I could have. Rage at my own physical and mental weakness tore through me as I stared at the thatched shelter above my head.

|||| |||| |||| |||| |||| |||| |||| ||||
||

By morning the pain had pretty much gone. I just felt drained. The one thing that consoled me was that I'd made the decision last night *not* to leave the island. The doctor had said that the fact that my stomach was gurgling was a good indication that there wasn't a blockage. The pain had become less and less frequent. He had thought that I might have a virus. I was sure that I wasn't absorbing the nutrients from the food that I ate. Everything was flushing straight through me in three vast dumps a day.

I eased my way back into work by making new flights for my arrows. My mark one flights had dried and curled over and so needed replacing. I opted this time for coconut palm leaves that had already dried flat. It wasn't hard to cut a few from the roof and tie them on.

By early afternoon, however, the pain was returning, and in my state of frustration this calmed me as it suggested that I'd perhaps not been such a hypochondriac after all. My stomach was bloated again and I was streaming with sweat.

Then something happened that changed my experience on the island more than I could have imagined. Between my camp and the beach, among the decaying coconuts under the trees, was a coconut crab. Up until now I had thought that hermit crabs were big. This thing caught me off guard as it was the biggest crab I had ever seen – even in pictures. The beast was well over a foot long and looked more like a lobster on steroids than a crab. I swiftly brought my heel on to the back of its head and it was dead. No fight at all. I lifted it to reveal a vast warm abdomen hanging from its twitching body.

During my journey from ex-army captain to who I am today, I have seen and experienced many things that don't make much sense. As I have also said, I have felt that someone is looking after me. Outside religion, that doesn't translate to a western mindset, but it started in the Amazon and it hasn't left me. In my weakened, malnourished state I had been given a meal that was beyond my wildest expectations.

I laid the exoskeleton on the fire to roast and salivated at the prospect of what all that protein and fat would do for my body and soul. Energy not yet restored, I lay down in expectation of the best meal of my life. My stomach was still jabbing me but I felt like I had the antidote. So I waited.

Was it the antibiotics attacking my illness or the fact that I knew something had been done about it? Had my prayers been answered or had I just ridden out a tough time to find better fortune?

Whatever it was, my strength started to return before I even tasted a single mouthful. As the meat barbecued, the gases that had been trapped in the shell escaped and I started to pick at the smaller bits. The texture of proper food for the first time in forty-two days was extraordinary. I broke open the claws to reveal the largest steaming slabs of white meat, each a meal in themselves.

Then there was the abdomen. I have already explained how the taste of the hermit crab abdomen had become a delicacy to me, but this one was the size of a melon. I broke it free from the body and it acted like a cup that I sat in the embers. After I had had my fill of meat I hung enough crab meat in the rafters to last for supper and breakfast. Wrapping the green shirt around my hand, I lifted the oily cocoon out of the fire and set it down in front of me to cool. I could smell coconut oil rising from the abdomen and impatiently I lifted the hot Holy Grail to my lips.

The warm oil that passed over my tongue and down my throat was life itself. I am certain that it would have been too rich and fatty for anyone to ingest in this raw state unless you were seriously depleted of nutrients and you were locked on absorption mode. I have never, ever experienced drinking oil as being so wonderful. And the amount was vast, too. Over a pint of pure coconut fat medicine filled my belly and glowed inside me. I could not stop smiling. I was so, so happy.

I grabbed my refurbished arrows and strode up the hill like a gladiator. With a grace that I'd not felt on the island before, I notched the arrow, drew the string back and released such a straight powerful shot that it embedded half the nail in a tree. With some effort, I heaved the arrow free with the realisation that I had been given new hope, new possibilities. I was standing atop the island with energy, motivation and a lethal weapon that had finally come of age.

'Not as good as sticking in a goat, obviously,' I reported, but for the first time I had a spark inside me that gave me the confidence that I really could now catch a goat.

CHAPTER 6
THRIVING

~~||||~~ ~~||||~~ ~~||||~~ ~~||||~~ ~~||||~~ ~~||||~~ ~~||||~~ ~~||||~~
|||

I slept extraordinarily well and ate the crab claws for breakfast. They were nothing short of phenomenal. The crab had done me for three meals now — twenty-four hours of amazing food from a single catch. The meat wasn't smelly like seafood can be — it was as clean and nutritious and as tasty as a large fillet of poached salmon in coconut oil.

Whether it was the physical nutrients or the psychological boost I'm not sure but I vowed that it was up to me to pick myself up. This wasn't a prison, this wasn't a scheme devised by someone else to test me; it was my idea, my dream, and it was totally and utterly up to me to approach however I wanted.

The massive log on the fire smouldered away and the scene reminded me of an indigenous village in the Amazon — crude but simple and efficient. I was starting to look like I knew what I was doing.

Now more in control than ever before, I skipped up the hill and set the goat trap in seconds. I think the antibiotics did have an effect. The lethargy had gone. I had energy and spark.

I had to carry out my daily seafood forage round the island and gathered my stuff together. The temptation, for this everyday and uneventful task, was to go light, just the GoPro and coconut palm leaf basket, and get back in time to do something worth filming. But the coconut crab had taught me that I needed to expect the unexpected and be ready to capture events at all times and so I grabbed my spear, one of the bigger video cameras, the Cinesaddle and all the spare batteries and CF cards that I needed to film. My old Scout motto, *Be Prepared*, echoed in my head.

Fully kitted up and loaded down, I turned left out of camp heading south down the beach. The sun was not yet at its hottest and, on the western shore, still partially hidden by the island. Decaying green coconuts lay in the sand to remind me of every nourishing drink I had smashed from the trees. I was alert as I approached the usual places where crabs ventured far enough from their protective rocks and I was ready to crush an unsuspecting creature at every opportunity. My feet were now tough and leathery. The coconut crab meat made me feel strong and robust. I was back in control and proactive. I was now convinced that I was the only person who would decide the quality of my existence on this island; I felt I was at last shedding the apathy and near-despair caused by my being unwell.

The tide was low and exposed the large flat reefs that stretched out into the sea like waterlogged football pitches after a monsoon. These were home to the bigger, tougher crabs that defiantly stood their ground and snapped ferociously at me — until, that is, I unceremoniously stamped on them with my bare feet. I built up a respectable number of crabs and collected two pots of larger snails that would provide me with my basic protein needs for the day. Nothing spectacular — but it would do. I knew the importance of using every small success to bolster my new positivity.

I was calm as I circled the island, my head in a good place. I was able to find fun in my situation and was planning to set the goat trap again. Killing a goat was my ultimate, elusive goal, the one that I'd still not yet achieved. I rounded the northern point of the island on to the firewood beach and immediately found that my mind was playing tricks on me again.

A large piece of driftwood had washed up into the bottom of one of the trees and the silhouette was the shape of a goat. I shook my head and cursed under my breath, looking away, suppressing the frustration at the reminder of what I'd so far failed to catch. As I looked away a desperate and frightened bleating rang out across the beach.

My head snapped back towards the tree line to confirm the impossible. I squinted to focus on the subject and felt all my senses sharpen at the significance of what I was now registering. The petrified goat bleated again.

I had come too close too many times to leave anything to chance. Nothing could have distracted me from the immediacy of what was happening. Point-of-view GoPro on – 'beep'. Main camera on. Radio mic on – 'check check'.

I approached the distressed animal with the stealth of an old lion that has not eaten for weeks. Nothing was more important than this moment. As I closed in I could see that the goat had initially got its horns tangled in the vines but that it had clearly panicked and had now trapped its whole neck in the thick fibrous chains. It was Black Stripe, the big-testicled billy goat. He jumped and bucked powerfully as I drew closer, screaming like a mother whose child's pushchair has been trapped in the closing doors of a departing underground train. Both the goat and I knew exactly what was happening.

My immediate concern was that the increased panic would enable Black Stripe to free himself, so I had to grab his horns while he was still trapped. As I did so I could feel a muscular explosion of energy as he kicked back fiercely, only just missing my own legs. With one horn in each hand, and standing beside the desperate beast as if I were wheeling a bicycle, I allowed myself time to think.

'Breathe, Stafford — reassess the situation.'

The goat was going nowhere. As strong as it was, the vines were as thick as boa constrictors and, if anything, appeared to be tightening around Black Stripe's throat. I had time. What did I have with me? I immediately realised that my new knife was back in camp. Could I go back and leave the goat here? No fucking way. I was not allowing any possibility of this animal escaping. I would not take my eyes off this creature until it was dead. All I had was the crude spear that I was using to smack eels and to lever crabs out of tight spaces.

I had never killed a goat before. I had never experienced the strength of a trapped animal like this. I tried to break its neck by wrenching it back but could tell immediately that this would not work. I dug my fingers into the goat's windpipe and clamped down on the airway. The goat wheezed but I could not close the airway enough to starve it of oxygen. I am not proud of this, but I considered all the vulnerable entrances to the animal that would allow me to dispatch it quickly. I took my stick and drove it into the goat's eye to try and pierce its brain. The blood-curdling scream was terrifying as the animal was blinded but the stick snapped and I knew it would not die this way. My last option was brute force: I stepped over the goat as if I was riding it and, with my left hand holding the animal's left horn, I brought my clamshell down with my right hand on to its forehead.

From the first strike it took fifteen minutes for the animal to die, battered to death by a giant clamshell. I hate cruelty to animals and I am not proud of doing this, but I had to eat.

Still tangled in the vines, the bloody goat hung limply from the tree. It was primal instinct maybe, but I was happier than at any previous moment on the island. I had meat. I had a skin. I had achieved what I had been dreaming of for forty-three days. My torso and arms were spattered in blood as I hacked through the vines with the clamshell to free the carcass. Once free, it fell to the floor and I attempted to move it for the first time. It was incredibly heavy – around fifty kilos, I would guess – and I used every ounce of energy to haul the beast up on to my shoulders to take it back to camp. As I strained under the weight of the warm meat I felt like a giant. To the tune of 'Peaches' – 'Movin' to the country – gonna eat a lot of peaches' – I sang, 'Got myself a goat – gonna eat a lot of goat meat' over and over again.

(Hardly surprisingly, two months later Discovery Channel would take one look at this footage and inform me that it was not transmittable. It was horrific, bloody and prolonged. I could only console myself that I had killed the goat as quickly as I could in the circumstances. If I had not been on the island the animal would have remained trapped and died of thirst – a far more drawn-out death.)

My legs were quivering under the strain as I let the goat fall from my shoulders and slam down hard on to the forest floor outside my shelter like a boxer hitting the canvas.

Despite the fact that I'd spent over ten minutes carrying the dead animal, I still worried as I headed back to get my camera equipment from the north of the island that the goat would be gone when I got back. This was too good to be true. Was it definitely dead? Had I dreamed the whole incident? Was I mad and I would get back and find nothing there? The blood on my arms reassured me that I could believe what was going on. I really had killed a goat.

Sure enough, the carcass was still there when I returned and I set up the cameras to record the lengthy process of cutting up the animal. I knew that in this tropical heat the meat would not last a day unless I cured it so I had to work fast. It was mid-morning and I could not afford to have any meat lying around or not ready by nightfall.

First I had to skin the animal. The hide could be used as a blanket to keep me warm at night or even a poncho-like cloak if it was supple enough. I retrieved my knife and hauled the large whetstone from the shelter and sat down to sharpen my most precious tool. Slow rhythmical figures of eight acted as a head-clearer for the labour-intensive task that lay ahead. I'd never skinned anything bigger than a rabbit or a large snake before and so this was using basic skills and just applying them to a bigger project.

I rolled the goat on to its back and worked back and forth just under the animal's sternum to make a longitudinal cut through the skin. The knife required a sawing action to work through the tough hide and once I'd made a hole I began to cut from the sternum to the genitals, carefully lifting the fur from the belly so that I didn't cut into any internal organs. Every two minutes or so the blade would become dull and I had to break off and spend thirty seconds sharpening it. I just had to accept the limitations of the poor-grade metal and settle into a routine of cutting and sharpening.

I gently sawed around the genitals and began to cut a line up each of the back legs to the knee joints. At each knee I then cut a ring around the joint.

Returning to the sternum, I sliced up to the throat and then sawed off the head whole. I had to use a clamshell to smash the knife through the spinal cord to sever the head completely from the body. Once removed, I tossed the head to one side.

I made further cuts up the forelegs and around the knees and then I began the process of peeling back the skin from the dead body. The aim was to remove the hide in one large piece so that I could lift the skin and gently slice the membrane attaching the skin to the muscle. The slightly blunt knife was perfect for this as it was forgiving and I only made one small cut through the hide in the entire process of removing it.

Without keeping a note of the time taken, I would say it must have been early afternoon by the time the skin was completely freed from the animal. I hung it over a branch to deal with later and it immediately started to attract flies.

I'm no butcher but I've gutted fish, tortoises and one tapir (not killed by me) in the Amazon, so the next task was to remove the stomach, bowel and intestines. Being herbivores, goats have vast stomachs and so this required a fair bit of yanking and cutting to free the huge sacks of digesting vegetation and shit. Invariably some of the excrement leaked out of the bowel as I removed it so I hauled the entire carcass down to the water's edge to wash it with seawater.

I piled the intestines up and put them to one side as I suspected there might be some use for these non-edible parts later. Then I had the very physical but relatively simple task of cutting up the remaining carcass into manageable portions. Each leg took about ten minutes to hack off with my blunt tools. I dunked them in the sea and placed them on some palm leaves. I managed to snap and twist one rack of ribs off the spine but the other side was impossible as I no longer had any torsion to apply. I settled for leaving that part of spine and the second rack of ribs joined together. Then I was left with all the regular cuts of meats that make various steaks. There was so much meat that I started to worry that I was not going to get it all cut up before it got dark.

With the sun now very low in the sky, and firewood still to collect, I loaded all the meat into a jerrycan with the top cut off that I had salvaged. I dunked it all in seawater and scrubbed it clean as best I could. I then hauled the meat-filled tub and the legs back to my shelter. To get the meat off the floor I cut it into shoe-sized chunks and hung it from the coconut palm spines of my shelter. The thatch made a perfect hanging rack with ready-made slats and I collected beach hibiscus bark to tie it all to the thatch directly above the fire.

By dusk I had managed to hang the last piece of meat above the fire. 'I just caught a goat! I just killed and skinned and quartered a goat. I have four legs, two racks of ribs, two big slabs of meat, all hanging above the fire.'

I knew that the heart, kidneys and liver would not last and so these were my supper. In the dark I chopped the internal organs into small pieces with the knife, using the camera case as a chopping board. A splash of seawater and a covering of rainwater and they were boiled in the huge soybean can.

The result was a vast steaming meal that I placed on the ground between my legs. With my scavenged spoon I scooped up a chunk of meat in the poor light, not knowing what I was going to get. It was a lucky dip of three distinct flavours: liver, heart and kidneys — which would it be?

Memories of me as a seven-year-old at school in the dinner queue came swimming back as I bit through a large chunk of tender liver and the meaty juices filled my mouth. Never a huge fan of liver, the taste was familiar and yet here elevated to the food of the gods. The texture was soft and giving, but the flavour was a work of art: rich and fine. I let out an unconscious moan of sheer pleasure and my eyes filled with tears of happiness. Forty-five days without red meat is a very long time and my sense of appreciation was nothing short of extraordinary.

I considered the number of things that had had to be in place for this day to have worked. I could not be cooking the meal without the recently salvaged larger soybean tin pot. I had most definitely needed the knife to skin and cut up the carcass. Both were relatively recent acquisitions. Had all the waiting been part of the grand plan? Was this always going to be the day when I caught the goat? I blinked at the magnitude of what I was contemplating.

That night I offered thanks for the food with every ounce of my body. It was incredible. 'Coconut crab for breakfast – goat kidneys for supper. Life, quite possibly, could not get any better.'

Right then, all things considered it couldn't.

~~||||~~ ~~||||~~ ~~||||~~ ~~||||~~ ~~||||~~ ~~||||~~ ~~||||~~ ~~||||~~
||||

I was aware that my grazed and cut hands were sore before I even opened my eyes. When I did, a sense of gratitude swept warmly through my torso. A whole goat's worth of meat was swaying in the smoky breeze above me. I'd tied the head to the side of the shelter, out of the smoke, and the skull spun ominously on its hibiscus cord warning any other animals that I was now in kill mode.

I untied a rack of ribs the size of one of those early laptops and placed it on the embers for breakfast. As I sat there turning my ribs occasionally I noticed that the spines of each thatched palm tile that ran horizontally above me were already stained brown from the permanent exposure to the fire's smoke. Its alternative use as a drying and smoking rack should work perfectly.

The morning was to be all about efficiency. Although I'd got the meat chopped into vast slabs and hung them over the fire overnight, they must now be cut into much finer strips in order to allow them to dry out and to expose the flesh to the curing properties of the smoke. The camera case was being used as a chopping board again but today was not one for considering the morality of this. Yes, I'd brought it with me. No, it wasn't something that I'd found in Lemon Camp. Yes, I would use it. I utilised the expanse of flat black plastic to assist me in chopping up the vast amount of meat. Every two or three minutes I would grind a fine edge back on to my knife to ensure that it slid cleanly through the red flesh. Essentially, I carved the entire body of the animal into long thin strips. Each strip was then dunked in a bucket of seawater to add salt and then carefully hung in the smoke above the fire to dry and for the outer layer to carbonise.

The flavour of the smoky ribs made me shudder with ecstasy. I tore the barbecued meat from each bone with the delight of a hungry dog and yet my whole situation was becoming increasingly civilised with each day. I realised that without decent food I had simply begun to shut down. I was aware enough of my body to physically feel the proteins entering my muscles and beginning to repair them. I had estimated that the ribs would last three meals but I seemed to polish them off by mid-morning and so put the lower spine on the coals for lunch.

The key thing was to ensure that none of the meat went to waste. Every strip was cut as thin as possible and I could tell that this jerky was going to work well. I stood back to admire my wall of perfectly sliced meat curing in the lazy smoke of the fire.

For someone who had lived off raw snails for two weeks it was quite a sight.

Calmly and peacefully I then went for a morning swim. By now I realised that stopping for five minutes to really have a nice time by doing something like swimming was very beneficial to my mental health. Dripping and clean, I emerged from the water charged with energy and life.

I needed to do something with the goatskin quickly, as it was covered in flies. In order to process rawhide into a more supple leather I knew that I had to soak it in the brains of the animal as I'd tried to do with the dead kid. But untying the goat's head immediately revealed maggots between the flaps of neck flesh. On day two! I hoped desperately that this was because it wasn't hung above the fire with the other meat, but the rate of decomposition was startling. It meant that I needed to work fast.

I smashed at the skull on Snail Rock to make a hole big enough to allow me to scoop the brains out with my fingers. The resulting goo I then mixed with seawater and submerged the hide in it using the cracked plastic jerrycan. This helped keep away the flies as the hide was weighed down with a rock below the level of the liquid.

Lunch was ongoing and constant — I munched the lower spine like a doner kebab, eating the cooked meat and then placing the carcass back on the fire to cook the now exposed uncooked flesh.

I heaped the offal from the goat into a pile to see if any animals would come and eat it. Lungs, oesophagus, stomach, intestines and testicles. I added the smashed-up head, too, and noted that it was mainly flies and tiny hermit crabs that were interested.

Not wanting to put all my eggs in one basket, I decided I would cook the legs in an underground oven. I was bored with cutting up strips of meat and if that didn't work it would be pretty disastrous if I'd cured the entire animal to no avail. So, on my hands and knees, I dug a pit the diameter of a large dustbin lid and collected non-porous, apple-sized stones with which to line it. I knew that to heat the rocks to glowing red hot I had to have a fire that was roaring and long-lasting so I also collected a huge amount of firewood. By mid-afternoon it was raining and my pit was filling with water. I couldn't have dug it under the shelter as the fire that I was planning to light would have been too big and I would have risked burning the whole thing down.

My worry was that the legs would go off before I cooked them but I did the maths and worked out that I had to wait until morning now anyway, unless I wanted to be roasting in the dark. With a bit of luck the morning would be dry.

That afternoon I also found a sea snake. I chucked a rock at it and, amazingly, killed it with one blow. I threw it in the basket as an appetiser before supper.

My plan for tomorrow was strict. I wanted to eat the slow-cooked goat legs at 4 p.m. so, allowing four hours of a roaring fire to heat the rocks and a further four hours of cooking, I had to have a fire going by 8 a.m. Everything in my control was accounted for. Now I just needed the rain to stop.

I lay in bed slightly worried that the legs would already have gone off. But then I considered that all over the world meat was hung to make it more tender and this had been hanging in smoke for the whole day so it had no flies on it. I also comforted myself with the fact that the first strips of jerky were drying well and tasted fantastic and crisp. I had done well and should relax — the legs would be cooked just fine, too.

|||| ||||| ||||| ||||| ||||| ||||| ||||| |||||
|||||

Breakfast, as if I need to say it, was the second rack of ribs. I had to admit that it was a bit gamey and I worried that the legs might be, too. I was enjoying gorging myself on goat meat and my body was absorbing absolutely everything. I felt amazing but, strangely, I was doing smaller poos than I had on coconut and snails. My body seemed to know that none of these nutrients should go to waste.

The jerky was now dry to the touch on the outside after a day of hanging, but I still wasn't totally convinced it had worked. It was my first attempt at curing meat without a big bag of salt.

Outside, the air was crisp and the morning was, thankfully, dry. I transferred embers from my fire and then emptied the cave of my emergency firewood. Emergencies seemed a thing of the past right now. I then spent the next few hours collecting and adding huge pieces of wood to the growing bonfire. All morning I dragged log after log and kept the temperature very hot indeed.

I *loved* that morning. Collecting firewood had become therapeutic so I just set myself the single challenge and brought back logs so big that I could hardly wrap both arms around them. Vast chunks of wood burned long and hot. It was great fun and I was achieving a furiously hot fire. Then, for the last hour of burning, I allowed the fire to burn down and turn into a red bed of embers.

While collecting driftwood, I also found a section of plastic piping. I immediately realised that I could employ this and a short section of bamboo in order to utilise the huge surface area of the roof for rain collection. I also found another flip-flop so I now had two working (but odd) pairs. 'One for Sunday best!' I laughed and reflected on how much of what I was using was actually man-made stuff that had been dropped or washed up on the beach. Plastic bottles were so abundant that I'd stopped picking them up now. I had *forty litres* of reservoir capacity and I simply didn't need any more.

By lunch the jerky had further dried out. If there were bits that had a 'belly' on them (i.e. they were too fat and not drying out inside) I just took them down and split the thicker meat with the knife to allow the smoke to carbonise the internal, wetter bit.

The waste pile was decomposing at an astonishing rate. The neck of the goat was a sea of writhing maggots but the flies had largely disappeared as it seemed to have gone beyond that stage. The difference between my cured meat and this unprotected pile was astounding. I would not feed this meat to my worst enemy's dog. I was so chuffed considering I had no prepared salt and no refrigeration. My meat was curing really well.

I cleared away the burning logs and, with a stick, brushed aside the embers to reveal the rocks below. As it was midday, and the sun was bright, I could not see if they were glowing red but I could tell they were bloody hot. I laid the legs directly on to the rocks like sardines in a tin, alternately, head to toe, like Charlie's four grandparents in bed together before they found Willie Wonka's golden ticket. I covered them under blankets of coconut palm leaves twelve deep to keep in the moisture. Finally, I heaped back the excavated soil on top to further block any steam that tried to escape. There wasn't enough soil to do this task well and so I ferried a further two bucketfuls of sand from the beach and dumped it on top for good measure. As I stood back, my gut instinct told that this was going to work. By the time the sun got low in the sky I would excavate the roasting parcel and see what we had.

My only concerns were, first, that the meat was a bit gamey and, second, whether or not I should have put a couple of leaves on the rocks before I laid the legs on them. I hoped the bottom side wouldn't be burned.

Dark Stripe's stunning rawhide had been submerged in seawater and brains. It was soft and wet but needed a thorough clean in the shallows. I soon realised that the skin wouldn't be as clean as a piece of clothing might be. The membrane and bits of fat were too firmly attached to remove and so I set about mounting it on a frame to dry. I began by envisaging a square frame and then realised that a square has a tendency to skew and go out of shape. A triangle wouldn't do that – I rationalised – and it would be much stronger.

And so I laid my wet goatskin on the forest floor and found three of the longest of the various boat poles that I'd brought back to camp. As well as being a good length, they were also clean – but not massively strong, as I'd learned from the goat trap – but for this non-contact sport they would work just fine. I lashed the ends together around the skin, leaving a nice gap around the hide – my triangular frame must have been about twice the surface area of my soon-to-be blanket.

Then, using only the offcuts from earlier hibiscus string making, I began to tie the skin to the frame. I would make a small incision using my knife and then thread the string through the hole and attach it to the frame with a clove hitch.

Then I'd go for the diametrically opposite side of the skin and attach that. Slowly the hide began to get tighter and more taut as it began to resemble the skin of a drum. The result of my first ever hide stretch was very rewarding. The skin was now taut enough for me to work on it with the blade and to remove any membrane, fat or even small patches of flesh that were still attached.

As the evening drew in I attached it to the underside of the shelter so that it sat flush with the thatch. It was above the wood pile rather than the fire as I did not want it to dry too quickly, but it was out of the rain and, in my eyes, a real success. I clicked my tongue against the roof of my mouth approvingly.

After three and a half hours I uncovered the goat legs.

'Oh, my God – I think these are going to be incredible!' I spluttered as steam wafted out from the shallow pit.

'We have success. All four legs are cooked to perfection!' The sun cut through the palm trees, highlighting the wisps of smoke coming off the fire. I couldn't stop laughing as I ate the meat. It was so tender that I could have bitten chunks off with my lips. 'That is extraordinarily good. I have to say that is better than oven-roasted – anything! I never thought I'd be eating this well on the island.'

Today I felt like I was living the dream. The birds were chirping and the waves were lapping the beach. I hung the slow-cooked goat legs above the fire to store. In the smoke they should last me about five days. What a beautiful day.

'Day forty-five has made me come alive. What a day. *What a day ...*'

卌 卌 卌 卌 卌 卌 卌 卌
卌 |

My nose streamed in the morning smoke and, closing off one nostril with my finger, I fired the contents of my sinuses on to the floor like a bullet. The snot rocket – a wonderful evolution from the handkerchief.

'The only problem with the legs is that they might not last five days because they taste really good and in the night I keep getting up and eating them!' I admitted. 'Do you know what? Every single bit of the edible meat is going to be eaten. I think that's really cool.' I was going to eat a leg a day but I decided to throw caution to the wind and make hay while the sun shone. No more silly rules and constraints – I would eat whatever I wanted until it was all gone. The meat was still utterly delicious thirty-six hours after killing the goat.

'Today I am going to look for bamboo to drag back to a point where I will build a raft. Then I will be able to get off the island, into the reef, and try and fish.'

Bamboo isn't indigenous to the island but there were several lengths washed up above the high-tide mark. In fact, the tide was too high to collect bamboo so I headed inland. I decided instead to use the elevation of the rocky outcrop to plan where I was going to build my raft and determine the shortest distance out to the edge of the reef.

From the top I examined the structure of the reef. It wasn't a thin line circling the island; it was a large rough expanse that also filled much of the lagoon. It could provide potential fishing opportunities without my going all the way out to the edge of the deep Pacific Ocean.

It was a sparkling sunny day and I recognised that I was comfortable in the direct sun and not getting burned any more. I had no need for clay and wondered whether the coconut oil in the food I ate was oiling and protecting my skin. As I gazed down into the lagoon I was conscious of the huge waves and the drop off beyond the reef. Sharks would surely be loitering around the spot where the ocean rises to the reef. I also spotted an area where, at low tide, I might be able to wade over the shallow reef all the way out to the ocean barrier.

'I know there are lobsters out there.' I salivated at the thought. 'Octopuses, I've been told, hide in the holes in the reef, too. I can grab them by the top of the head! Turtles, too ...' There would also be a lot of bigger fish. I debated where I should build the raft. It was high tide and I noticed schools of larger fish and small sharks in the pools below me. It was clearly time to harvest the ocean.

The goat trap was still set and I decided I was going to leave it like that. If I got another goat that would be a dream come true. That said, I'd seen neither sight nor sound of a goat since my first catch. Up until then I'd been seeing them three or four times a day. It was strange — as if they now knew to stay away from me.

The hide was definitely leaning towards being rawhide rather than buckskin. Maybe the goat hadn't had sufficient brains. But I continued to clean and dry it on its rack each day. I didn't know anything about this stage of processing but the hide looked great and, even if it was a tad stiff, would be a perfect warm rug to sleep on at night.

One of the biggest success stories of the goat was the jerky. Every time I went anywhere I took with me a strip of pure protein. They were brilliant. Slightly salty, quite chewy, and full of smoky, fatty flavour.

The waste, however, was now truly disgusting. As I passed the decomposing mess one eye socket was fluid with maggots contesting their prize.

As my stock of meat began to diminish, I considered the hooves and the shins of the goat and decided that if chicken foot soup was regarded as a delicacy in some parts of the world, then there had to be more nutrients in a goat's hoof. So I made up a big hoof stock for supper to get the bones soft enough to eat.

The result was fatty and sticky like bone marrow and I could tell it had loads of goodness in it as I licked my sticky, fatty fingers. It also felt good not to be wasting a single morsel.

In my now quite casual meanderings I returned to the headland in the afternoon to observe the scene at low tide. I specifically looked for pools in which fish might congregate. I looked down for ten minutes but there were no fish at all. Remarkably slowly I began to join up the dots. I finally worked out that I had to catch the fish that were coming in at high tide. That was when they were abundant. Might it be possible to make a rock corral that trapped some of these plentiful fish as the tide went out? That way they would be contained in a restricted pool and, importantly for me, would be accessible at *low* tide. I identified two rock pools at low tide that, from the high rock lookout, looked as if they would be damable. I waited and spotted some schools of fish coming in with the new tide, which confirmed my theory.

I liked having time on the beach at sunset. I loved that time of day. I'd done my exercises, had a swim and a wash. Tomorrow I would make my raft. It was going to take me two days and no more.

The evening brought a feather-cloud sky, purple and gold. I was at peace. For the moment.

𝐇𝐇𝐓 𝐇𝐇𝐓 𝐇𝐇𝐓 𝐇𝐇𝐓 𝐇𝐇𝐓 𝐇𝐇𝐓 𝐇𝐇𝐓 𝐇𝐇𝐓 𝐇𝐇𝐓 𝐈𝐈

'Good morning. What an appalling night's sleep,' I moaned. It had been light for a while and I still hadn't bothered to get out of bed. There was less than two weeks to go and I was dreaming of being at home. What breakfast cereal was I going to eat? All of them — every single one ever known to Kellogg's.

I spent all night thinking about TV ideas, buying a flat, spending time with the family. All night I had wallowed in the excitement of going back to my life.

I was going to build a raft today. One straightforward task.

'Let's get some fish, Staffs.' I brushed myself down. 'Let's get some fish.'

Not surprisingly, as it had been high tide in the morning yesterday, and that had stopped me collecting bamboo for the raft, it was roughly the same time today, too, and so I had the same issue. Rethink needed.

Instead I made my guttering, in order to make use of the huge surface area of my thatched roof. My longest section of bamboo was too strong and I couldn't split it to create the 'U' that I needed. I placed it to one side to use on the raft. A smaller section broke more easily, however, and I knocked out the internal nodes between each partition to create one long natural channel.

I used the fire to heat up another bent scrap of metal (presumably from the same outboard motor) to a temperature that could cut through plastic. I then used this hot metal to lop off the top off the second jerrycan and to split the circular black plastic tube into two U-shaped guttering sections. With patience, going back and forth to the fire using the green T-shirt to stop my fingers burning, the tasks were both completed efficiently and to a good standard.

I lifted the palm thatching and tied the guttering directly on to the frame. Then, ensuring that the drip would be directly over the centre of the bamboo I ran along the entire length with my knife, cutting the thatch into a sharp fringe. The result was very professional and looked as close to a roof edge and guttering as I could ever have hoped. I poured some seawater on to the thatch and it dripped into the channel and ran into the decapitated jerrycan. It worked, but the real test would be when it rained properly for the first time. I then made repairs to the area below the guttering, which now had a few holes in it, with fresh green coconut leaves. 'Job's a good 'un,' I admired smugly.

By now the tide had gone out so my thoughts turned to building some sort of rock corral in which to trap fish. A rock corral is made simply by damming any holes in an existing rock pool to form a large cordoned-off area from which fish cannot escape when the tide recedes. Once in a contained area they can be clubbed, stoned or simply cornered and lifted out of the water.

I would need to bait the area with chum (waste food, rotten fruit, etc.) and I immediately thought of my decaying pile of maggots. I wanted to bait the area in advance of building the actual corral so as to entice fish to the site. On dipping my hands into the seething mass of maggots I was struck by its warmth. I collected two full hair gel container pots, screwed the lids on tightly and walked up the beach to the rock pools.

I emptied the maggots into a prospective corral and watched the small fish swarm to the area. I added a mature coconut for good measure and decided that this was a possible success story in the making. The water was clear and fresh. Small colourful sprats nibbled at my maggots. I would come back and dam this pool.

For now I returned to my original focus of the day as the tide was now lower. I would make my raft on Komo beach, the beach beyond Bravo Beach to the south that faced Komo. There was a lot of driftwood on this southern tip of the island and, once constructed, I would easily be able to paddle the raft around to where the coral was closest to the shore.

I dragged back the five best bits of bamboo on the island. I could haul three at a time but they were heavy and so I wedged them under my arms and dragged the long lengths over the rocks and the sand. I listened to the different noises that the bamboo made over different surfaces as I plodded on. It's amazing what grabs your attention when you're totally alone.

I opted for a conventional long thin raft with five parallel poles. I considered a triangle (following the success of my stretching rack for the goat hide) but decided it would not be manoeuvrable enough for a raft. With cross struts and diagonals my design would work just fine, I was sure. I chucked the bamboo into the trees above the high-tide line so that they would not be gone in the morning and went home for supper. Tomorrow I would lash it all together.

I made myself 'surf and turf' for supper. Although I had one leg left I opted to eat all the little crabs that I'd found along the coast. I added a strip of jerky for a salty, smoky flavour. The result was fantastic and crunchy as I munched through the pot of whole crabs.

So it had been a good day. Amazing weather. I had attached the guttering. I had collected all the poles to build a raft. I was in a really healthy, positive state of mind. And, for the first time on the island, it seemed stable and constant. I wasn't having to check in at all. No panic, worries or calming myself down in the stone circle. The very fact that I'd decided to leave the stones in the cave rather than move them to the shelter showed that I was growing out of these armbands that had so successfully kept me afloat. Now I was simply living – brimming with ideas and enthusiasm.

卌 卌 卌 卌 卌 卌 卌 卌
卌 |||

'That was the most incredible night's sleep. The best night's sleep in a long while and I feel like I've just had sex, I enjoyed it so much!' Too much information, Ed, but I had been a long time away from home. The sleep was offputtingly good – amazingly good. I sat and grinned at how good I felt. Recharged. Positive. Happy.

There was still loads of jerky left so I munched on a couple of sticks. I saw no need to extend my shelter any more. I loved the openness and the light afforded by the single-sided home. It was good for filming, too, as it let in light and allowed me to get wide shots of myself working indoors. It would be a waste of time and energy to do any more. 'So that's that settled then. No more construction work!'

There was no beach hibiscus left on my side of the island any more. I'd used half an island's worth. So, with the high tide, I walked via the Faraway Tree to Lemon Camp to collect some bark to lash the raft together. I knew how long tasks could take and so I wanted to be there and back in two hours and raced over to cut the poles, strip them of their bark in Lemon Camp, coil the bark up and throw it over my shoulder. I was back in my shelter within the allotted time. Legend.

I wolfed down some of the last leg of goat and a few sweet chunks of coconut and slung the hibiscus over my shoulder again to go and build the raft. No rest for the wicked on this island. It was non-stop from dawn till dusk. The hibiscus around my neck was like a wooden scarf that weighed about as much as a Rottweiler. The skies were greyer today, which was fine for getting a task like this done on a beach with no shade. I was in sync – it was appropriate. I felt solid and worked nimbly to get the raft built.

I knelt down in the sand and set to work. Each square lashing was tight and secure. My mouth was dry and parched and I was utterly exhausted but the raft was complete in three hours and I dragged it into the tree line ready to be launched another day.

Building the wall for my fish trap would also have to wait for another day. I could only do so much and my days were now packed and positive. I wasn't worried at all – just happy to be home in time for tea.

<del>HH</del> <del>HH</del> <del>HH</del> <del>HH</del> <del>HH</del> <del>HH</del> <del>HH</del> <del>HH</del>

<del>HH</del> IIII

caught six crabs while on the beach sending the 'All OK' message on the InReach device. I had no goat leg left and so this was easy and most welcome. I was looking forward to the pleasant change of a crab broth once again.

With a smile on my face I shouted, 'I want to get out! I want to get off this island!' then to the camera I countered this with 'Don't count the days – make the days count.' A wise man, Muhammad Ali.

I would launch the boat tomorrow, as I wasn't quite ready to go to sea. First I made another spear to replace the one that I had broken in the goat's eye. It was simple, with a fire-hardened tip. I enjoyed making a paddle using the chopping board bit of plywood that was spliced into a four-foot section of boat pole and bound, as ever, with hibiscus bark.

After four days of drying and scraping, the hide was now ready. I untied all of the strings and freed it from the triangular frame. I decided that sewing wasn't an option but that if I made one alteration to the hide I would have a simple, functional garment. I made a foot-long slit in the centre, big enough to put my head through, and slipped the skin over my head with the fur next to my skin. I used the hibiscus that had held the hide to the frame to wrap the whole thing tight around my body like a furry corset.

'Do you know what? Fashion aside, I've got myself a warm top! Rather Fred Flintstone, isn't it?' The fur was trapping all the warm air next to my skin. 'That's really cool – it's a grey, drizzly day and I'm warm!' I beamed, with tufts of goat hair stuck in my big wiry beard.

Day forty-nine meant that it was the end of week seven so I did my end-of-week exercises. I had managed eighteen chin-ups three weeks ago, then I only competed ten the following week, and last week I had skipped them entirely because I was ill.

'Eighteen again!' I gasped as I dropped to the ground and bent over, panting. 'That was good, though – I feel strong.' It was my current limit and I knew it. At least I'd got back to my full strength after my illness. I was duly happy.

By now I was changing shape. My muscles felt full and hard. I had long ago shed my beer belly and I imagined that, had I been a boxer, I was now at my fighting weight.

On the way home I decided to dig up a dead plant that I'd passed every week for the past seven. As soon as I started digging I could see tubers – and lots of them. It was a 'kowai', not taro but a similar Pacific plant that produces a crop of potato-like tubers, too. The leaves were unrecognisable from the vine that I'd been shown. It was just a mass of dead vines.

I got to eleven large starchy corms and I almost started to cry with happiness: twelve, thirteen and on it went. This one is enormous! In the end I managed to excavate a big pile of potatoes – twenty-two in total – and as I had eleven days left that gave my morale an enormous boost. I had two whole potatoes per day for the rest of my time here. It was beyond incredible. Even with gorging on goat meat I'd still had relatively heavy legs due to the lack of complex carbs. This could be my ticket to real energy for the remaining days.

Once in my shelter it began to rain. As it grew heavier I could hear the sound of water trickling into my rain collecting bucket. 'The guttering is working!' I shrieked. The water was red thanks to the smoke that had stained the thatch but otherwise it was pure and uncontaminated because it fell from the sky.

'Soooo nice not have to suck water from clamshells through a straw any more. It just collects in a bucket from falling on the roof above my head.'

Ten minutes of a medium-heavy downpour has provided half a bucket. Fourteen bottles of fresh rainwater wasn't bad. And I'd not had to move a muscle.

The kowai was good but needed a lot more boiling than the taro, a good half an hour to get it to the point where it was soft enough to eat.

At the end of week seven I pressed my abraded fingers into the pulse at my wrist and used the video camera to time one minute. My resting heart rate was sixty-four – higher than when I'd started. Slightly confused, as I felt fit and strong, I put it down to the mountain of red meat that I was now consuming.

In the dark I summarised my current status. 'I feel like I've proved that you can come on to an island, with absolutely nothing, and survive. Everything is improving and life is becoming easier. There is, annoyingly, a rat on my right foot, and one behind me. Come on, guys. They don't do any harm …' I rationalised. Then I remembered the bubonic plague.

The night before I'd dreamed that an Arab woman in a head-scarf was cutting my nails. Every time I tried to pull my fingers away she looked really offended and carried on. When I woke up I realised that rats had been nibbling at the tips of my fingers where they could smell coconut. Surely the only sensible interpretation of such a dream was that I should make myself a bed and get off the floor?

'If I do make a bed I need to get some more beach hibiscus,' I rambled … 'I've never done that before. Perhaps it will take me an hour to collect poles, perhaps it will take twenty minutes to strip them of bark and then a further twenty minutes to strip the bark into string …' I cut myself short. 'Go to sleep, Ed.'

In the night the rats ate all my coconut that I had left roasting beside the fire, so there was nothing to chew on when I woke up sporadically, which disturbed my habitual pattern. I could collect more tomorrow, but my nightly ritual was upset. My body felt battered on the hard floor. I had my goatskin, which was soft, but I drifted off again dreaming of a foam mattress.

卌 卌 卌 卌 卌 卌 卌 卌
卌 卌

A night of drizzle brought me a further five or six litres of water in my bucket. It amazed me that this had happened while I slept.

I didn't launch the raft because of blustery weather. The trees were groaning and tormented and rain further served to smother any hope I had of fishing. I feared the ocean enough when it was flat and calm and had no intention of fighting nature's grander plans.

As a result, day fifty was a naked day. I forgot about the camera and just did the grunt work needed to keep things moving forward. I collected firewood, palms and beach hibiscus to make my bed. And because the camera was off there was absolutely no need to get dressed.

卌 卌 卌 卌 卌 卌 卌 卌
卌 卌 I

I woke up very early on the morning of day fifty-one. I wasn't sure how much I'd slept. My internal body clock knew that I needed to launch the raft before the tide started to rise.

A quiet thought crept into my head: nine days to go.

I experimented with heating up the jerky by resting it on a smouldering log, and it crackled enticingly. The fat was being cooked for the first time and the strip doubled over and crinkled up like bacon. The result was utterly delicious. Crisp, smoky meat and sizzling fat that melted between my teeth.

If it ever seems like I am overdoing it about how good something tasted, I can only assure you that I am not. In a world bereft of physical contact with others, pleasure seemed to come from a small handful of things. Accomplishment, and feeling that I was winning, were big internal ones, but I also found that enormous pleasure was to be taken in awakening my senses. As a result, swimming and eating had become my top two pastimes. I cannot overstate the effect that both had on me.

Turning to today's activity, I was quite concerned about my own safety as I'm a terrible swimmer. The beach was fresher and cooler at this early hour and the wind stripped away my night-time snugness. With goose bumps on my arms I added large plastic bottles (the two- or three-litre ones) and washed-up floats to the raft to increase the buoyancy. I then warmed up by using all of my lean muscle mass to drag the rectangular vessel down to the sea. I worried that the whole boat would dissolve in the water as I'd not tested the beach hibiscus bark lashings to see if they held fast when they were saturated. The test would be ongoing when I was on the ocean, relying on them for survival. I reduced the risk by taking some extra bark on the boat with me to conduct emergency repairs if necessary.

My green shirt wrapped round my head like a shepherd in a nativity play, I now felt like a hardened islander. The elastic strap of the GoPro camera that held it in place was perhaps less biblical, but needs must. Deeply tanned, with lean delineated muscles, I scoffed at the memory of the white arse-cheeked flabby Londoner who had arrived here eight weeks ago. Did I fancy myself? Well, there had to be some compensation for all this hardship.

I entered the water and, as the cold waves lapped at my thighs, making me stand on tiptoes to protect my balls that were now tight from the cold, I remembered the first day when I had stepped off the boat naked and terrified of what I was about to put myself through.

The raft floated beside me and so I swung a leg on top and gently eased my weight over the craft and lowered myself to a kneeling position. I was at sea! I took the now obviously very small paddle in two hands and ploughed it down into the water on alternate sides of the boat like an Amazon native in a dugout canoe. But paddling seemed to get me nowhere. I was using all my energy doing deep hard thrusts into the water but it might as well have been a stationary exercise rower. The onshore wind and the prevailing currents dictated that I could not move far off the shore. Feeling about as penetrative as a marshmallow drill bit, I walked the raft round to the more sheltered side of the island in the shallows.

Once more I clambered atop the floating platform and attempted to take control but the currents took me out of my depth and I felt so vulnerable to the whim of the ocean that I jumped off and swam the raft back in until I could stand again. The swimming used all of my energy and I was shaking with exhaustion.

Panting, I took in the scene. The waves were thundering into the reef and if I'd had hair it would have been billowing behind me. I'd been so blinkered in my urge to get out to sea that I'd ignored the weather conditions and attempted the apparently impossible. The short period during which I had been tugged away from the beach had given me a slap round the face and woken me up. I could so easily have been swept out to sea, surrounded by sharks, with no possibility of turning the craft around.

'It is buoyant. It is stable. But, my goodness it is not manoeuvrable.' I gave up the hope of fishing on the reef for the day and put it down to a good lesson learned. The raft was still in excellent condition and I decided to let the incoming tide move it up the beach. The wet weight of the bamboo was now far too heavy for me to drag through the sand.

I ate my last ever meal of goat meat. Adding my penultimate, then ultimate, strips of jerky to my snail and crab broth, my rafters were now bare. I dried my radio mic on a rock by the fire, knowing in my heart that it was long dead. My grass skirt, sodden from my hour in the water, was also hung from the empty thatch in the smoke to dry it out and reduce the weight. Kowai bubbled in the pot for forty-five minutes. The rainy season had begun and I had guttering and a collection tank so I could be relaxed about the amount of water I was using. The final goat meat was especially tender as well, thanks to the long cooking time.

Day fifty-one was a great day as far as I'm concerned. The boat was very difficult to keep in one line but at least it floated and I had learned a lot in one simple outing. A calmer, less windy day may prove more successful. I desperately wanted to access seafood from the reef.

None of the goat meat that was edible had perished. It had all lasted me all the way through. Nine plentiful days of eating as much red meat as I could had left me strong, but if I had one aim in the next nine days it was to catch some bigger fish.

Looking back, I really did think that at times I'd been very ill with a viral infection. My grumbling stomach slightly unnerved me as I lay down to sleep.

'I enjoyed today – a lot,' I said, ignoring my stomach.

~~HHt HHt HHt HHt HHt HHt HHt HHt~~
~~HHt HHt~~ ||

I woke up to sharp stomach cramps and explosive diarrhoea on the beach. Mouth hanging open, gasping, I didn't want to admit I might be ill again. I couldn't let myself slip into sick mode, though, and so fishing was the order of the day.

I had seen shoals of fish swimming just off the beach at high tide in the shallows. I had heard about the local Fijian women using palm leaves tied together as a giant noose to trap fish in shallow water and I thought the method might just work for me.

I had to make a palm frond line to act as a noose for the fish. I knew I would have to daisy-chain all the palms together and really hoped I could do that by using the palm leaves themselves (rather than collecting even more beach hibiscus to use as cordage). In an hour I had cut thirty-two palm leaves and dragged them to a pile at the top of the shallow beach.

I scooted directly up the side of the huge rocky headland. I'd not been up this way before, considering it too steep, and the journey had been taking me about an hour from my camp via the Faraway Tree and the woodland slopes. But after nine days eating goat meat I climbed the steep slope in no time at all, perhaps five minutes, and realised I'd been making an absurdly convoluted journey. It's a funny feeling when you realise that you've been doing something the hard way for such a long time. Part of you is thrilled that you now have an easier method and the other is pissed off that you hadn't worked it out sooner. I laughed at my cautiousness. 'I'm never coming up the other way again!'

The tide was relatively high now and there was a much better view from the top as to where fish might be. I could see that the fish weren't where I'd piled up the palm leaves. They appeared to be swimming over the large flat rocks of the wave-cut platform – the large area of flat rock the size of a baseball field at the base of the cliff. It was worth spending some time up here observing the general movements of the fish. Several black-tipped sharks swam in single file through the rock pools. If I was going to spend valuable time making a thirty-palm-leaf line, I wanted to know what the fish were doing.

The problem I faced was that the area in which the sharks were swimming was too deep for the palm-leaf line to work. As I hauled it in and constricted it they would just swim under the line, so I decided I would work on the huge rock platform. It looked as if the line would work a treat there.

I moved my pile of palms, realising that they would be easier to shift while they were still not joined together. This was all very experimental – I'd never done this sort of fishing before. Above the high tide I then tied the palms together using just the palm leaves themselves to make a mammoth snake-like line that must have stretched over some forty metres.

I headed back to the shelter and reflected to the camera that some people function well on their own. They may even prefer their own company. I admired that. Explorers who never faltered on a solo journey to the poles or rowing across an ocean. That stood for everything that was strong and independent about mankind. Didn't it? I now considered I wasn't that abnormal in the fact that my enjoyment was somewhat qualified because I missed all the people that I love so much. I no longer saw that as a weakness – it was just an indicator of what mattered to me most.

What is life anyway? Is it going out on your own trying to prove something to yourself or to others? Selfishly seeking just one more adrenaline rush? Seeking the approval or admiration of others? Or is it spending time with the people you truly care about and looking after them? Maybe I'm not ungrateful after all. Maybe I'm just growing up.

At times my weeks spent on the island felt like irrelevant nonsense, while on the other side of the fence was a fulfilling, meaningful life at home. 'Days like today I just think – really? You're thirty-seven years old, Ed. You have people in your life who you adore and who love you – why would you choose to go away from them for so long? Why would you do that?' The silence told me that I still hadn't quite worked it out. And I wouldn't tonight.

'Soul-searching over. Good night,' I sighed and switched off the camera.

꿰뚫 ꒐꒐꒐ꓕꓕ ꒐꒐꒐ꓕꓕ ꒐꒐꒐ꓕꓕ ꒐꒐꒐ꓕꓕ ꒐꒐꒐ꓕꓕ ꒐꒐꒐ꓕꓕ ꒐꒐꒐ꓕꓕ
꒐꒐꒐ꓕꓕ ꒐꒐꒐ꓕꓕ ꒐꒐꒐

A week today I leave the island. Home …

My morning ramblings were rudely interrupted by the need to run. Diarrhoea was dribbling out as I ran to the beach and lost control. On all fours at the water's edge a colonic wave of pain overcame me, followed by a breathtaking release. The unwelcome stomach cramps returned undiminished but my body stood firm, repelled the attack and expelled the interlopers once more. I gasped as if I'd been submerged under water for the entire time.

My faeces at the top of the beach were quite processed and brown. At the bottom of the beach they were just unprocessed coconut that had gone straight through me. I wondered if I should make a drama out of it, and then just accepted that I was losing nutrients once more. For some reason my food was travelling through me faster than tea through a strainer.

I built the rock wall at the entrance to the rock pool to make my corral. I also tried the palm fishing line on the rocks but the force of the shallow water just ripped the line to pieces. The surge of the water coming in washed the line into the rocks and then, when the water was dragged out, the line snapped like cotton thread. I rubbed my temples and put down the failure to yet another learning experience. I expelled the air from my lungs and allowed my shoulders to sag. Once I had repaired the line, I would just have to revert to my original plan of using it on the shallow beach.

Like a child at the end of double maths, my island lesson had been going on far too long and my ability to take in any more information was fast fading.

꜏꜏꜏ ꜏꜏꜏ ꜏꜏꜏ ꜏꜏꜏ ꜏꜏꜏ ꜏꜏꜏ ꜏꜏꜏ ꜏꜏꜏

꜏꜏꜏ ꜏꜏꜏ ꜒꜏꜏

baited the rock corral with chum (maggots and coconut in this case) at low tide and sat high up on the beach and watched the tide start to come in. I didn't need to wait, of course – this sort of trap could be left to its own devices. I knew I wouldn't in any way influence a fish into being trapped by sitting there. But as I gazed at the water flooding into the new pools, turning miniature mountains into an underwater world of shrunken canyons, I acknowledged a certain weariness.

I was comfortable now. I wasn't worried about water, fire or shelter — I'd long ago mastered them all. And, although I was for ever seeking new and more abundant sources of food, I think I felt that I'd made it. There were six days left now and my motivation to run around and try new things was dwindling. I felt like an old man at the end of his life who can see only his own death. He no longer travels or seeks new experiences; he feels like he has experienced his life and is ready to be taken away. I was in my twilight years on the island now and I was aware of it.

'Take me now!' I said to myself mockingly and decided to go for a stroll. Not a hunting mission or a firewood collecting trip but a walk for the sake of the pleasure of walking. I moved slowly and peacefully, one soft footstep after another, and felt the sand between my toes and the sun's warmth and wind's cooling on my bare back. Without thinking about it, I did collect more than enough food for supper — mainly crabs, snails and mussels — but it didn't make me speed up or stop enjoying the walk. I allowed myself to feel. I was tired and I was bored of being alone. I felt as if I'd put my body on the line. But these were superficial feelings — thoughts of the now less influential *ngan duppurru* mind. The walk allowed me to go to a level deeper where something more had been stirred. Dare I say it? In the calm I was also beginning to feel proud.

I returned to the corral once the tide had gone out but there were no fish in it.

I smiled. I really wasn't bothered at all.

~~IIII~~ ~~IIII~~ ~~IIII~~ ~~IIII~~ ~~IIII~~ ~~IIII~~ ~~IIII~~ ~~IIII~~ ~~IIII~~ ~~IIII~~ ~~IIII~~

baited the rock corral again, and this time, when I returned after the tide had dropped, I noticed the head of a larger fish poking out from behind a large flat rock. I jumped into the rock pool and moved the rock to see a ten-inch black fish dart up to the end of the pool. I had trapped a fish! I staggered back and forth attempting to corner the fish but it kept swimming back between my legs, making me feel clumsy and inept. Then I started simply to throw stones at the fish. I hurled large rocks hard at the water but that didn't quite seem to work either. Eventually the fish almost grounded itself in panic and I grabbed the body firmly. I really had caught my first fish! I banged the head with a rock until it was dead and chucked the prize in my basket.

The method had worked. It meant a huge amount to me as it proved that I had devised a method of fishing without a hook, line or net that could trap bigger fish and concentrate them in a small enough space for me to kill them. Triumphantly I carried my catch back to camp.

I scaled and gutted the fish in the shallows with my knife. It brought back memories of the Amazon. Scaling and gutting dinner each day had been such a familiar task. But back then I'd had fishing hooks and a net — this was an especially proud moment as I'd caught this fish using my brains and my bare hands. I chopped it up and had an early lunch of fish broth.

The taste, too, took me right back to the Amazon again. The fish oils transformed the broth into a healthy cure for lethargy

and I could feel brain cells being elbowed awake by their neigh-
bours. I blinked as if resurfacing from a deep sleep. I felt very
much alive.

卌 卌 卌 卌 卌 卌 卌 卌
卌 卌 卌 |

As I'd spent time making the long palm-leaf 'net' I decided
that I should have one last go at using it. I tied one end
around a small rock at the end of my beach and, as I did so, I
could see a school of small dark fish loitering in the shallows. I
realised that if I played my cards right this might actually work.

I walked the free end of the line straight out into the sea,
slowly and quietly, and then walked behind the place where I'd
seen the fish and crept back to the shore, encircling the area.
From the beach I could see that about twenty or so of the three-
inch fish were within my enclosure. I drew in the line slowly so
as to tighten the area and concentrate the fish. The idea was that
the fish would be scared enough by the line to turn away from
it and swim the other way. It wasn't a net, of course — more like
a herder — but the fish certainly saw it as a barrier. The noose
grew tighter and tighter and I envisaged that they would eventually all beach themselves neatly in front of me. I would be able
to just scoop them up and throw them further up the sand
where they couldn't escape. But at the last minute they simply
swam through the line — that had, of course, always been pene-
trable — and calmly swam away from me.

Far from being discouraged, I found this to be a far more
successful experience than I'd expected. The system did work;

perhaps I just needed to be a touch slower at drawing the line in. Perhaps, if the fish hadn't clocked on that they were in danger, they wouldn't have felt the need to try and escape.

I copied my first attempt time and time again until I could feel the red heat in my shoulders under the direct glare of the sun. Try as I might I never entrapped a shoal of fish again.

I spent a couple of hours making a bed using beach hibiscus and some long poles. It looked good enough propped up vertically against a tree. Then, when I picked it up, the frame skewed and all the hibiscus just fell off it.

~~HH~~ ~~HH~~ ~~HH~~ ~~HH~~ ~~HH~~ ~~HH~~ ~~HH~~ ~~HH~~
~~HH~~ ~~HH~~ ~~HH~~ II

managed nineteen chin-ups at the end of week eight. 'Nineteen! YEESSS!!' I roared as I dropped from the high branch. With three days to go I was physically stronger than I'd ever been on this island.

I made another bed (mark two) that this time was braced so that it couldn't skew. The lashings that were to act as the canvas between the poles were also tied on much more strongly so I carried it to my shelter and put it in place. I used some rocks to rest the frame upon to ensure it was horizontal and laid the rawhide from the goat on top for added comfort. Gingerly I laid my tired body on the bed for the first time. I was off the floor! I was fully outstretched and supported and comfortable. The sensation was like being cradled and it felt magical, like a world I had known long ago where it was normal to be free from discomfort.

'I'm going to sleep like a baby tonight.'

Then, as if Olorua was having the last laugh, I found a mango tree. The twist was that the mangos were not yet ripe. I didn't care: I hauled down a small bunch of hard green fruits and bit into them. They smelled like mangos but tasted like, and had the consistency of an unripe hard fruit. I knew that I could still enhance my diet by eating them and getting the vitamins they contained, so I chomped through about five in one sitting and promptly snapped my false tooth in two. I shook my head at the gap-toothed reflection in the camera screen. Who cared what I looked like by this stage? I didn't need the denture and, frankly, who cared if I now had a lisp.

I was eating so well – taro leaf, two crabs, snails, mango. Life after the goat was still good. I was ticking along very nicely and if I were to stay longer many more fruits would surely come into season and I would be eating fruit and fish like a king.

卌 卌 卌 卌 卌 卌 卌 卌

卌 卌 卌 |||

I awoke from the deepest sleep in a state of near-bliss. The tonnage of my body sank deep into the folds of my bed as if I were a Goliath engulfed in Bavarian goose down. I wanted this warm, supported sensation to last for ever. A burst of caramel-ised coconut fuelled my first creaky movements of the day. I rolled my log-like legs off the bed to pendulum myself upright. Head in hands, I sat planted on the side of the bed as if the night's recharge had doubled the force of gravity. My connection to the earth was palpable; I had roots that penetrated the ground and my bare feet allowed energy to flow upwards into my body and fill me with strength and life. This was no metaphor. This was real.

I chuckled like a drunken hobo at the absurdity of not having made myself a bed earlier. Who cared? I'd done it now and was reaping the revitalising rewards. I saw clearly the need to learn this lesson, to look after myself and provide myself with comfort and support in all walks of life. I made a pledge that when I got off the island I would slow down and take the time to care more for myself and for others.

I reflected on all the things I could have done to make my life more comfortable – such as not spending *seven bloody days* flogging myself on the goat trap in the rain. I had gently to chide myself at my mistakes so as to take in the lessons. When I had thrown myself into a busy self-absorbed world I had chosen to be on my own. I had been battling and I had struggled to stay calm. But when I elected to stop, lift my head, open my eyes and really connect to everything around me I had support, composure, joy even. In this latter state I had reconnected to a bigger force that would always support me, and I knew that now. It wasn't even as if I'd opened up and allowed luck to strike. I no longer believed in luck – there was a clear purpose to this force.

As the penny dropped I couldn't stop smiling. I was so elated that I radiated gratitude and happiness, the whites of my eyes shining like wet moons. I saw how I'd always been trying to get somewhere else, never satisfied with who I was or where I was. But the moment I stopped trying so hard I came to understand what I'd already got. On the island I had so much: reliable food, a rainwater collection tank, life-giving fire, a sturdy home, a magical garden and a gargantuan swimming pool. Off the island I had all these things and more. I had every opportunity in the world. I had my health; I had a fantastic career, and, most importantly, I had true love from Amanda and the children. All I had to do to be genuinely happy was to stop and appreciate the things I already had. The peace and clarity of the moment told me it was true.

With the morning sun cutting through the highest branches, life really was that simple.

The day's events were bright and vivid. I collected the best bone-dry firewood I'd ever collected. I swam in the lagoon and let the water wash me clean of myself. I ate good food and I drank crystal-clear rainwater. I took my time over everything and found I had still more time to rest, to relax, to enjoy. The hurrying seemed done with. The eternal fog of unrest to get somewhere else had burned off. I had everything I needed.

卌 卌 卌 卌 卌 卌 卌 卌
卌 卌 卌 ||||

When I returned to camp for my final night, after another peaceful day on the island, guilt, my old acquaintance, crept into my shelter, unbuckled his belt and pissed on my fire. 'Shit!' I sat up. 'I need to get off this bed and do stuff!' – the way I had always reacted to make this uncouth intruder leave.

Then I remembered what I'd learned, laughed, and guilt skulked off without even having to be asked. I lay back down on my luxurious bed and watched the treetops stir in the breeze. I'd worked hard. I'd put myself through one of the toughest experiences of my life and I wasn't going to allow guilt to control my last days. The aim had been to make myself comfortable, to do more than just survive but to thrive. As I lay by the fire I realised that the very fact that I had the option to relax and do nothing meant that I'd achieved that. I'd put in the hours, days of toil, to reach a stage where I was comfortable and relaxed. I would let myself enjoy that very fact.

Having used the lagoon as a bidet for perhaps the last time, I looked out at the sea and acknowledged that I'm not really a survival expert. Sure, I could survive, I'd proved that, and I wasn't blind to the fact that many people with fewer survival skills than me would continue to claim the title 'expert'. But this acknowledgement wasn't about them; they could say what they liked. *I* certainly didn't feel like an expert. I'm not a bushman or a tribal member, I'm a pale-skinned westerner who can get by – that's it. I reminded myself that I'd dreamed up the entire experience to test my own boundaries, put myself through challenges that I hadn't got the answers to, and I certainly felt like I'd been pushed mentally and physically to my absolute limits.

I realised that just getting through my time on the island had, in fact, been a success. The experiment had been designed to show me – if I placed myself in an ultimate survival situation without anything or anybody to help – how I would cope. Despite flirting with desperation and near-madness on several occasions I had come out the other side. I *had* coped. But beyond that I had also grown up. I wasn't the same person who had set foot on the island fifty-nine days ago. I had been ravaged by self-realisation and by a necessity to readdress the way I dealt with the world. It had been relentless and unforgiving and I had often resented the experience. But in the serenity of the aftermath – in the peace of the fruition – I knew it had been worth it. Beyond televisual success, beyond survival success, I had learned lessons in sixty days that 860 days in the Amazon had failed to teach me and it was that which was giving me a satisfied sense of growing confidence once more. The long-ago extinguished candle of self-worth had been unearthed, dusted off and lit once more. It felt good to be home again.

卌 卌 卌 卌 卌 卌 卌 卌
卌 卌 卌 卌

'**M**orning! Day sixty – it's day sixty! I'm going home.' I didn't have to pretend to be utterly elated at the prospect. There was a sense of relief that could have erupted into uncontrollable sobs if I'd let myself drop my guard now that I'd reached the end of the road. Was there any rush to get out of bed? No – none whatsoever. I shut my eyes and decided to have a final lie-in.

My experience had always had a soundtrack, and the last morning had a new song that I not played myself before. The melancholy tones of 'Every Rose Has Its Thorn' vibrated through my heart and my eyes opened once more to a sense of sad admission to the thorn of the rose. It had been hard for me, of course, but now I sensed more than ever that it had been really hard for Amanda. I longed for her to be happy and well and yet I was apprehensive about speaking to her. Had the separation damaged our relationship? Were we going to be OK?

I was so excited about seeing Amanda again, sharing moments together, eating food together, laughing together. I hoped from the bottom of my heart that she was all right.

The warmth of the fire and the familiar sound of the birds brought me back to the present. It was over. I'd made it. I was about to go home.

My more banal brain grasped a simpler theme and my first verbalising to the camera was the bastardised lyrics to the English football anthem: 'We're going home, we're going home, we're going, Eddy's going home.' The words were an insult to how I really felt.

I creaked and pulled myself up off the bed that had provided such comfort in the past few nights. All I had to do was stumble on to the beach and be picked up.

Simple.

'It's done me very well, this shelter. I've been very comfortable and very content in this shelter. Cheerio.' The observational commentary didn't touch the powerful emotions that were fighting to be heard. I was elated and shattered, sad and deeply satisfied, too. Was that possible?

Was I happy it was over? Yes − no question. Was I proud of what I'd achieved? Yes − I thought so − but last night's pride wasn't high in my list of emotions now. Pride could wait.

The pick-up was scheduled for mid-morning. A production message in the dropbox had given me the heads-up about how I would be taken off Olorua but my heart had already left and I had a little time to do something that I had resisted the temptation to do for the last sixty days.

I had to call Amanda.

I took out the clunky Iridium satellite phone, still covered in sand from my conversation with Dr Sundeep in the rain, and brushed the keypad clean with my fingers. I held the alien machine in my hand and was terrified to open the door. Every bit of my journey suddenly felt so selfish and I felt unprepared to deal with life outside my world. I keyed in her number and, after a long pause, pressed the call button. The British dial tone twisted my stomach.

'Hi, my love, it's me.' I ventured tentatively.

'Oh, my God! Hi, babe! It's so good to hear your voice.' The soft, familiar tones immediately started to unravel me. An unstoppable wave of emotion cracked my defences and I broke down. I sobbed powerfully out of love, pain and the knowledge that Amanda was still there. We couldn't begin to explain to each other what we'd both been through, but, for now, who cared? We would be together again soon and that was what mattered to me more than anything in the world. I had tried to hold on to an emotional connection to her for the entire time but neither of us was blind to the fact that I'd really left her to fend for herself.

I hung up and broke down again. Loud raw sobs that I didn't fight but embraced. I allowed the release. It felt good to let go. To allow myself to crumble at last.

I lowered my skinny frame to the sand and sat waiting for the crew to arrive. 'Would I do that again? No. No. Never.' I sank my fingers into my thick wiry beard and blinked, absorbing the end of something that would never need to be repeated.

Resorting to trivia, I began to chat to the camera. 'Lost a bit of fat and a tooth. Gained quite a bit of hair and a beard. I don't think there is a snail left on this island!' I'd eaten over 800 snails since the goat meat ran out so I calculated I'd eaten easily over a couple of thousand in total. I was sure they'd helped keep me strong throughout.

It seemed there were fewer unknowns now. This was my little island and I knew every inch of her. As I sat facing the sea I felt connected to her energy as if she was my horse on a long journey. I had tried to steer and influence the experience as well as I could but she had the real power to decide where I went or what I'd found. In many ways I had simply been a passenger.

Olorua was also me, I knew that now. Sure, she could always be viewed as being isolated and exposed, battling the Pacific storms, but that was only part of her story – the obvious, superficial part. Below the surface she was physically connected to, and an integral part of, the earth. She was a peaceful entity that didn't need to fight for her survival. She would always be there. She would always be safe. She wasn't alone.

I was interrupted by an alien noise. 'That is the sound – not of a boat – but a helicopter!'

The heli's round belly lowered on to the sand by Snail Rock. Camera in hand, I got a thumbs-up from the pilot and hurried to the escape pod. As I got to the door I saw Steve Rankin's familiar round face sitting in the back, filming. 'Hello, mate!' I smiled, genuinely thrilled to see him.

After having some pictures taken, I climbed into the helicopter and sat heavily on the soft, cushioned seat. The pilot turned around and asked me to put my seat belt on. I pulled the stiff nylon across my bare chest and clipped it in at the edge of my grass skirt. The engine rose in pitch and intensity and the aircraft roared and rose from the beach. As I gazed out of the glass bubble at the treetops I could see Olorua in all her splendour. My mental picture of the island had been almost exactly correct and I was in awe at sights that, while familiar from the ground, fascinated me from this new perspective.

The rocky outcrop; the amphitheatre; was that the Faraway Tree? The lush green-quilted island now seemed nothing short of magical. She had protected me and taught me so much and I knew I would never see her again. As we drew higher and further away she began to shrink into the distance. I was sad but I also knew that she would always be there and always be within me. We had been through something unique together and, like a World Cup-winning rugby team, we had shared an experience that was beyond words. She would always be visible in my eyes.

I turned away from the window and gave out a long, tired sigh. 'Mission accomplished.' The weariness on my face said it all. I'd done it.

I stepped out of the helicopter on the island of Komo to the most incredible reception from the Komo women, who embraced me, kissed me and covered me in colourful flower garlands. From the Fijian men, I was struck by their genuine appreciation of just how hard it must have been. I could see in the wise old faces that somehow they understood and it moved me to tears.

Back in the privacy of the painted wooden hut, I took off my coarse grass skirt and let it drop to the floor for the last time. I pulled on my khaki shorts and laughed at the gaping waist. The rusty old scales flickered at seventy-nine kilos. I'd lost almost ten.

I felt emotionally in better shape too. The experience seemed to have shown me what really mattered in life. Before, I'd been all about proving myself, achieving goals, seeking recognition and the approval of others. Now I could concentrate on just being myself and, at last, enjoy what I already had.

As I prepared to come home I felt I'd come a long way. I could no longer go through life without being accountable for everything that I did. In taking back this responsibility I'd in turn found a new strength. Everything was in my power and I would not so easily give that away now.

卌 卌 卌 卌 卌 卌 卌
卌 卌 卌 卌 卌 卌 卌
卌 卌 卌 卌 卌 卌 卌
卌 卌 卌 卌 卌 卌 卌
卌 卌 卌 卌 卌 卌 卌
卌 卌 卌 卌 卌 卌 卌
卌 卌 卌 卌 卌 卌 卌
卌 卌 卌 卌 卌 卌 卌
卌 卌 卌 卌 卌 卌 卌
卌 卌 卌 卌 卌 卌 卌
卌 卌 卌 卌 卌 卌 卌
卌 卌 卌 卌 卌 ||

Epilogue

One year, two months and twenty-one days after day sixty.
5 January 2014

'Ed, is there a bit of you that would be relieved if I rang the doctor?' Amanda asked, as I lay, deflated, on our king-size bed in the middle of the afternoon. I was due to depart to film episode six of my new series for Discovery Channel in the Golden Triangle the next day. I hadn't packed. I felt weak. Christmas and New Year had been shit. It had been my fault. I was confused.

'Yes,' I replied softly into the pillow, tears once more forming in my eyes.

'Stay there. I'll call Kenric now.' Amanda left me and I could hear her ankle socks tiptoeing down the wooden stairs.

What was going on? What was wrong with me? I felt like I was unravelling again. When was this island nightmare going to end?

I was so sensitive I could have cried at the slightest thing. Equally I could take offence and just as easily become angry and frustrated. Was I paranoid? Was I finally going mad? I was scared of going away again. Of taking my clothes off yet again. Of being put in the position where I had to start from scratch *yet again*.

I could hear the gentle footsteps once more. 'Eddy S, are you awake, my love?' I cocked my head and gazed at the woman I love, the woman for whom I had caused so many problems, the woman who, despite my destructive behaviour, was still sticking with me. Standing there, she was the embodiment of kindness. Her face was tired but compassionate, her eyes windows into a world of sacrifice, of having to be patient and strong.

'They are sending a specialist, a psychiatrist; he's coming from Chiswick and he'll be here in half an hour.'

Nowhere to hide now, Stafford.

Fuck me.

Thirty minutes later, I heard the doorbell ring. Amanda answered it and I walked through to the kitchen as if I was being brought into the headmaster's office after he had found out that I had somehow got away with being a truant for months on end. I shook hands with the grey-haired man, a psychiatrist named Mike, and showed him through to the lounge while Amanda made us coffee.

'You must be Ed,' he said.

'Do you mind sitting there?' asked Mike. 'I normally sit at forty-five degrees to my patients.' I dutifully obeyed, having already acknowledged that I was handing over the controls to this well-mannered man. I was relieved to do so.

Mike asked many questions. When he had finished he looked up, put his pen down and cleared his throat. He described what I had been feeling as if he had known me for years. It was both disarming and utterly reassuring at the same time.

'Do you know what the best method of torturing people is?' he opened. I visualised James Bond strapped down with a laser pointing at his privates; or sitting naked on a chair with the seat cut out ready to be whipped from below. 'Solitary confinement,' Mike went on. 'It's the ultimate punishment in prison and it's the best guaranteed way to break somebody. Thumbscrews came about because of pressure to get results fast – but, if you've got the time, the best way to turn a perfectly healthy man's brain to mush is to lock him in a dark room and leave him alone for two months.' I logged the timespan he referred to. Sixty days in isolation. He continued: 'After this time I could be your worst enemy but you would beg to be my friend. You would be putty in my hands.

'Take Terry Waite – he and his family suffered hugely after he came back because of all kinds of symptoms that are very similar to you. Did you also know that many Auschwitz survivors developed eating disorders after they became free?' I winced at the pain of acknowledging how much of a pickle I'd got into about food. It occupied my brain for much of every day and I couldn't look in the mirror without seeing an excess of fat around my waist. I sometimes weighed myself more than twice a day and made sure that I put the scales back exactly as I'd found them so that no one knew I'd done it. What an admission for a thirty-eight-year-old man.

'There is no doubt that what you are experiencing is the effects of psychological torture. The unique thing about your case is that you *opted* to be put in this situation.'

Winding back the extremity of his comparisons, Mike continued. 'There is a reason that lighthouse managers are hard to come by. And why few of them remain in their job for more than a year. Most of us do not function very well on our own – and the fact that you've experienced these effects actually makes you 100 per cent normal.' He smiled and I could feel a cool breeze of relief beginning to stir.

'It is my opinion that those who experience no emotional stress when isolated have something missing in them. Some of the greatest explorers do not require an emotional connection to be happy and as a result have the ability to do extraordinary things without any particular psychological issues. But I would suggest that if you looked at their family life you might find that their relationships were detached and dysfunctional. There is a cost to such cold independence.'

When you already know something to be true you absorb it there and then. There is no need for deliberation or analysis and I could tell I was hearing a wise voice of experience who had dealt with the minds of many people who had undergone periods of intense mental trauma.

'Take Bradley Wiggins,' Mike continued. 'He will never do another Tour de France. He spent a year in the mountains away from his family and friends, drinking sports drinks and training every hour of the day. It worked – he won the Tour de France – but at what cost?'

My eyes were welling up again. The fact that someone sitting in front of me was recognising the extent of what I felt was happening to me was a phenomenal relief. I wasn't going mad after all. These were *expected* side effects of isolation and if I *hadn't* suffered them it would have made me abnormal.

I looked at Amanda and felt how much sadness I had caused by not facing up to what was going on and trying to cover up for my deteriorating mental state by pretending to be fine. No wonder she felt desperate and had had to reach out for help. What a woman. I welled up again; this time tears spilled down my cheeks.

As I write, two months have passed. I've been signed off as having fully recovered by Mike, and I feel rebuilt and stronger than ever. But there is a reason this book does not have the fairytale ending that might have been expected – I felt a compulsion to be honest right to the end. If you sit in front of the TV and admire adventurous people who seem to have a far more exciting life than you, I urge you to consider the following.

Having a *moderate* amount of adventure in your life is healthy – the last thing I want to encourage people to do is sit on the couch playing computer games all day. Of course there is also scope once in a while to have *a lot* of adventure in your life. But if adventure *becomes* your life you have lost something. You have become addicted to a thrill, a rush, and have lost sight of balance, responsibility and meaning. You have become a serial escape artist and need to stop and work out what you are escaping from.

It seems the more I tried to escape my own pain and problems the more complicated and unhappy life got and the more I felt the need to escape and destroy everything around me out of blind frustration to find a scapegoat. And somehow, despite all the experiences on the island, I still hadn't managed to face my own demons.

You can't avoid pain, and to do so would be to stop growing, to stop learning and seek a life of avoidance. Addressing and working through our problems and our pain makes us wise. I did everything on that island to stay busy and keep myself away from my own inner pain. In everyday life my distraction techniques could have been excessive exercise, smoking, chocolate-chip cookies, or perhaps binge drinking – but in such an exposed existence I found myself creating my own drama in order to perpetually live in my tangled thoughts, as neurotic as they were, because at least it meant I was distracted from my real darkness.

And so despite the experience on the island and the lessons it taught me I realised that I still must have issues to face – and face them I had to. It was the only way to heal and the only way I would ever be able to live a good and honest life.

There is a theory that every adopted child experiences trauma as a result of the separation from their mother at birth. A newborn baby is inherently dependent; it cannot move or feed itself. The *only* thing it can do in order to survive is to form a bond to its mother. As a result separation is said to be experienced as a suffering of the same magnitude as death. This pre-memory experience becomes the blueprint for how the child learns to manage in life: deeply traumatised – feeling abandoned and worthless. If left unaddressed this will never change.

They say we subconsciously recreate situations in our lives, even negative ones, because it's what we know and we naturally seek out familiarity. Victims of domestic violence often unconsciously seek out new abusive partners. Crazy, but sadly true. I was adopted as a baby and I think it is no coincidence that, as a man in his late thirties, I somehow construed my job as being abandoned naked on an island with no meaningful contact with the outside world for two months. It's laughable – but it wouldn't be funny if there wasn't an element of truth in it.

So I had my issues to confront. Who doesn't? I needed to know I could survive on my own in life and yet at the same time I acknowledged that I also wanted the sympathy of the televisual onlooker. My insecurity was so deep I needed the world to see that I could thrive on my own in the most extreme of circumstances.

Mike clearly did his job, for which I am very grateful, but to put my entire recovery down to CBT and psychiatric sessions alone would be a disservice to my family and friends who are listed below in the acknowledgements. There are also some unsung heroes here who, out of respect for who they are and what they do, shall remain deliberately unsung.

We can all get by in life muddling through, doing a bit of unconscious grumbling, and catching fleeting moments of fun and happiness, often with the help of a couple of drinks. But for me, something deep within me wanted to understand more. Why did I have a tendency to judge people or situations? Why was I not content with what I had? What was the underlying restlessness all about? I had to know and I hoped that such an isolated experiment would surely give me the opportunity to turn myself inside out and find some answers.

We live in a world of ego, consumption and accumulation of wealth. But there is an inherent incompleteness to such a life. To desire to own something or someone, to grab onto it or them, is a needy and insecure place to live and it is a poor substitute for real happiness. Go sit on an uninhabited island in that state, I dare you. The removal of all the crutches is terrifying. I was left with a giddying, maddening sense of 'Who *the fuck* am I?'

But in the same way as I felt I had no option but to expose my struggles, I feel compelled to share my own personal realisations too. It seems almost too simplistic, but the ability to just sit back and let go of everything has been infinitely more valuable to me than anything money could buy. This could only come about after a painstaking look deep inside, a reconnection to everything that I know to be true, and a new-found love for myself as a part of this world. Nothing and noone could make me happy until I was honest with myself and prepared to face parts of me that were not at all pretty.

I worked through layer after layer of neurotic behaviour until I eventually got to a true place of self. And despite never having lived in such a clean place I immediately knew this me so well. The good person that I've always protested to be. The conscience that has soaked through all the layers from time to time. The light, funny, confident me. The loving me.

Paradoxically, by letting go of my frantic struggle to keep things as I wanted them, the people and things that I had clung onto so desperately remain there with no forced effort. I have more in my life than I ever did.

Does this change who and what I love? No – not one bit. We are who we are. I never want to lose my rage, I love the reprobate in me, I love my adventures, I love to push myself hard, and most of all I love to come home again. My family is the core of who I am and they are what gives me a purpose. The only change is that everything comes without fear, guilt or struggle. Life, quite simply, feels great.

Survival in this world is not a lone battle. It is about respect for, and acknowledgement of, a higher consciousness that oversees everything and has everyone's best interests at heart. I know it will carry me where I want to go and protect us all on our journey through life as it guided me in the Amazon and on Olorua. Nobody has told me this – I just feel it. This universal force flows through, and is part of, us all. All we need to do is acknowledge it, surrender to it, and laugh.

But don't try and work that out with your logic brain – it will send you bloody mad.

Acknowledgements

To Craig Langman, with whom, over a cup of Lady Grey tea, I conceived this thunderously life-changing experiment. It seemed like a simple fun idea at the time …

To Julian Bellamy, Dan Korn, Liz McIntyre, Helen Hawkins and all at Discovery for commissioning and facilitating the entire experiment. Thank you for believing in me.

To Dick Colthurst, Steve Rankin, Steven Ballantine and everyone at Tigress Productions for making the entire experience physically happen. You were the guys who took the dream and turned it into a reality. Thanks so much.

To Ed Faulkner at Virgin Books in London, Phil Budnick at Penguin Books in New York, and Julian Alexander at the LAW Agency for allowing this book to happen and encouraging me to write it honestly. You have all been a tremendous help.

To Dr Mike McPhillips and Mal Kahn for patiently listening and gently pointing me in a less destructive direction.

To Karen, Tony, James and Robert Lovell, my birth mother, birth father and two full-blood brothers whom I never knew I had until two years ago. Thank you for understanding and giving me space when I needed it. I love you all and hope to see more of you.

To Harold Tayley. For your big heart, timeless understanding and eternal wisdom. Much love!

To Jeremy Donovan for everything. I will never forget your warrior-like love and support for Amanda and myself, often at your own expense. I am always there for you, *bunji*.

Gigi and Baba, for the love and support you've given me. For the openness of your hearts and the wisdom of your experience. I respect and love you both enormously. Don't let the buggers get you down, FB!

To my sister, Janie Stafford, and my two nephews Archie and Rupert. I love you all and hope you are happy. Family is everything.

To my dad, Jeremy Stafford, for the continuing moral guidance you have always imparted. May I always follow your impeccable lead. I love you, Dad.

To my mum, Barbara Stafford, for your love throughout everything. I love you unconditionally and always will.

Amanda's kids — Frederick and Coco — for staying strong and looking after your Mummy. For the love and happiness you have brought into my life. You have been my best teachers. I will always love you both enormously.

To Amanda — the woman who came into my life with an open heart – for all the things that you went through and sacrificed for me. I am humbled by your love and care. I support you in everything that you are and everything that you want. Our lives were destined to be interwoven. Wherever I am on this Earth I will always be able to feel you in my *gupanyung* – my heart. May our souls dance together in the dreaming where time doesn't exist. Walk in beauty, my love – just as you are.